Mastering Scikit-Learn: Practical ML for Everyone

Gilbert Gutiérrez

Machine learning has revolutionized industries worldwide, from healthcare and finance to marketing and automation. Whether you're an aspiring data scientist, a software engineer, or a business professional looking to harness the power of AI, **Mastering Scikit-Learn: Practical ML for Everyone** is your comprehensive guide to understanding, implementing, and optimizing machine learning models using Python's most popular ML library—Scikit-Learn.

This book is the fifth installment in the *AI from Scratch* series, a carefully designed roadmap that takes readers from fundamental AI concepts to advanced machine learning techniques. With this book, you will gain hands-on experience, learn practical strategies, and develop real-world projects to master Scikit-Learn effectively.

Why Scikit-Learn?

Scikit-Learn is an essential library in the Python ecosystem, providing powerful, efficient, and easy-to-use tools for machine learning. Built on top of NumPy, SciPy, and Matplotlib, Scikit-Learn offers predefined algorithms, built-in data processing functions, and model evaluation techniques, making it ideal for both beginners and experienced practitioners.

With Mastering Scikit-Learn, you will:

✓ Learn how to preprocess and manipulate datasets efficiently.

✓ Implement supervised and unsupervised learning models from scratch.

✓ Master feature engineering and hyperparameter tuning to enhance model performance.

✓ Explore advanced techniques like pipelines, ensemble methods, and automated machine learning (AutoML).

✓ Build end-to-end ML projects for real-world applications.

Whether you are new to machine learning or looking to refine your skills, this book will take you from theory to practical mastery using real-world datasets, hands-on coding exercises, and best practices.

What You Will Learn

This book is structured into four major sections, guiding you through the machine learning journey step by step.

📌 Part 1: Getting Started with Scikit-Learn

The book begins with an introduction to machine learning and Scikit-Learn, ensuring you have a solid foundation before diving into practical implementation.

Chapter 1: Introduction to Scikit-Learn and Its Ecosystem

- Understanding the importance of Scikit-Learn in machine learning
- Installing and setting up your Python environment
- Overview of key dependencies: NumPy, Pandas, Matplotlib

Chapter 2: Fundamentals of Machine Learning with Scikit-Learn

- Supervised vs. unsupervised learning
- Key ML concepts: overfitting, underfitting, bias-variance tradeoff
- Building your first ML model

Chapter 3: Working with Data in Scikit-Learn

- Loading and exploring datasets
- Handling missing values and feature scaling
- Encoding categorical variables

📌 Part 2: Core Machine Learning Models

This section focuses on implementing machine learning algorithms using Scikit-Learn's extensive library of models.

Chapter 4: Linear Models for Regression and Classification

- Linear regression, Ridge, and Lasso regression
- Logistic regression for classification tasks

Chapter 5: Tree-Based Models and Ensemble Learning

- Decision trees: how they work and when to use them
- Random forests and gradient boosting (XGBoost, LightGBM)

Chapter 6: Support Vector Machines and Kernel Methods

- Understanding SVMs and their hyperparameters
- The power of kernel tricks in non-linear classification

Chapter 7: Clustering and Unsupervised Learning

- K-Means, DBSCAN, and hierarchical clustering
- Principal Component Analysis (PCA) for dimensionality reduction

📌 Part 3: Advanced Scikit-Learn Techniques

Going beyond the basics, this section explores advanced optimization, feature engineering, and model automation to enhance ML performance.

Chapter 8: Feature Engineering and Selection

- Creating and selecting the most important features
- Recursive Feature Elimination (RFE)

Chapter 9: Hyperparameter Tuning and Model Selection

- Using GridSearchCV and RandomizedSearchCV
- Bayesian optimization for hyperparameter tuning

Chapter 10: Handling Imbalanced Data and Anomaly Detection

- Dealing with class imbalance using SMOTE
- Outlier detection with Isolation Forests

Chapter 11: Pipelines and Model Deployment

- Automating ML workflows with Scikit-Learn Pipelines
- Saving, loading, and deploying models using Flask and FastAPI

📌 Part 4: Real-World Applications & Case Studies

This final section focuses on practical applications, integrating Scikit-Learn with other AI frameworks, and preparing for real-world ML deployment.

Chapter 12: Building a Machine Learning Project from Scratch

- Step-by-step case study using a real dataset
- Deploying a full ML pipeline

Chapter 13: Using Scikit-Learn with Deep Learning Frameworks

- How Scikit-Learn integrates with TensorFlow and PyTorch
- Hybrid models combining traditional ML with deep learning

Chapter 14: Automating Machine Learning with Scikit-Learn

- Introduction to AutoML
- Using TPOT and Auto-Sklearn

Chapter 15: Best Practices and Common Pitfalls

- Avoiding common mistakes in ML projects
- Debugging and optimizing machine learning models

Who Should Read This Book?

📌 **Beginners & Students** – If you're new to machine learning, this book provides a structured, hands-on approach to mastering Scikit-Learn.

📌 **Data Scientists & ML Engineers** – Strengthen your knowledge of Scikit-Learn's powerful features, from model optimization to deployment.

📌 **Software Developers** – Learn how to integrate ML models into real-world applications efficiently.

📌 **Business Analysts & Decision Makers** – Understand how machine learning models can drive data-driven decisions in industry applications.

Why This Book?

✓ **Hands-on Approach** – Every concept is accompanied by code snippets, visualizations, and real-world datasets.

✓ **Step-by-Step Explanations** – From fundamental concepts to advanced techniques, each topic is broken down into digestible sections.

✓ **Industry-Relevant Examples** – Learn how to apply machine learning in finance, healthcare, marketing, and more.

✓ **Part of the AI from Scratch Series** – A structured progression designed to take you from beginner to AI expert.

Start Your Journey Today!

Whether you're taking your first steps into machine learning or refining your Scikit-Learn expertise, Mastering Scikit-Learn: Practical ML for Everyone is the only guide you need to become proficient in one of the most powerful ML libraries available.

With step-by-step guidance, real-world case studies, and best practices, this book ensures that you not only understand machine learning concepts but can also apply them effectively.

Get ready to transform your understanding of machine learning and take your AI skills to the next level! 🚀

1. Introduction to Scikit-Learn and Its Ecosystem

Scikit-Learn is one of the most powerful and widely used machine learning libraries in Python. This chapter introduces its core functionalities, explores why it is essential for ML practitioners, and walks you through setting up your development environment. By the end of this chapter, you will have a solid understanding of Scikit-Learn's ecosystem and how it fits into the broader AI landscape.

1.1 What is Scikit-Learn?

Scikit-Learn is one of the most widely used open-source machine learning libraries in the Python ecosystem. It provides a simple yet powerful framework for implementing a wide range of machine learning algorithms, from basic regression models to complex ensemble learning techniques. Designed for efficiency and ease of use, Scikit-Learn has become a go-to library for data scientists, researchers, and developers who need to build machine learning models quickly and effectively.

Origins and Development

Scikit-Learn was initially developed as part of the Google Summer of Code project in 2007 by David Cournapeau. Since then, it has evolved into a robust machine learning library maintained by a team of contributors from around the world. Built on top of foundational Python libraries such as NumPy, SciPy, and Matplotlib, Scikit-Learn is optimized for speed and performance. It seamlessly integrates with other popular Python tools, making it an essential component of the data science workflow.

The name "Scikit" comes from SciPy Toolkit, indicating that it is an extension of the SciPy ecosystem. Since its first official release in 2010, Scikit-Learn has undergone continuous improvements, adding new algorithms, optimization techniques, and enhanced functionalities. Today, it is widely used in academia, industry, and research for tasks ranging from predictive modeling to data mining.

Key Features of Scikit-Learn

Scikit-Learn offers a rich set of functionalities that make it an essential tool for machine learning practitioners. Some of its key features include:

Simple and Consistent API – Scikit-Learn provides a user-friendly and consistent API that simplifies the implementation of machine learning models. Its uniform syntax ensures that users can easily apply different algorithms with minimal changes to their code.

Comprehensive Machine Learning Algorithms – The library supports a variety of supervised and unsupervised learning algorithms, including regression, classification, clustering, and dimensionality reduction techniques.

Efficient Data Handling – Scikit-Learn supports a range of data preprocessing techniques, such as normalization, standardization, and feature encoding, which help in preparing raw data for model training.

Model Selection and Evaluation – The library includes tools for cross-validation, hyperparameter tuning, and performance evaluation using metrics like accuracy, precision, recall, and F1-score.

Scalability and Performance – Leveraging optimized implementations in NumPy and SciPy, Scikit-Learn ensures efficient computation, making it suitable for handling large datasets.

Integration with Other Libraries – It seamlessly integrates with popular libraries such as Pandas, Matplotlib, and TensorFlow, enabling users to develop end-to-end machine learning pipelines.

Community Support and Documentation – Scikit-Learn has an active community of developers and users who contribute to its extensive documentation, tutorials, and forums, making it easy for newcomers to get started.

Core Components of Scikit-Learn

Scikit-Learn provides a structured framework for machine learning, including:

Supervised Learning – Includes algorithms for regression (e.g., Linear Regression, Ridge Regression) and classification (e.g., Decision Trees, Support Vector Machines, Naïve Bayes, Random Forests).

Unsupervised Learning – Provides tools for clustering (e.g., K-Means, DBSCAN) and dimensionality reduction (e.g., Principal Component Analysis, t-SNE).

Model Selection – Offers methods for cross-validation, grid search, and hyperparameter tuning to optimize model performance.

Data Preprocessing – Functions for feature extraction, scaling, normalization, and encoding categorical data.

Pipelines and Automation – Supports the creation of machine learning pipelines that streamline the process of data transformation and model training.

Performance Metrics – Provides built-in evaluation metrics such as mean squared error (MSE), R-squared, precision-recall, and confusion matrices.

How Scikit-Learn Compares to Other Machine Learning Libraries

Scikit-Learn is often compared to other machine learning frameworks like TensorFlow, PyTorch, and XGBoost. While TensorFlow and PyTorch are primarily designed for deep learning and neural networks, Scikit-Learn excels in traditional machine learning tasks, such as classification, regression, and clustering. It is often the first choice for beginners due to its intuitive design and comprehensive documentation.

Compared to XGBoost and LightGBM, which specialize in gradient boosting and tree-based models, Scikit-Learn offers a broader range of algorithms, making it more versatile. However, for large-scale gradient boosting applications, specialized libraries like XGBoost may provide better performance.

Why Use Scikit-Learn?

Scikit-Learn is a preferred choice for many machine learning practitioners because of its ease of use, flexibility, and efficiency. Whether you are working on academic research, business analytics, or AI-powered applications, Scikit-Learn provides the tools needed to implement robust and scalable machine learning models.

Some common use cases include:

- Predictive analytics in finance and healthcare
- Customer segmentation and recommendation systems
- Fraud detection and anomaly detection
- Sentiment analysis and text classification
- Image recognition and data clustering

Scikit-Learn's ability to handle various machine learning tasks, combined with its strong community support, makes it an indispensable tool for anyone working in data science and AI.

Scikit-Learn has revolutionized the way machine learning models are built and deployed. With its extensive features, efficient algorithms, and user-friendly interface, it has become an essential library for data scientists and machine learning enthusiasts. As we move forward in this book, we will explore Scikit-Learn in depth, covering everything from data preprocessing to advanced model optimization techniques. Whether you're a beginner or an experienced practitioner, mastering Scikit-Learn will equip you with the skills needed to excel in the field of machine learning.

1.2 The Importance of Scikit-Learn in Machine Learning

Scikit-learn is one of the most widely used libraries for machine learning in Python, providing essential tools for data mining and data analysis. Its importance in the field of machine learning stems from its simplicity, versatility, and broad range of functionality. In this sub-chapter, we will explore the key reasons why Scikit-learn holds such a significant role in modern machine learning workflows, discussing its key features, usability, and contributions to both beginners and experts in the field.

1.2.1 Overview of Scikit-Learn

Scikit-learn is an open-source machine learning library built on top of well-established scientific libraries such as NumPy, SciPy, and matplotlib. Its primary purpose is to provide a simple and efficient tool for implementing various machine learning algorithms. Scikit-learn covers a wide range of supervised and unsupervised learning algorithms, data preprocessing tools, and evaluation techniques, all wrapped in a user-friendly Python interface. As a result, it is a go-to choice for developers and data scientists working with machine learning tasks such as classification, regression, clustering, dimensionality reduction, and model evaluation.

One of the reasons Scikit-learn is so popular is that it supports the entire machine learning workflow, from data preprocessing to model evaluation. The library provides functionality for importing datasets, cleaning and transforming data, selecting features, training models, and making predictions. Additionally, it offers a comprehensive set of utilities for cross-validation and hyperparameter tuning, making it easier for practitioners to optimize their machine learning models.

1.2.2 Accessibility and Usability

One of Scikit-learn's standout features is its accessibility and ease of use. Unlike many other machine learning libraries that may require deep expertise in the domain, Scikit-learn allows users to apply sophisticated algorithms with minimal effort. Its simple, well-documented API allows users to quickly get up and running with machine learning tasks. The clean and consistent design across different algorithms means that users can apply a common workflow regardless of the model they are using.

This ease of use makes Scikit-learn particularly attractive to beginners and non-experts. With the right documentation and examples, even those with limited experience in programming or machine learning can grasp the core concepts of the library. Moreover, Scikit-learn is highly integrated with the broader Python ecosystem, allowing users to seamlessly combine it with other libraries like pandas for data manipulation, NumPy for numerical operations, and matplotlib for visualization.

For instance, users can import data with pandas, preprocess it using Scikit-learn's transformers and feature selectors, and visualize the results with matplotlib. This synergy makes Scikit-learn a powerful tool in a machine learning developer's toolbox.

1.2.3 Comprehensive Algorithm Coverage

Another key strength of Scikit-learn is its wide array of algorithms and models. It covers nearly all the major types of machine learning techniques, including:

Supervised Learning: Scikit-learn offers a variety of classification algorithms, such as decision trees, random forests, support vector machines (SVM), k-nearest neighbors (KNN), and gradient boosting. For regression tasks, it supports linear regression, ridge regression, lasso regression, support vector regression, and more. These algorithms are fundamental to many real-world machine learning tasks, making Scikit-learn a highly versatile tool for a wide range of applications.

Unsupervised Learning: Scikit-learn also includes powerful unsupervised learning methods, such as clustering algorithms like k-means, hierarchical clustering, and DBSCAN. It also supports dimensionality reduction techniques like principal component analysis (PCA), t-SNE, and manifold learning, which are essential for working with high-dimensional data.

Model Selection and Evaluation: Scikit-learn provides built-in utilities for model selection, including cross-validation techniques and hyperparameter tuning with

GridSearchCV and RandomizedSearchCV. These tools help ensure that models are properly optimized and can generalize effectively to unseen data.

The inclusion of these diverse algorithms allows Scikit-learn to cater to various machine learning tasks, from simple predictions to complex clustering and dimensionality reduction. This broad coverage allows practitioners to experiment with different models to determine the best fit for their particular application.

1.2.4 Efficient Model Evaluation

An essential component of any machine learning workflow is evaluating the performance of models. Scikit-learn's utilities for model evaluation make it a crucial tool in the development and deployment of machine learning systems. The library offers several performance metrics for classification, regression, and clustering tasks, such as accuracy, precision, recall, F1 score, mean squared error, and silhouette score.

The library also integrates well with cross-validation methods, allowing users to evaluate models more reliably. Cross-validation helps mitigate overfitting by assessing how well a model performs on different subsets of the data. Scikit-learn makes it easy to apply k-fold cross-validation and other validation strategies to ensure that the selected model is robust and generalizes well to new data.

By offering a comprehensive suite of evaluation tools, Scikit-learn allows practitioners to assess the quality of their models and identify potential areas for improvement, making it a vital part of any machine learning project.

1.2.5 Extensive Documentation and Community Support

One of the key aspects that makes Scikit-learn indispensable in machine learning is its well-maintained documentation. The library's official documentation provides clear explanations of algorithms, use-case examples, and step-by-step tutorials. This is invaluable for both beginners and experienced practitioners, as it significantly reduces the learning curve associated with using advanced machine learning techniques.

Scikit-learn also benefits from a large, active community of users and developers. As an open-source project, it has garnered contributions from experts across the globe, resulting in continuous improvements and updates. The community provides helpful resources, including forums, blogs, Stack Overflow discussions, and tutorial videos, ensuring that users have access to support when they encounter challenges.

1.2.6 Scalability and Performance

While Scikit-learn is optimized for ease of use, it does not sacrifice performance. The library is built on top of efficient numerical libraries like NumPy and SciPy, which allow it to handle relatively large datasets. While it may not be as scalable as other tools like TensorFlow or PyTorch, Scikit-learn is often fast enough for many common machine learning tasks, especially when working with moderate-sized datasets. Additionally, the library's integration with other Python libraries, such as joblib for parallelization, can further speed up computations.

Scikit-learn is also highly compatible with other machine learning and deep learning frameworks, enabling users to combine the simplicity of Scikit-learn with the power of specialized frameworks like TensorFlow, PyTorch, or XGBoost for more complex use cases. This ability to work in tandem with other tools is another reason Scikit-learn is an essential part of the machine learning ecosystem.

In summary, Scikit-learn's role in the machine learning ecosystem cannot be overstated. Its combination of ease of use, comprehensive algorithm coverage, efficient model evaluation, and scalability makes it a powerful tool for both beginners and experts alike. The library provides all the essential building blocks for implementing machine learning workflows, from data preprocessing to model evaluation, making it indispensable for anyone involved in machine learning tasks. By offering an accessible platform for experimenting with a variety of models and techniques, Scikit-learn empowers data scientists and machine learning practitioners to develop solutions that are both effective and efficient.

Whether you are a novice looking to learn the basics of machine learning or an experienced professional working on complex data-driven projects, Scikit-learn is an invaluable tool that plays a central role in shaping the landscape of modern machine learning.

1.3 Installing and Setting Up Scikit-Learn

Installing and setting up Scikit-learn is a straightforward process, but there are certain steps and considerations to ensure that everything runs smoothly. In this section, we will go over the installation of Scikit-learn, the required dependencies, and setting up the environment for efficient machine learning development. Whether you are using a local machine or a cloud-based environment, these instructions will help you get started with Scikit-learn quickly.

1.3.1 Prerequisites for Installing Scikit-Learn

Before installing Scikit-learn, you need to ensure that your environment has Python and several essential libraries installed. Scikit-learn relies on other Python libraries like NumPy, SciPy, and joblib for numerical operations, scientific computing, and model persistence. These dependencies must be installed in advance for Scikit-learn to function properly.

Python: Scikit-learn requires Python 3.7 or later. It is essential to have a working version of Python installed. If you do not have Python installed yet, you can download it from the official Python website.

pip: Scikit-learn is distributed as a Python package and can be installed using pip, the default Python package manager. Ensure that pip is installed and up to date by running the following command:

python -m pip install --upgrade pip

Additionally, if you're working on machine learning projects, it's recommended to have NumPy, SciPy, and matplotlib installed. These libraries provide the numerical and scientific computing functionality needed for data manipulation, linear algebra, and plotting.

1.3.2 Installing Scikit-Learn Using pip

The easiest and most common way to install Scikit-learn is by using pip, Python's package installer. This method ensures that Scikit-learn is installed along with its dependencies in a consistent and efficient manner.

Open a terminal or command prompt on your system.

To install the latest stable version of Scikit-learn, run the following command:

pip install scikit-learn

This command will automatically install Scikit-learn along with the required dependencies like NumPy, SciPy, and joblib.

1.3.3 Installing Scikit-Learn in a Virtual Environment

For most machine learning projects, it's a best practice to work within a virtual environment. Virtual environments provide isolated environments for your projects, which help avoid conflicts between dependencies required for different projects.

To set up a virtual environment, follow these steps:

Create a virtual environment: In your terminal or command prompt, navigate to your project directory, and run the following command to create a virtual environment:

python -m venv myenv

Here, myenv is the name of your virtual environment. You can choose any name you prefer.

Activate the virtual environment:

On Windows, activate the environment using:

myenv\Scripts\activate

On macOS or Linux, activate the environment with:

source myenv/bin/activate

Install Scikit-learn within the virtual environment:

pip install scikit-learn

By installing Scikit-learn in a virtual environment, you can ensure that the specific versions of libraries used in a project do not interfere with other projects or system-wide packages.

Deactivating the virtual environment: When you are done working, you can deactivate the virtual environment with:

deactivate

1.3.4 Installing Scikit-Learn Using Conda

Another popular way to install Scikit-learn is using Conda, which is a package manager and environment manager for Python. Conda is often preferred for data science workflows because it handles binary dependencies more effectively, especially when working with large datasets and complex dependencies.

To install Scikit-learn with Conda:

Install Anaconda or Miniconda if you do not already have it. Anaconda is a complete distribution of Python and R for scientific computing, which includes Conda, as well as popular data science libraries. Miniconda is a minimal version of Anaconda, which installs only Conda and lets you install libraries as needed.

You can download Anaconda from the official website, or Miniconda from the Miniconda download page.

Create a new Conda environment:

conda create --name myenv python=3.8

This will create a new environment called myenv with Python 3.8. You can specify another Python version if required.

Activate the Conda environment:

conda activate myenv

Install Scikit-learn:

conda install scikit-learn

Conda will handle the installation of Scikit-learn and its dependencies, ensuring that all the necessary libraries are installed correctly.

1.3.5 Verifying the Installation

Once Scikit-learn is installed, it is important to verify that the installation was successful. To do this, you can open a Python interactive shell (by typing python in your terminal or command prompt) and try importing Scikit-learn:

import sklearn

print(sklearn.__version__)

If the import is successful and the version number is printed without any errors, your Scikit-learn installation is complete.

1.3.6 Troubleshooting Installation Issues

While installing Scikit-learn is generally straightforward, you may run into some common issues during installation. Here are a few common problems and their solutions:

Dependency Conflicts: Sometimes, you may encounter errors related to incompatible versions of libraries like NumPy or SciPy. If this happens, try updating those libraries first using:

pip install --upgrade numpy scipy

Outdated pip version: If you are using an old version of pip, it may fail to install Scikit-learn correctly. To upgrade pip, run:

python -m pip install --upgrade pip

Permission Issues: On some systems, especially macOS or Linux, you may need to use sudo to install packages system-wide. However, it is recommended to use a virtual environment to avoid permission issues and conflicts.

Installing and setting up Scikit-learn is a straightforward process that can be done using pip, Conda, or within a virtual environment. Once installed, Scikit-learn provides a user-friendly interface to a wide range of machine learning algorithms and utilities. Whether you're working in a local development environment or using cloud-based tools, Scikit-learn is easy to integrate into any machine learning workflow.

By following the steps outlined in this section, you will have Scikit-learn up and running, ready to build and evaluate machine learning models with ease. The next step is to dive into the actual usage of Scikit-learn, starting with loading data and applying machine learning algorithms to solve real-world problems.

1.4 Understanding Scikit-Learn's API and Design Principles

Scikit-learn is widely praised for its clear and consistent application programming interface (API), which provides a user-friendly approach to building machine learning models. A key aspect of Scikit-learn's success lies in its intuitive and well-structured design principles, which enable practitioners, both beginners and experts, to quickly implement machine learning algorithms and integrate them into a broader data analysis workflow. Understanding how Scikit-learn's API is organized, as well as the core design principles behind it, is essential to becoming proficient in using this powerful library.

1.4.1 Scikit-Learn's API Structure

At the heart of Scikit-learn's design is its simple, consistent, and predictable API. The API is structured around several key concepts, including estimators, transformers, and predictors. These concepts unify how different machine learning models and data processing methods are applied in Scikit-learn. Let's break down the core components of the API and their relationships.

Estimators: The Core Building Blocks

In Scikit-learn, estimators are the primary objects used for both machine learning models and data preprocessing steps. An estimator is a general term for any object in Scikit-learn that learns from data. Estimators are used to fit models and transform data, and they share a consistent set of methods and attributes, making it easy to work with different types of models using the same interface.

Fit: The fit() method is used to train a model or learn parameters from the data. It takes input data (features) and, in most cases, the corresponding target labels (in supervised learning tasks) and learns the necessary patterns. This method is implemented by almost all Scikit-learn algorithms and transformers.

Example:

model.fit(X_train, y_train)

Predict: Once an estimator has been trained using fit(), it can make predictions on new data using the predict() method. This is particularly useful in supervised learning tasks, where the goal is to predict labels or values for unseen data.

Example:

predictions = model.predict(X_test)

Estimators include machine learning algorithms such as classification models (e.g., Support Vector Machines, Decision Trees, K-Nearest Neighbors) and regression models (e.g., Linear Regression, Ridge Regression).

Transformers: Preprocessing and Dimensionality Reduction

Transformers are a type of estimator specifically designed for data preprocessing tasks. These include operations like scaling features, encoding categorical variables, or reducing the dimensionality of data. Transformers modify the input data and return a transformed version.

Fit and Transform: Transformers implement the fit() method to learn necessary statistics (e.g., mean and standard deviation for scaling), and the transform() method to apply the learned transformation to the data.

Example:

```
from sklearn.preprocessing import StandardScaler
scaler = StandardScaler()
X_scaled = scaler.fit_transform(X_train)
```

Pipeline Integration: Transformers are commonly used in pipelines (discussed below) to streamline workflows involving multiple preprocessing steps.

Predictors: Combining Estimators and Transformers

Predictors combine the functionality of both estimators and transformers. A predictor is an estimator that can fit data, transform it, and make predictions. In Scikit-learn, many models like decision trees, random forests, and support vector machines are both estimators and predictors.

In practice, the terminology of "predictor" is usually interchangeable with "estimator" when discussing models that can predict outcomes. These predictors can be easily combined into pipelines, which makes the process of preprocessing and predicting seamless.

Model Evaluation and Metrics

Scikit-learn provides tools for model evaluation through various metrics and utilities. For supervised learning tasks, these include accuracy, precision, recall, F1 score, confusion matrix, and mean squared error (for regression). Evaluating models is an integral part of any machine learning workflow, and Scikit-learn standardizes this process through consistent methods like cross_val_score(), train_test_split(), and metrics submodules.

Example:

from sklearn.metrics import accuracy_score
accuracy = accuracy_score(y_true, y_pred)

1.4.2 Core Design Principles

Scikit-learn's API is designed with several guiding principles that focus on simplicity, flexibility, and ease of use. These principles ensure that Scikit-learn remains a powerful yet user-friendly tool for machine learning tasks.

Consistency

One of the core strengths of Scikit-learn is its consistent API design. Whether you're working with a simple model like K-Nearest Neighbors or a more complex model like Random Forests, the interface remains the same. All estimators follow a unified structure, with common methods like fit(), predict(), and score(). This consistency ensures that once you learn the API for one model, you can easily transfer that knowledge to other models.

For example, training a model in Scikit-learn typically follows this basic pattern:

model = SomeModel()
model.fit(X_train, y_train)
predictions = model.predict(X_test)

This predictable structure makes Scikit-learn intuitive and reduces the learning curve.

Simplicity

Scikit-learn is designed to be simple and intuitive for users with varying levels of expertise. Its API emphasizes minimalism and avoids unnecessary complexity. Users can quickly apply algorithms to real-world problems by following straightforward, high-level commands.

Scikit-learn's reliance on Python's native data structures (such as NumPy arrays or pandas DataFrames) further simplifies the experience, as users are not required to learn complex new data structures to use the library effectively.

Additionally, many machine learning algorithms can be implemented in just a few lines of code, making Scikit-learn a great tool for both beginners and experienced data scientists.

Extensibility

While Scikit-learn is simple to use, it is also highly extensible. Scikit-learn's modular approach allows users to easily integrate custom components, such as custom transformers, models, and evaluation metrics. For instance, users can create their own transformer by subclassing the BaseEstimator and TransformerMixin classes.

This extensibility is key for more advanced applications, where users may need to tailor their machine learning workflows or create new models. Scikit-learn also supports parallel processing for certain tasks, such as cross-validation and grid search, which helps improve performance for large datasets.

Reusability

The library's design encourages reusability. Once a model is trained, it can be reused to make predictions on new data or saved and loaded for later use. Scikit-learn supports model persistence using the joblib library, allowing users to save models to disk and reload them when necessary. This capability is essential for deploying machine learning models to production environments.

Example:

```
from joblib import dump, load
dump(model, 'model.joblib')  # Save model
model = load('model.joblib')  # Load model
```

Pipelines for Workflow Automation

A key feature of Scikit-learn's design is the Pipeline class, which allows users to bundle multiple steps of a machine learning workflow into a single object. This is especially useful when you need to perform several preprocessing tasks (such as feature scaling, encoding, or dimensionality reduction) in sequence before training a model. By using pipelines, users can automate these steps, reduce redundancy, and ensure that transformations are applied in the correct order.

Example:

```
from sklearn.pipeline import Pipeline
from sklearn.preprocessing import StandardScaler
from sklearn.linear_model import LogisticRegression

pipeline = Pipeline([
    ('scaler', StandardScaler()),
    ('model', LogisticRegression())
])
pipeline.fit(X_train, y_train)
```

This ensures that the scaling operation is applied to both the training and testing datasets in the same manner.

Scikit-learn's API is one of the defining features of the library, and its thoughtful design principles contribute to its widespread adoption among data scientists and machine learning practitioners. The consistent, simple, and extensible structure of the API makes it easy to implement and experiment with machine learning models, while also providing flexibility for more advanced applications. Understanding Scikit-learn's design and core API components is essential for leveraging its full potential, and it lays the foundation for building efficient, reusable, and maintainable machine learning workflows.

2. Fundamentals of Machine Learning with Scikit-Learn

Before diving into Scikit-Learn, it's important to grasp the fundamentals of machine learning. This chapter covers key ML concepts such as supervised vs. unsupervised learning, bias-variance tradeoff, overfitting, and the essential steps of a typical machine learning workflow. You'll also build your first ML model using Scikit-Learn to get hands-on experience.

2.1 Understanding Supervised and Unsupervised Learning

Machine learning, as a subfield of artificial intelligence, revolves around algorithms that enable computers to learn from data and make predictions or decisions. At the heart of machine learning, two main paradigms—supervised learning and unsupervised learning—play crucial roles in solving real-world problems. Understanding the distinction between these two types of learning is foundational to selecting the right approach for various machine learning tasks.

In this section, we will explore the key differences between supervised and unsupervised learning, their applications, and the types of algorithms commonly used in each paradigm.

2.1.1 What is Supervised Learning?

Supervised learning is the most widely used paradigm in machine learning, where the model is trained on labeled data. Labeled data means that the dataset contains both input features and the corresponding output labels or targets. The primary goal of supervised learning is to learn a mapping from input data (features) to output labels (targets), which can then be used to predict the labels of unseen data.

In supervised learning, the algorithm learns from the training data by finding patterns that link the inputs to their corresponding outputs. Once trained, the model can make predictions on new, unseen data by applying the patterns it learned during training.

Types of Supervised Learning

Supervised learning is generally divided into two main categories based on the nature of the target variable:

Classification: In classification tasks, the target variable is categorical. The goal is to assign data points into predefined classes or categories. For example, in an email spam filter, the algorithm is trained to classify emails as either "spam" or "not spam."

Example problems: Email spam detection, sentiment analysis, image classification (e.g., identifying whether an image contains a cat or a dog), medical diagnosis (e.g., classifying whether a tumor is benign or malignant).

Regression: In regression tasks, the target variable is continuous. The goal is to predict a continuous value based on the input features. For example, predicting the price of a house based on features like the number of rooms, location, and square footage.

Example problems: Predicting stock prices, forecasting weather, estimating real estate prices, or predicting sales revenue.

Key Concepts in Supervised Learning

Training Data: This is the dataset that includes both the input features and the correct output labels. The model learns from this data.

Testing Data: This is a separate dataset that the model has not seen during training. It is used to evaluate the performance of the trained model by checking how well it generalizes to new, unseen data.

Loss Function: In supervised learning, the loss function measures the difference between the predicted output and the actual output. The goal is to minimize the loss, which is typically done using optimization algorithms like gradient descent.

Overfitting and Underfitting:

- Overfitting occurs when a model learns the training data too well, capturing noise and irrelevant patterns, which leads to poor generalization on new data.
- Underfitting occurs when a model is too simple to capture the underlying patterns in the data, resulting in poor performance on both the training data and unseen data.
- **Example**: Supervised Learning with Scikit-Learn

A common example of supervised learning is using a classification algorithm to predict whether a passenger survived or not on the Titanic. The dataset might include features like age, class, and gender, and the goal is to predict whether the passenger survived (target label).

```
from sklearn.model_selection import train_test_split
from sklearn.ensemble import RandomForestClassifier
from sklearn.metrics import accuracy_score

# Sample Titanic dataset
X = df[['Age', 'Pclass', 'Sex']]  # Features
y = df['Survived']  # Target variable (Survived or not)

# Split the dataset into training and testing sets
X_train, X_test, y_train, y_test = train_test_split(X, y, test_size=0.2, random_state=42)

# Initialize a classifier
clf = RandomForestClassifier()

# Train the model
clf.fit(X_train, y_train)

# Make predictions
y_pred = clf.predict(X_test)

# Evaluate the model
accuracy = accuracy_score(y_test, y_pred)
print(f'Accuracy: {accuracy}')
```

In this example, a random forest classifier is trained to predict the likelihood of survival based on input features, and its performance is evaluated using accuracy.

2.1.2 What is Unsupervised Learning?

Unsupervised learning, in contrast to supervised learning, is a machine learning paradigm where the model is trained on unlabeled data. In unsupervised learning, there is no target variable or output labels. The goal is to find patterns, structures, or relationships within the input data, such as clustering similar data points or reducing the dimensionality of the dataset.

Since there are no predefined labels, unsupervised learning algorithms attempt to explore the inherent structure of the data. It is used when the task is more exploratory, and there is no clear outcome or prediction.

Types of Unsupervised Learning

Clustering: Clustering involves grouping similar data points together based on some measure of similarity. The objective is to find patterns or structures in the data without knowing the exact categories beforehand. The model tries to partition the data into distinct clusters that share similar characteristics.

Example problems: Customer segmentation in marketing, grouping articles based on topic, identifying patterns in biological data, market basket analysis.

Dimensionality Reduction: In dimensionality reduction, the goal is to reduce the number of input features while retaining as much relevant information as possible. This is particularly useful when dealing with high-dimensional data (e.g., images, text data) and aims to simplify the data, remove noise, or make it easier to visualize.

Example problems: Visualizing high-dimensional datasets, compressing images, reducing the feature space for supervised learning.

Key Concepts in Unsupervised Learning

Unlabeled Data: In unsupervised learning, the model is given data without any target labels. The model's task is to find structure, relationships, or groupings within the data based on the input features alone.

Cluster Centroids: In clustering algorithms, the cluster centroids represent the "center" of each cluster. These centroids are used to measure the similarity between data points and the cluster they belong to.

Principal Components: In dimensionality reduction techniques like PCA (Principal Component Analysis), principal components are the new axes that capture the most variance in the data.

Example: Unsupervised Learning with Scikit-Learn

A common application of unsupervised learning is clustering. For example, using the K-Means algorithm to cluster customers based on purchasing behavior:

```
from sklearn.cluster import KMeans
import matplotlib.pyplot as plt

# Sample dataset: Customer features (e.g., annual income, spending score)
X = df[['Income', 'SpendingScore']]

# Initialize KMeans algorithm
kmeans = KMeans(n_clusters=3)

# Fit the model
kmeans.fit(X)

# Predict the clusters
y_kmeans = kmeans.predict(X)

# Plot the clusters
plt.scatter(X['Income'], X['SpendingScore'], c=y_kmeans, s=50, cmap='viridis')
plt.show()
```

In this example, the K-Means algorithm is used to group customers into three clusters based on their income and spending behavior. The model does not have any labeled target but instead identifies inherent groups in the data.

2.1.3 Key Differences Between Supervised and Unsupervised Learning

Aspect	Supervised Learning	Unsupervised Learning
Data Type	Labeled data (input-output pairs)	Unlabeled data (only inputs)
Goal	Learn a mapping from inputs to outputs	Find patterns or structures in data
Types of Problems	Classification, regression	Clustering, dimensionality reduction
Output	Predicted labels or continuous values	Groupings, reduced data representations
Examples	Spam detection, price prediction	Customer segmentation, anomaly detection
Evaluation	Accuracy, F1 score, RMSE, etc.	Internal measures (e.g., cluster purity, silhouette score)

Supervised and unsupervised learning are two of the most important paradigms in machine learning, each suited to different types of problems. In supervised learning, we aim to learn a mapping from inputs to outputs, while in unsupervised learning, the focus is on uncovering hidden structures or patterns within the data. Understanding these fundamental concepts is essential for selecting the right approach for a given machine learning task.

By gaining a deeper understanding of both paradigms, machine learning practitioners can apply the appropriate techniques to solve real-world problems, whether it's classifying data, predicting outcomes, clustering similar items, or reducing dimensionality for further analysis.

2.2 Key Machine Learning Concepts (Bias-Variance Tradeoff, Overfitting, etc.)

Machine learning (ML) is a complex field, and understanding some of its core concepts is essential for developing effective models and ensuring their generalizability to unseen data. Among these concepts, the bias-variance tradeoff, overfitting, underfitting, and several other key principles play a crucial role in how machine learning models behave and perform. In this section, we will explore these concepts in depth, explaining their significance, how they interrelate, and how to manage them to build robust models.

2.2.1 Bias-Variance Tradeoff

The bias-variance tradeoff is a fundamental concept in machine learning that describes the tradeoff between two sources of error in a model's predictions:

Bias: Bias refers to the error introduced by making assumptions about the data. A model with high bias typically makes strong assumptions about the underlying patterns in the data, leading to an oversimplified model. This can cause the model to miss important nuances and result in underfitting (more on that shortly). Models with high bias tend to perform poorly on both the training data and unseen data because they fail to capture the true complexity of the problem.

Variance: Variance refers to the error caused by the model's sensitivity to small fluctuations in the training data. A model with high variance is highly flexible and can fit the training data very well, but it may fail to generalize to new, unseen data. High variance typically leads to overfitting. In this case, the model learns not only the underlying patterns in the training data but also the noise or irrelevant details, which reduces its ability to generalize.

The bias-variance tradeoff occurs because reducing one type of error often increases the other. For example, if we use a very simple model with a strong assumption (high bias), it may perform poorly on both the training and testing data. On the other hand, if we use a very complex model with a lot of parameters (high variance), it may fit the training data perfectly but perform poorly on the testing data due to overfitting.

The goal is to find a balance between bias and variance that minimizes the total error, which includes both bias and variance. This is often achieved by selecting the appropriate model complexity and using techniques like cross-validation to assess model performance on unseen data.

- **High Bias, Low Variance**: A simple model (e.g., linear regression) that may not capture the underlying complexity of the data, leading to underfitting.
- **Low Bias, High Variance**: A complex model (e.g., deep decision trees) that fits the training data very well but is prone to overfitting.
- **Low Bias, Low Variance**: An ideal model that captures the underlying patterns in the data without overfitting or underfitting.

Visualizing Bias-Variance Tradeoff

One common way to visualize the bias-variance tradeoff is by plotting the model error as a function of model complexity. As model complexity increases, bias decreases but variance increases, leading to an optimal point where total error is minimized.

2.2.2 Overfitting and Underfitting

Two common issues that arise during the training of machine learning models are overfitting and underfitting.

Overfitting occurs when a model becomes too complex and learns not only the underlying patterns in the training data but also the noise and random fluctuations. An overfit model fits the training data almost perfectly, but when evaluated on new, unseen data (such as the test set), its performance deteriorates significantly. This happens because the model has learned specific details that do not generalize to other data points.

Symptoms of Overfitting:

- Extremely low error on the training data, but high error on the test data.
- The model is too complex or has too many parameters relative to the amount of data available.

How to Avoid Overfitting:

- Use simpler models (e.g., linear regression or decision trees with limited depth).
- Regularization techniques such as L1 (Lasso) and L2 (Ridge) can penalize large model coefficients to prevent overfitting.
- Use cross-validation to assess the model's performance on different subsets of the data.
- Increase the amount of training data to help the model generalize better.
- Pruning decision trees to limit their complexity.

Underfitting occurs when a model is too simple to capture the underlying patterns in the data. An underfit model will have high bias and will likely perform poorly on both the training and test data. Underfitting is usually a result of using overly simplistic models, insufficient training, or inadequate feature engineering.

Symptoms of Underfitting:

- High error on both the training and test data.
- The model fails to learn the relationships in the data and is too simplistic.

How to Avoid Underfitting:

- Increase model complexity (e.g., use more complex algorithms like random forests or neural networks).
- Add more features that better represent the data.
- Train the model for more epochs if using iterative algorithms like gradient descent.

2.2.3 Regularization

Regularization is a technique used to prevent overfitting by adding a penalty to the model for having overly large or complex parameters. This technique helps balance the bias-variance tradeoff by encouraging simpler models. Common regularization methods include:

L1 Regularization (Lasso): This technique adds a penalty equal to the absolute value of the coefficients. It can drive some coefficients to zero, effectively performing feature selection and creating sparse models.

L2 Regularization (Ridge): This technique adds a penalty equal to the square of the coefficients. It does not necessarily eliminate features but rather reduces the magnitude of the coefficients, making the model simpler and less prone to overfitting.

Elastic Net: A combination of L1 and L2 regularization that balances the benefits of both methods.

2.2.4 Cross-Validation

Cross-validation is a technique used to evaluate the performance of a machine learning model on multiple subsets of the dataset. Instead of splitting the data into just one training set and one test set, cross-validation divides the data into several smaller subsets (or folds). The model is trained on a combination of these folds and tested on the remaining fold. This process is repeated multiple times, and the model's performance is averaged across all iterations.

K-fold cross-validation is the most commonly used method. For example, in 5-fold cross-validation, the dataset is split into five parts, and the model is trained five times, each time leaving out a different fold as the test set.

Cross-validation helps to ensure that the model's performance is consistent and generalizes well to unseen data. It also provides a more reliable estimate of model performance than using a single train-test split.

2.2.5 Model Evaluation Metrics

To assess how well a machine learning model is performing, several evaluation metrics can be used. These metrics vary depending on the task (classification or regression) and the goals of the model.

For Classification:

- **Accuracy**: The proportion of correct predictions made by the model.
- **Precision**: The ratio of true positive predictions to all positive predictions made by the model.
- **Recall**: The ratio of true positive predictions to all actual positives in the data.
- **F1-Score**: The harmonic mean of precision and recall, providing a balance between the two.
- **Confusion Matrix**: A table that visualizes the performance of a classification algorithm, showing the counts of true positives, true negatives, false positives, and false negatives.

For Regression:

- **Mean Squared Error (MSE):** The average of the squared differences between predicted and actual values.
- **Root Mean Squared Error (RMSE):** The square root of MSE, which gives error in the same units as the target variable.
- **R-Squared (R²):** A measure of how well the model's predictions match the actual values, with higher values indicating better performance.

Key machine learning concepts like the bias-variance tradeoff, overfitting, underfitting, and regularization are critical for building effective and robust models. Striking the right balance between bias and variance is essential to avoid both underfitting and overfitting. Understanding these concepts helps practitioners to choose appropriate models, tune hyperparameters, and apply techniques such as cross-validation and regularization to achieve good generalization performance. By applying these principles, machine learning practitioners can build models that not only perform well on the training data but also generalize effectively to new, unseen data.

2.3 Steps of a Typical Machine Learning Workflow

A typical machine learning (ML) workflow involves a series of well-defined steps aimed at transforming raw data into actionable insights or predictions. From problem definition to model deployment, each step is crucial for building a successful machine learning solution. In this section, we will outline the key steps of a standard machine learning workflow, emphasizing best practices and methodologies used by practitioners in the field.

2.3.1 1. Defining the Problem

The first and most important step in any machine learning workflow is to clearly define the problem you are trying to solve. This step helps to understand the context and objectives of the project, guiding the choice of data, algorithms, and evaluation metrics.

Business Understanding: Understand the broader business or research goals. Are you trying to predict a specific outcome, classify categories, or uncover patterns in the data? The problem definition will help determine the type of machine learning approach (supervised, unsupervised, reinforcement learning) you should take.

Feasibility Check: Assess whether it is feasible to solve the problem with the available data and resources. If not, you may need to collect more data or rethink the approach.

Example: If you're building a model to predict customer churn, the problem is clearly defined as a binary classification task. The goal is to classify customers as either likely to churn (leave the company) or not.

2.3.2 2. Data Collection

Once the problem is defined, the next step is to gather the relevant data needed for training and evaluating the machine learning model. Data collection can take many forms, such as pulling data from internal databases, gathering data via APIs, web scraping, or using publicly available datasets.

Source Identification: Identify where the data will come from. Will you rely on structured data from databases, unstructured data (e.g., text or images), or a combination of both? Ensure the data is relevant and representative of the problem at hand.

Data Quantity and Quality: Ensure that the dataset is large enough to capture the patterns in the problem domain. It is equally important that the data is clean, free from errors, and accurately reflects the real-world scenario.

Example: In the customer churn prediction example, data may be collected from CRM systems, such as customer demographics, account details, usage patterns, and previous interactions with the company.

2.3.3 3. Data Preprocessing

Once you have collected the data, the next crucial step is to preprocess it. Raw data is often messy, inconsistent, and contains errors, missing values, or irrelevant information. Preprocessing involves cleaning and transforming the data to make it suitable for machine learning algorithms.

Handling Missing Data: Missing data can be filled in using techniques like imputation, or rows/columns containing missing values can be removed entirely, depending on the dataset and the significance of the missing data.

Data Cleaning: Removing duplicates, correcting errors, and handling outliers to prevent them from negatively affecting model performance.

Feature Engineering: Creating new features or transforming existing ones to improve the model's predictive power. This could include encoding categorical variables, normalizing numerical features, and creating interaction features.

Feature Selection: Reducing the number of features used in the model to eliminate irrelevant or redundant variables. Feature selection can improve model efficiency and generalization.

Splitting Data: Divide the data into training and testing sets to ensure that the model is evaluated on unseen data. A common split is 80/20 or 70/30, where 80% of the data is used for training and 20% for testing.

Example: In the churn prediction example, you might encode categorical variables such as customer region or plan type into numerical values (using one-hot encoding), fill missing values in customer usage data with the mean, and remove features that do not seem relevant, such as a customer's favorite color.

2.3.4 4. Choosing a Model

Once the data is prepared, the next step is to choose a machine learning model that best fits the problem. The choice of model depends on the type of problem (classification, regression, clustering), the amount of data, and the model's interpretability.

Supervised Learning Models: If you have labeled data, consider supervised models like:

- **Classification Models (for categorical outcomes):** Logistic regression, decision trees, random forests, support vector machines (SVM), and neural networks.
- **Regression Models (for continuous outcomes):** Linear regression, decision trees, and ensemble methods like gradient boosting.

Unsupervised Learning Models: If you have unlabeled data, you may want to explore unsupervised learning techniques like clustering (e.g., K-means) or dimensionality reduction (e.g., PCA).

Hyperparameter Tuning: While choosing a model, you also need to decide on the model's hyperparameters, such as the depth of a decision tree or the learning rate of a neural network. These hyperparameters affect how well the model performs and must often be fine-tuned.

Example: In the customer churn prediction example, since we are predicting a binary outcome (churn vs. non-churn), we could start with a classification model like logistic regression or random forests.

2.3.5 5. Model Training

After selecting a model, the next step is to train it on the training data. During this step, the machine learning algorithm learns the relationship between the input features and the target labels (in the case of supervised learning) or tries to identify patterns in the data (in the case of unsupervised learning).

Model Fitting: The model's parameters are adjusted based on the training data to minimize the error between the predicted and actual values. This process is typically done iteratively using an optimization algorithm, such as gradient descent.

Cross-Validation: Use techniques like k-fold cross-validation during training to validate the model's performance on multiple subsets of the data. This helps ensure that the model generalizes well and is not overfitting to one particular subset of data.

Example: In the churn prediction model, during training, the logistic regression model would learn the best coefficients for the features (e.g., customer age, plan type, usage patterns) that predict customer churn.

2.3.6 6. Model Evaluation

Once the model is trained, it's important to evaluate its performance using the test data. The purpose of evaluation is to assess how well the model generalizes to unseen data and to determine whether the model is suitable for deployment.

Evaluation Metrics: The evaluation metrics will vary depending on the type of problem you are solving. For classification tasks, common metrics include accuracy, precision, recall, F1-score, and the ROC-AUC score. For regression tasks, metrics such as mean squared error (MSE) and R-squared are often used.

Confusion Matrix: In classification problems, a confusion matrix helps you understand the types of errors the model is making, such as false positives and false negatives.

Model Comparison: If multiple models were tested, compare their performance based on the evaluation metrics. Choose the model that performs best according to the problem's requirements.

Example: In the churn prediction task, you would assess the model's accuracy, recall (for detecting churners), and precision (for minimizing false positives) to determine if it meets the required performance criteria.

2.3.7 7. Model Tuning and Improvement

After evaluating the initial model, it's often necessary to fine-tune or improve it. This step involves adjusting hyperparameters, improving feature selection, or trying different models to see if performance can be enhanced.

Hyperparameter Tuning: Use techniques like grid search or random search to explore a wide range of hyperparameters and identify the combination that produces the best performance.

Ensemble Methods: Consider combining multiple models using techniques like bagging, boosting, or stacking to improve performance.

Example: In the churn prediction case, you could try tuning the regularization parameter in logistic regression or use a more complex model like random forests to improve accuracy.

2.3.8 8. Model Deployment

Once the model is performing well, it is time to deploy it in a real-world setting. This can involve integrating the model into an existing application or building a new system for predictions.

Model Deployment: Deploy the trained model to a production environment where it can make predictions on new data in real-time or batch mode.

Monitoring and Maintenance: Continuously monitor the model's performance to ensure it remains accurate as new data is introduced. Retrain the model periodically if its performance starts to degrade.

Example: In the churn prediction example, once the model is deployed, it could be used to predict which customers are likely to churn, allowing the company to proactively offer retention incentives.

The typical machine learning workflow involves a series of steps that transform raw data into valuable insights. By following these steps—defining the problem, collecting data, preprocessing, selecting and training the model, evaluating and tuning the model, and deploying it—you can systematically approach any machine learning task and ensure that the resulting model is both effective and reliable. Each step builds upon the last, ensuring that you are taking the necessary actions to address the problem at hand while maximizing the potential for success.

2.4 First Machine Learning Model in Scikit-Learn

Scikit-learn is one of the most popular and versatile machine learning libraries in Python, designed to be simple and efficient for data analysis and modeling. In this section, we will walk through the process of building your first machine learning model using Scikit-learn. We will cover everything from loading a dataset, preparing the data, to training and evaluating a model. For simplicity, we will focus on a basic classification task using a well-known dataset — the Iris dataset.

2.4.1 Overview of the Iris Dataset

The Iris dataset is a classic dataset in machine learning, often used for demonstrating classification algorithms. It consists of 150 samples from three different species of Iris flowers (setosa, versicolor, virginica). Each sample contains four features:

- Sepal Length (cm)
- Sepal Width (cm)
- Petal Length (cm)
- Petal Width (cm)

The goal is to predict the species of the Iris flower based on these four features. This is a classification problem where the output variable (target) is categorical, consisting of three classes.

2.4.2 Importing Libraries and Loading the Data

First, let's start by importing the necessary libraries and loading the Iris dataset. Scikit-learn provides a simple function to load this dataset directly from the library.

```
# Import nooocssary libraries
import numpy as np
import pandas as pd
from sklearn.datasets import load_iris
from sklearn.model_selection import train_test_split
from sklearn.preprocessing import StandardScaler
from sklearn.linear_model import LogisticRegression
from sklearn.metrics import accuracy_score, confusion_matrix, classification_report
```

- **load_iris():** This function loads the Iris dataset as a dictionary-like object containing both the features and the target labels.
- **train_test_split():** This function splits the dataset into training and testing sets to evaluate the model's performance.
- **StandardScaler():** This is used to scale the features so that all of them have the same standard scale, improving the model's performance.
- **LogisticRegression():** A simple machine learning algorithm that can be used for classification tasks.
- **accuracy_score(), confusion_matrix(), classification_report():** These are evaluation metrics used to assess the model's performance.

2.4.3 Loading the Iris Dataset

Let's load the Iris dataset and take a look at the first few records to understand the structure of the data.

```
# Load the Iris dataset
iris = load_iris()

# Convert the data into a Pandas DataFrame for easier manipulation
df = pd.DataFrame(data=iris.data, columns=iris.feature_names)

# Add the target variable to the DataFrame
df['species'] = pd.Categorical.from_codes(iris.target, iris.target_names)

# Display the first few rows of the dataset
print(df.head())
```

This will print a table with the first five rows of the Iris dataset, showing the features (sepal length, sepal width, petal length, and petal width) along with the corresponding species for each sample.

2.4.4 Splitting the Data into Training and Testing Sets

Before training the model, we need to split the data into a training set (to train the model) and a testing set (to evaluate the model). Typically, we use a 70/30 or 80/20 split for training/testing. Scikit-learn's train_test_split() function makes this task easy:

```
# Split the data into training and testing sets (80% training, 20% testing)
X_train, X_test, y_train, y_test = train_test_split(iris.data, iris.target, test_size=0.2, random_state=42)

# Check the shapes of the resulting splits
print(f"Training features shape: {X_train.shape}")
print(f"Testing features shape: {X_test.shape}")
```

Here:

- X_train and X_test are the feature matrices (inputs).
- y_train and y_test are the target labels (species) corresponding to each sample.
- We use test_size=0.2 to specify that 20% of the data will be reserved for testing.

2.4.5 Scaling the Data

Machine learning models typically perform better when features are on the same scale. In this case, we will standardize the data by using the StandardScaler. This ensures that each feature has a mean of 0 and a standard deviation of 1, which helps many machine learning algorithms (like logistic regression or support vector machines) converge faster and perform better.

```
# Initialize the StandardScaler
scaler = StandardScaler()

# Fit the scaler to the training data and transform both training and test data
X_train_scaled = scaler.fit_transform(X_train)
X_test_scaled = scaler.transform(X_test)
```

- **fit_transform():** This fits the scaler to the training data and scales it.
- **transform():** This scales the test data based on the parameters learned from the training data.

2.4.6 Building and Training the Model

Next, we choose a machine learning model to train. For simplicity, we'll use Logistic Regression, which is a commonly used algorithm for binary and multiclass classification problems.

```
# Initialize the Logistic Regression model
model = LogisticRegression(max_iter=200)

# Train the model using the scaled training data
model.fit(X_train_scaled, y_train)
```

- **fit():** This method fits the model to the training data by learning the relationships between the features and the target labels.

2.4.7 Evaluating the Model

Once the model is trained, we evaluate its performance on the test data using several metrics. First, we make predictions using the predict() method, and then we evaluate the model using accuracy, confusion matrix, and classification report.

```
# Make predictions on the test data
y_pred = model.predict(X_test_scaled)

# Evaluate the model
accuracy = accuracy_score(y_test, y_pred)
conf_matrix = confusion_matrix(y_test, y_pred)
class_report = classification_report(y_test, y_pred)

# Print the evaluation results
print(f"Accuracy: {accuracy:.2f}")
print("Confusion Matrix:")
print(conf_matrix)
print("Classification Report:")
print(class_report)
```

- **accuracy_score():** Measures the proportion of correct predictions.
- **confusion_matrix():** Shows a matrix that helps evaluate classification performance, indicating how many predictions were correct or incorrect for each class.
- **classification_report():** Provides precision, recall, and F1-score for each class.

2.4.8 Interpreting the Results

The evaluation metrics will give you insights into how well the model is performing:

- **Accuracy**: This tells you the proportion of correct predictions, though it may not always be reliable if there is class imbalance.
- **Confusion Matrix**: This matrix helps you identify how many false positives and false negatives occurred for each class.
- **Classification Report**: This includes precision, recall, and F1-score for each class, providing a more detailed evaluation than accuracy alone.

2.4.9 Example Output

Here's what the output might look like after running the code:

```
Accuracy: 1.00
Confusion Matrix:
[[14  0  0]
 [ 0 13  0]
 [ 0  0 13]]
Classification Report:
              precision    recall  f1-score   support

      setosa       1.00      1.00      1.00        14
  versicolor       1.00      1.00      1.00        13
   virginica       1.00      1.00      1.00        13


    accuracy                           1.00        40
   macro avg       1.00      1.00      1.00        40
weighted avg       1.00      1.00      1.00        40
```

In this case, the model achieved perfect accuracy (1.00), which is common for this simple dataset with a logistic regression model. However, in real-world scenarios, you may not always achieve perfect accuracy, and the confusion matrix and classification report will help identify any areas where the model can be improved.

In this section, we've gone through the process of building and evaluating your first machine learning model using Scikit-learn. We used the Iris dataset for classification, applied basic preprocessing (scaling the data), trained a logistic regression model, and evaluated its performance using accuracy, confusion matrix, and classification report. This simple workflow demonstrates how accessible machine learning can be with Scikit-learn and sets the foundation for building more complex models and solving real-world problems.

3. Working with Data in Scikit-Learn

Data is the foundation of every machine learning model. In this chapter, you'll learn how to load, clean, and preprocess datasets efficiently. We will cover techniques for handling missing values, encoding categorical variables, normalizing features, and splitting data for training and testing, ensuring your models receive high-quality inputs.

3.1 Loading Datasets from Scikit-Learn and External Sources

One of the key steps in building machine learning models is obtaining the right dataset. Scikit-learn, one of the most widely used libraries for machine learning in Python, offers a wide range of built-in datasets that can be accessed easily for experimentation and model development. Additionally, data may be stored in various external formats, such as CSV, Excel, SQL databases, and more. In this section, we will explore how to load datasets both from Scikit-learn and from external sources, with practical examples.

3.1.1 Loading Datasets from Scikit-Learn

Scikit-learn provides several built-in datasets that are great for learning and practicing machine learning algorithms. These datasets are categorized into three groups:

- **Toy Datasets**: Small datasets like the Iris, Wine, and Boston Housing datasets.
- **Real-World Datasets**: Larger datasets like the 20 Newsgroups dataset or the California Housing dataset.
- **Generated Datasets**: Datasets that are generated for specific use cases, such as blobs, circles, and moons.
- **Example**: Loading the Iris Dataset

The Iris dataset is one of the most popular datasets for classification problems. It consists of 150 samples of Iris flowers, with four features each (sepal length, sepal width, petal length, and petal width), and three target classes (species: setosa, versicolor, and virginica).

Here's how to load and explore the Iris dataset in Scikit-learn:

```
# Import necessary libraries
from sklearn.datasets import load_iris
import pandas as pd
```

```
# Load the Iris dataset
iris = load_iris()

# Convert the dataset into a Pandas DataFrame for easier exploration
df = pd.DataFrame(iris.data, columns=iris.feature_names)

# Add target column (species) to the DataFrame
df['species'] = iris.target

# Display the first few rows of the dataset
print(df.head())
```

Explanation:

- **load_iris():** This function loads the Iris dataset and returns a dictionary-like object containing both the data and the target labels.
- **iris.data**: A NumPy array containing the feature values.
- **iris.target**: A NumPy array containing the target labels (species).
- **iris.feature_names**: The names of the features (sepal length, sepal width, petal length, petal width).

Example: Loading the Wine Dataset

The Wine dataset is another classification dataset, with 13 features describing various chemical properties of wines from three different cultivars. Here's how to load it:

```
# Import necessary libraries
from sklearn.datasets import load_wine

# Load the Wine dataset
wine = load_wine()

# Convert the dataset into a Pandas DataFrame
df_wine = pd.DataFrame(wine.data, columns=wine.feature_names)

# Add target column (wine class) to the DataFrame
df_wine['class'] = wine.target

# Display the first few rows of the dataset
```

```
print(df_wine.head())
```

Explanation:

load_wine(): Loads the Wine dataset, which has 13 features and 3 possible target classes (wine cultivars).

3.1.2 Loading Datasets from External Sources

While Scikit-learn offers many built-in datasets, real-world machine learning projects typically involve working with data from external sources. Data can be stored in various formats such as CSV files, Excel files, SQL databases, JSON files, and more. In this section, we will explore how to load data from some common external sources.

Loading Data from CSV Files

CSV (Comma Separated Values) is one of the most common formats for storing datasets. You can easily load a CSV file into a Pandas DataFrame, which is a versatile structure for data manipulation.

Here's an example of how to load a CSV file:

```
# Import necessary libraries
import pandas as pd

# Load a CSV file into a Pandas DataFrame
df_csv = pd.read_csv('path_to_your_file.csv')

# Display the first few rows of the dataset
print(df_csv.head())
```

Explanation:

- **pd.read_csv():** This function is used to load data from a CSV file into a Pandas DataFrame.
- The path provided can either be an absolute path or relative to the current working directory.
- Once the data is loaded into a DataFrame, you can use Pandas functions to explore and manipulate it.

Loading Data from Excel Files

Excel files (XLSX format) are another common format for storing data. To load data from Excel, you can use the read_excel() function from Pandas. First, ensure that you have the required library installed (openpyxl or xlrd), as they are needed to read Excel files.

Here's how to load data from an Excel file:

```
# Import necessary libraries
import pandas as pd

# Load an Excel file into a Pandas DataFrame
df_excel = pd.read_excel('path_to_your_file.xlsx', sheet_name='Sheet1')

# Display the first few rows of the dataset
print(df_excel.head())
```

Explanation:

- **pd.read_excel():** This function reads an Excel file and loads the specified sheet into a DataFrame. You can specify the sheet name or the sheet index (default is 0).
- You may need to install dependencies like openpyxl for reading .xlsx files.
- Loading Data from SQL Databases

In many real-world applications, data is stored in relational databases like MySQL, PostgreSQL, or SQLite. To load data from a SQL database into Python, you can use the pandas.read_sql() function, along with a connection to the database.

Here's an example of how to load data from a SQL database:

```
# Import necessary libraries
import pandas as pd
import sqlite3

# Establish a connection to the database (replace with your database file)
conn = sqlite3.connect('your_database.db')

# Query the data and load it into a Pandas DataFrame
df_sql = pd.read_sql('SELECT * FROM your_table_name', conn)
```

```
# Display the first few rows of the dataset
print(df_sql.head())

# Close the connection
conn.close()
```

Explanation:

- sqlite3.connect(): Establishes a connection to an SQLite database. For other types of databases (like MySQL or PostgreSQL), you would use a different connector (e.g., mysql.connector or psycopg2).
- pd.read_sql(): Reads data from a SQL query directly into a Pandas DataFrame.
- conn.close(): Always close the connection once done.

Loading Data from JSON Files

JSON (JavaScript Object Notation) is a popular data exchange format, especially when dealing with web data. You can load JSON files into Python using Pandas as well.

Here's how to load data from a JSON file:

```
# Import necessary libraries
import pandas as pd

# Load a JSON file into a Pandas DataFrame
df_json = pd.read_json('path_to_your_file.json')

# Display the first few rows of the dataset
print(df_json.head())
```

Explanation:

pd.read_json(): This function is used to load data from a JSON file into a Pandas DataFrame.

3.1.3 Summary of Common Data Loading Methods

Data Source	Function to Load	Notes
Scikit-learn	`load_iris()`, `load_wine()`, etc.	These are built-in datasets for quick experimentation.
CSV File	`pd.read_csv()`	A common format for data storage, supported natively in Pandas.
Excel File	`pd.read_excel()`	Can load data from Excel (.xlsx) files.
SQL Database	`pd.read_sql()`	Allows querying and loading data from a SQL database.
JSON File	`pd.read_json()`	Used for loading data in JSON format, often used in web APIs.

In this section, we covered how to load datasets both from Scikit-learn (using built-in datasets like the Iris and Wine datasets) and from external sources like CSV, Excel, SQL databases, and JSON files. Scikit-learn's built-in datasets are ideal for learning and testing, while external sources allow for working with real-world data. Once the data is loaded, you can proceed with exploring, cleaning, preprocessing, and modeling it for various machine learning tasks.

3.2 Handling Missing Values and Data Cleaning

Data cleaning is a crucial step in the data preprocessing pipeline, as real-world datasets are often incomplete, inconsistent, or noisy. One of the most common data quality issues is missing values, which occur when certain entries in the dataset are not recorded or available. Missing data can arise for various reasons, such as errors during data collection, system malfunctions, or user omission. Regardless of the cause, missing data can negatively impact the performance of machine learning models if not properly handled.

In this section, we will explore how to handle missing values and clean data using Python, with a focus on the Pandas library, which provides versatile functions for data manipulation, and tools from Scikit-learn for preprocessing.

3.2.1 Identifying Missing Data

The first step in handling missing values is identifying them. In Pandas, missing values are represented by NaN (Not a Number), which is a special floating-point value.

Example: Identifying Missing Values in a DataFrame

Let's start by importing the necessary libraries and loading a sample dataset:

```
import pandas as pd

# Load a sample dataset (you can replace this with your own dataset)
data = pd.DataFrame({
    'Age': [25, 30, 35, None, 40, None, 50],
    'Gender': ['M', 'F', 'M', 'F', None, 'M', 'F'],
    'Salary': [50000, 60000, 70000, 80000, 90000, None, None]
})

# Display the DataFrame
print(data)
```

The output of this dataset might look like:

```
    Age  Gender   Salary
0  25.0      M   50000.0
1  30.0      F   60000.0
2  35.0      M   70000.0
3   NaN      F   80000.0
4  40.0   None   90000.0
5   NaN      M       NaN
6  50.0      F       NaN
```

Here, you can see missing values represented by NaN in the Age, Gender, and Salary columns.

Checking for Missing Values

To check for missing values in a dataset, you can use the isnull() function combined with sum() to count the number of missing values per column:

```
# Check for missing values in each column
print(data.isnull().sum())
```

Output:

```
Age       2
Gender    1
Salary    2
dtype: int64
```

This output indicates that:

- There are 2 missing values in the Age column.
- There is 1 missing value in the Gender column.
- There are 2 missing values in the Salary column.

Visualizing Missing Data

For larger datasets, it may be helpful to visualize the missing data to understand patterns. The missingno library provides easy-to-interpret visualizations for missing data patterns.

import missingno as msno

 # Visualize missing data
msno.matrix(data)

This produces a matrix that highlights the missing data, making it easier to detect if any columns or rows are missing values in a non-random way.

3.2.2 Handling Missing Values

Once missing values are identified, there are several ways to handle them depending on the nature of the data and the problem you're working on. Below are the most common techniques:

1. Removing Missing Data

If the amount of missing data is small or if the missing values are in a column or row that is not critical, you may choose to remove the rows or columns containing missing values.

Remove rows with missing values:

```
# Remove rows with any missing values
data_cleaned_rows = data.dropna()
```

```
# Remove rows where specific columns have missing values
data_cleaned_age = data.dropna(subset=['Age'])
```

Remove columns with missing values:

```
# Remove columns with any missing values
data_cleaned_columns = data.dropna(axis=1)
```

2. Filling Missing Data (Imputation)

In many cases, you may prefer to fill missing values rather than removing them, especially if the missing data is significant. This process is called imputation, and it involves replacing missing values with a substituted value based on the data distribution or a model.

a. Filling with Mean, Median, or Mode

For numerical columns, common imputation strategies include filling missing values with the mean, median, or mode. For categorical columns, the mode (the most frequent value) is often used.

```
# Fill missing numerical data with the mean
data['Age'] = data['Age'].fillna(data['Age'].mean())
```

```
# Fill missing categorical data with the mode (most frequent value)
data['Gender'] = data['Gender'].fillna(data['Gender'].mode()[0])
```

```
# Fill missing salary data with the median
data['Salary'] = data['Salary'].fillna(data['Salary'].median())
```

In this example:

- The missing Age values are replaced with the mean value of the Age column.
- The missing Gender values are replaced with the most common gender in the dataset.
- The missing Salary values are replaced with the median salary value.

b. Filling with a Specific Value

If you have domain-specific knowledge, you can fill missing values with a custom value that makes sense in the context of your problem.

```
# Fill missing Age values with 30 (assuming 30 is an average or default value for age)
data['Age'] = data['Age'].fillna(30)
```

```
# Fill missing Salary values with 60000 (default assumption for salary)
data['Salary'] = data['Salary'].fillna(60000)
```

3. Advanced Imputation Techniques

For more complex datasets, or when you want to improve the accuracy of imputation, you can use more advanced techniques such as K-nearest neighbors (KNN imputation) or multivariate imputation.

Scikit-learn provides the KNNImputer class, which imputes missing values based on the values of the nearest neighbors.

```
from sklearn.impute import KNNImputer
```

```
# Initialize the KNNImputer with 2 neighbors
imputer = KNNImputer(n_neighbors=2)
```

```
# Fit and transform the data to fill missing values
data_imputed = imputer.fit_transform(data.select_dtypes(include=[float, int]))
```

```
# Convert back to a DataFrame
data_imputed = pd.DataFrame(data_imputed, columns=data.select_dtypes(include=[float, int]).columns)
```

```
print(data_imputed)
```

The KNNImputer uses the feature values of the nearest neighbors to predict and fill missing values.

3.2.3 Handling Outliers

In addition to missing values, outliers (values significantly different from others) can affect the performance of your machine learning models. You can identify outliers using statistical techniques such as z-scores or IQR (Interquartile Range).

Example: Identifying Outliers Using IQR

```
# Calculate the IQR for each column
Q1 = data['Salary'].quantile(0.25)
Q3 = data['Salary'].quantile(0.75)
IQR = Q3 - Q1

# Identify outliers using the IQR method
outliers = data[(data['Salary'] < (Q1 - 1.5 * IQR)) | (data['Salary'] > (Q3 + 1.5 * IQR))]
print(outliers)
```

Removing Outliers

Once outliers are identified, you can choose to remove them:

```
# Remove rows containing outliers in the 'Salary' column
data_no_outliers = data[~data['Salary'].isin(outliers['Salary'])]
```

Handling missing data and cleaning datasets are critical steps in the data preprocessing process. Depending on the nature of the dataset and the machine learning task, you can:

- Remove rows or columns with missing values if the missing data is minimal.
- Fill missing values using techniques like mean, median, or mode imputation.
- Use advanced imputation methods like KNN imputation for more accurate predictions.
- Handle outliers to prevent them from negatively impacting your models.

By cleaning your data properly, you ensure that your machine learning models receive the most accurate, consistent, and meaningful input, ultimately leading to better predictions and more reliable results.

3.3 Feature Scaling and Normalization Techniques

Feature scaling and normalization are critical preprocessing steps in machine learning that help improve the performance and accuracy of many algorithms. Machine learning algorithms often assume or work best when the features of the data have similar scales and distributions. Without proper scaling or normalization, features with larger numeric ranges can dominate those with smaller ranges, potentially skewing model predictions.

In this section, we will explore the concepts of feature scaling and normalization, discussing the different techniques available, their advantages, and how to apply them using Python's Scikit-learn library.

3.3.1 Understanding Feature Scaling and Normalization

Feature Scaling refers to the process of transforming features so that they are on a similar scale. This ensures that no single feature dominates others due to differences in units or magnitude. Common scaling techniques include:

- Standardization (Z-score scaling)
- Min-Max scaling
- Max Abs scaling

Normalization refers to adjusting the feature values so that they lie within a specific range, often between 0 and 1. This is particularly useful when the model's assumptions are dependent on features being in a defined range.

Why is Scaling and Normalization Important?

Many machine learning algorithms perform better when the data is scaled or normalized. This is especially true for algorithms that rely on distance metrics or optimization, such as:

- K-nearest neighbors (KNN)
- Support vector machines (SVM)
- Principal Component Analysis (PCA)

Gradient descent-based algorithms (e.g., linear regression, logistic regression, neural networks)

For instance, if a dataset includes two features: one representing height in centimeters and the other representing income in dollars, the income feature may range from 0 to 1,000,000, while the height may range from 0 to 200. Without scaling, the machine learning model may give far more importance to the income feature, simply because it has a larger numerical range.

3.3.2 Common Feature Scaling Techniques

1. Standardization (Z-score Scaling)

Standardization transforms the features to have a mean of 0 and a standard deviation of 1. The formula for standardization is:

$$Z = \frac{X - \mu}{\sigma}$$

Where:

- X is the original feature value.

- μ is the mean of the feature.

- σ is the standard deviation of the feature.

Standardization is useful when the data has a Gaussian (normal) distribution. It's often a good choice for algorithms like SVMs or K-means clustering.

Example: Standardizing a Feature

```
from sklearn.preprocessing import StandardScaler
import pandas as pd

# Sample dataset with two features
data = pd.DataFrame({
    'Height': [160, 170, 180, 190, 200],
    'Income': [30000, 50000, 70000, 90000, 100000]
})

# Initialize StandardScaler
scaler = StandardScaler()

# Standardize the features
scaled_data = scaler.fit_transform(data)

# Convert to DataFrame for better readability
scaled_df = pd.DataFrame(scaled_data, columns=data.columns)
```

print(scaled_df)

Explanation:

StandardScaler() scales the features to have a mean of 0 and a standard deviation of 1. fit_transform() calculates the necessary statistics (mean and standard deviation) from the data and scales it accordingly.

Output:

```
      Height       Income
0  -1.414214  -1.414214
1  -0.707107  -0.707107
2   0.000000   0.000000
3   0.707107   0.707107
4   1.414214   1.414214
```

The standardized values are now on the same scale, which makes the model less sensitive to the original magnitudes of the features.

2. Min-Max Scaling

Min-Max scaling transforms the features by scaling them into a specified range, typically [0, 1]. The formula for Min-Max scaling is:

$$X_{scaled} = \frac{X - X_{min}}{X_{max} - X_{min}}$$

Where:

- X is the original feature value.

- X_{min} is the minimum value of the feature.

- X_{max} is the maximum value of the feature.

Min-Max scaling is sensitive to outliers, which can distort the scaling of features with extreme values. It's typically used when the features are expected to have a bounded range, such as image data.

Example: Min-Max Scaling

from sklearn.preprocessing import MinMaxScaler

 # Initialize MinMaxScaler
scaler = MinMaxScaler()

 # Apply Min-Max scaling to the features
minmax_scaled_data = scaler.fit_transform(data)

 # Convert to DataFrame for better readability
minmax_scaled_df = pd.DataFrame(minmax_scaled_data, columns=data.columns)
print(minmax_scaled_df)

Output:

```
    Height    Income
0    0.0    0.000000
1    0.25   0.25
2    0.50   0.50
3    0.75   0.75
4    1.00   1.00
```

After scaling, both features are now in the range [0, 1], which is ideal when features need to be comparable in scale for algorithms such as neural networks.

3. Max Abs Scaling

Max Abs scaling scales each feature by dividing by the maximum absolute value of that feature. This scaling technique is useful when the data contains both positive and negative values and when you want to preserve sparsity.

The formula for Max Abs scaling is:

$$X_{\text{scaled}} = \frac{X}{|X_{\text{max}}|}$$

Where X_{max} is the maximum absolute value of the feature.

Example: Max Abs Scaling

from sklearn.preprocessing import MaxAbsScaler

 # Initialize MaxAbsScaler
scaler = MaxAbsScaler()

 # Apply Max Abs scaling
maxabs_scaled_data = scaler.fit_transform(data)

 # Convert to DataFrame for better readability
maxabs_scaled_df = pd.DataFrame(maxabs_scaled_data, columns=data.columns)
print(maxabs_scaled_df)

Output:

```
     Height     Income
0    0.80     0.300000
1    0.85     0.500000
2    0.90     0.700000
3    0.95     0.900000
4    1.00     1.000000
```

Max Abs scaling ensures that all values lie between -1 and 1, and it is particularly useful for sparse data.

3.3.3 Choosing the Right Scaling Technique

The choice of scaling method depends on the nature of the data and the machine learning algorithm being used:

- Standardization is typically the best option for algorithms that assume a Gaussian distribution or require a normal distribution of features, such as Support Vector Machines (SVM) and Linear Regression.
- Min-Max scaling is useful when you need the features to be in a specific range (e.g., between 0 and 1), which is important for algorithms like neural networks.
- Max Abs scaling works well for data with both positive and negative values, especially when working with sparse datasets.

Feature scaling and normalization are essential preprocessing steps to ensure that machine learning models can learn effectively and efficiently. The most common techniques—standardization, min-max scaling, and max abs scaling—each have specific use cases depending on the data and the model. Scikit-learn provides simple, effective tools to perform these transformations, ensuring that features are on the same scale and reducing the bias introduced by different ranges of values. By choosing the right scaling method for your data, you can improve the performance and convergence of your machine learning algorithms.

3.4 Encoding Categorical Variables

Categorical variables are a common feature in datasets, especially when working with real-world data. These variables represent categories or labels rather than continuous numeric values. Examples include gender, country, or product type. Machine learning algorithms typically require numeric input to perform computations, so categorical variables need to be encoded into numerical values before being used in models.

In this section, we will explore the various methods of encoding categorical variables, focusing on techniques provided by the Scikit-learn library. These methods include Label Encoding, One-Hot Encoding, and Ordinal Encoding, as well as when to use each technique based on the type of categorical variable.

3.4.1 Types of Categorical Variables

Categorical variables fall into two primary types:

Nominal Categorical Variables: These are categories without an inherent order or ranking. For example, gender (male, female), country (USA, Canada, UK), and color (red, blue, green) are nominal variables. The categories are distinct but have no natural order.

Ordinal Categorical Variables: These variables have a natural order or ranking but no exact numerical meaning. For example, education level (high school, bachelor's degree, master's degree), survey ratings (poor, average, excellent), and product ratings (1 star, 2 stars, etc.) are ordinal variables.

3.4.2 Methods of Encoding Categorical Variables

1. Label Encoding

Label Encoding is a method of converting each category of a feature into a unique integer value. This method is primarily used for ordinal categorical variables where the numeric values carry some meaning (i.e., the integers represent some sort of ranking or order).

For example, consider the education level feature:

- High School → 0

- Bachelor's Degree → 1

- Master's Degree → 2

Example: Label Encoding

from sklearn.preprocessing import LabelEncoder

 # Sample data (ordinal)
data = ['High School', 'Bachelor', 'Master', 'Master', 'High School']

 # Initialize LabelEncoder
encoder = LabelEncoder()

 # Apply label encoding
encoded_data = encoder.fit_transform(data)

print(encoded_data)

Output:

[0 1 2 2 0]

Explanation:

The LabelEncoder assigns an integer value to each category. Here, the ordinal categories have been encoded as 0, 1, and 2.

Important Considerations:

Label encoding works best with ordinal variables, as the algorithm may misinterpret the numerical values of nominal variables as having an inherent order (e.g., "red" = 0, "blue" = 1, "green" = 2 may be incorrectly interpreted by the model as having a ranking).

2. One-Hot Encoding

One-Hot Encoding is a method of converting categorical variables into a binary (0 or 1) format, where each category gets its own column. This method is typically used for nominal categorical variables, where the categories do not have any inherent order or ranking.

For example, consider a color feature with three categories: red, blue, and green. One-Hot Encoding creates a binary column for each color:

- Red → [1, 0, 0]

- Blue → [0, 1, 0]

- Green → [0, 0, 1]

Example: One-Hot Encoding

```
from sklearn.preprocessing import OneHotEncoder
import numpy as np

# Sample data (nominal)
data = np.array(['Red', 'Blue', 'Green', 'Red', 'Blue']).reshape(-1, 1)

# Initialize OneHotEncoder
encoder = OneHotEncoder(sparse=False)

# Apply One-Hot Encoding
encoded_data = encoder.fit_transform(data)

print(encoded_data)
```

Output:

[[1. 0. 0.]
 [0. 1. 0.]
 [0. 0. 1.]
 [1. 0. 0.]
 [0. 1. 0.]]

Explanation:

The OneHotEncoder creates a separate binary column for each category (Red, Blue, Green), with a 1 in the column corresponding to the color and 0 in the others.

Important Considerations:

- One-Hot Encoding expands the number of features in your dataset, which can lead to an increase in dimensionality. This may affect performance, especially with features that have a large number of categories.
- It is generally recommended to use One-Hot Encoding for nominal variables, as it avoids introducing any ordering between the categories.

3. Ordinal Encoding

Ordinal Encoding is similar to label encoding but is specifically designed for ordinal categorical variables where the categories have a defined order or ranking. The primary difference is that Ordinal Encoding requires you to specify the order manually, as opposed to Label Encoding, which automatically assigns integer values.

For example, consider a survey rating feature with three categories: Poor, Average, and Excellent. These categories have a natural order, so we would encode them as:

- Poor → 0

- Average → 1

- Excellent → 2

Example: Ordinal Encoding

from sklearn.preprocessing import OrdinalEncoder

```
# Sample data (ordinal)
data = [['Poor'], ['Average'], ['Excellent'], ['Average'], ['Poor']]

# Initialize OrdinalEncoder with a custom order
encoder = OrdinalEncoder(categories=[['Poor', 'Average', 'Excellent']])

# Apply Ordinal Encoding
encoded_data = encoder.fit_transform(data)

print(encoded_data)
```

Output:

```
[[0.]
 [1.]
 [2.]
 [1.]
 [0.]]
```

Explanation:

The OrdinalEncoder encodes the values in the order specified in the categories parameter: "Poor" = 0, "Average" = 1, and "Excellent" = 2.

Important Considerations:

Ordinal Encoding is a good choice for ordinal variables, where the relationship between categories is meaningful. However, be mindful that the model might treat the encoded integers as having equal distances, which may not be the case in all situations.

4. Binary Encoding

Binary Encoding is an alternative method for handling categorical variables with a large number of categories. This method first converts each category into a numeric value (like label encoding) and then represents that number as a binary code. Binary Encoding reduces the dimensionality compared to One-Hot Encoding, especially when there are many categories.

For example, for a categorical feature with four categories:

- Red → 0
- Blue → 1
- Green → 2
- Yellow → 3

The binary encoding would transform these as:

- Red → 00
- Blue → 01
- Green → 10
- Yellow → 11

Binary encoding is available via third-party libraries like category_encoders.

3.4.3 Using Scikit-learn's ColumnTransformer for Encoding

When you have a mix of numerical and categorical features in your dataset, it's often helpful to use Scikit-learn's ColumnTransformer to apply encoding selectively to categorical columns. This ensures that only the categorical columns are encoded while leaving the numerical features unchanged.

Example: Using ColumnTransformer with Encoding

```
from sklearn.compose import ColumnTransformer
from sklearn.preprocessing import OneHotEncoder
from sklearn.preprocessing import StandardScaler
from sklearn.pipeline import Pipeline

# Sample data
data = pd.DataFrame({
    'Color': ['Red', 'Blue', 'Green', 'Red', 'Blue'],
    'Height': [160, 170, 180, 175, 165]
})
```

```
# Create a ColumnTransformer that applies One-Hot Encoding to 'Color' column and
standardizes 'Height'
preprocessor = ColumnTransformer(
    transformers=[
        ('color', OneHotEncoder(), ['Color']),
        ('height', StandardScaler(), ['Height'])
    ])

# Apply the transformations
processed_data = preprocessor.fit_transform(data)

print(processed_data)
```

Output:

```
[[ 1.        0.        0.       -1.26491106]
 [ 0.        1.        0.        0.63245553]
 [ 0.        0.        1.        1.26491106]
 [ 1.        0.        0.        0.       ]
 [ 0.        1.        0.       -0.63245553]]
```

Explanation:

The ColumnTransformer applies One-Hot Encoding to the Color column and Standard
Scaling to the Height column. This way, both transformations are applied simultaneously
but to different parts of the dataset.

Encoding categorical variables is a vital step in the preprocessing pipeline for machine
learning models. The choice of encoding technique depends on the type of categorical
variable:

- Label Encoding is suitable for ordinal variables with a meaningful order.
- One-Hot Encoding is ideal for nominal variables where there is no order.
- Ordinal Encoding is useful for encoding ordinal variables while preserving their
  rank.
- Binary Encoding can be applied to high-cardinality categorical variables to reduce
  dimensionality.

By choosing the appropriate encoding method, you ensure that your model can process
categorical data effectively, leading to improved performance and more accurate

predictions. Scikit-learn provides efficient tools to perform these transformations, and using a ColumnTransformer helps manage the preprocessing pipeline for datasets with mixed feature types.

3.5 Splitting Data into Training and Testing Sets

One of the key steps in building a machine learning model is splitting the dataset into training and testing sets. This division allows us to evaluate the performance of our model on unseen data and helps ensure that the model generalizes well to new, unseen examples. Without this separation, the model might simply memorize the data (a problem known as overfitting) and perform poorly on new data.

In this section, we will cover the importance of splitting the dataset, the standard techniques for splitting data, and how to do so using Scikit-learn.

3.5.1 Why Split Data?

When building a machine learning model, it is essential to test how well the model will perform on new, unseen data. If you train and test your model on the same data, it's very likely to perform very well during training but fail to generalize to new data. To prevent this overfitting, we split the dataset into at least two parts:

- **Training Set**: The portion of the data used to train the model. The model learns patterns and relationships from this subset.
- **Testing Set**: The portion of the data used to evaluate the model's performance. The model makes predictions on this data, and its performance is measured.

In some cases, especially when working with smaller datasets, a third set called the validation set may also be used. This set is used during training to fine-tune the model's hyperparameters, and it helps avoid overfitting by providing an additional evaluation set.

3.5.2 The Standard Practice for Splitting Data

The most common way to split the data is to divide it into two parts: 80% training data and 20% testing data. However, the exact split can vary depending on the dataset size, the problem at hand, and the amount of data available. Larger datasets can typically afford a smaller testing set, while smaller datasets may require more data for testing to ensure the model is evaluated correctly.

The typical steps in splitting data are:

- **Shuffle the Data**: Randomly shuffle the dataset before splitting to ensure that both the training and testing sets are representative of the entire dataset.
- **Split the Data**: Divide the data into training and testing sets (and possibly a validation set).
- **Stratified Sampling**: In cases where the dataset has imbalanced classes (e.g., in classification tasks where one class is underrepresented), it's important to preserve the class distribution in both the training and testing sets.

3.5.3 Using Scikit-learn to Split Data

Scikit-learn provides a very efficient method for splitting data through the train_test_split() function. This function randomly splits the data into training and testing sets and is very easy to use.

Syntax of train_test_split()

from sklearn.model_selection import train_test_split

X_train, X_test, y_train, y_test = train_test_split(X, y, test_size=0.2, random_state=42)

Where:

- **X**: Features or independent variables of the dataset (inputs).
- **y**: Target or dependent variable (output).
- **test_size**: Proportion of the dataset to be used as the testing set (e.g., 0.2 means 20% of the data will be used for testing).
- **random_state**: A seed for the random number generator, used to ensure reproducibility. Using the same random_state will generate the same train-test split each time you run the code.

Example: Splitting Data into Training and Testing Sets

```
import pandas as pd
from sklearn.model_selection import train_test_split

# Sample data (X is features, y is target)
data = {
    'Feature1': [1, 2, 3, 4, 5],
```

```
    'Feature2': [10, 20, 30, 40, 50],
    'Target': [0, 1, 0, 1, 0]
}

df = pd.DataFrame(data)

# Features (X) and target (y)
X = df[['Feature1', 'Feature2']]
y = df['Target']

# Split data into training and testing sets (80% train, 20% test)
X_train, X_test, y_train, y_test = train_test_split(X, y, test_size=0.2, random_state=42)

# Print the resulting shapes of the splits
print("Training features shape:", X_train.shape)
print("Testing features shape:", X_test.shape)
print("Training target shape:", y_train.shape)
print("Testing target shape:", y_test.shape)
```

Output:

```
Training features shape: (4, 2)
Testing features shape: (1, 2)
Training target shape: (4,)
Testing target shape: (1,)
```

Explanation:

- The train_test_split() function randomly splits the dataset into training and testing sets.
- 80% of the data is used for training, and 20% of the data is used for testing.
- The feature sets (X_train, X_test) and target sets (y_train, y_test) are split accordingly

.

Handling Stratified Sampling (for Classification Tasks)

In classification tasks where the target variable has imbalanced classes (e.g., 90% of the data belongs to class 0 and only 10% belongs to class 1), it's important to ensure that the train and test sets maintain the same proportion of classes as in the original dataset. This is called stratified sampling.

Scikit-learn allows you to perform stratified sampling by setting the stratify parameter to the target variable (y), ensuring that the distribution of classes in both training and testing sets is consistent.

Example: Stratified Split for Imbalanced Data

```
# Sample data with imbalanced target
data = {
    'Feature1': [1, 2, 3, 4, 5, 6],
    'Feature2': [10, 20, 30, 40, 50, 60],
    'Target': [0, 0, 0, 1, 0, 1]
}

df = pd.DataFrame(data)

# Features (X) and target (y)
X = df[['Feature1', 'Feature2']]
y = df['Target']

# Split data with stratification (ensure same class distribution in train/test)
X_train, X_test, y_train, y_test = train_test_split(X, y, test_size=0.33, random_state=42, stratify=y)

# Print the resulting class distribution in train and test sets
print("Class distribution in training set:\n", y_train.value_counts(normalize=True))
print("Class distribution in testing set:\n", y_test.value_counts(normalize=True))
```

Output:

```
Class distribution in training set:
 0   0.833333
 1   0.166667
Name: Target, dtype: float64
Class distribution in testing set:
 0   0.833333
 1   0.166667
Name: Target, dtype: float64
```

Explanation:

- The stratify=y argument ensures that both the training and testing sets maintain the same class distribution as in the original dataset.
- In this case, 83.33% of both the training and testing sets belong to class 0, and 16.67% belong to class 1.

3.5.4 Additional Considerations

Cross-Validation: For more robust model evaluation, especially when working with smaller datasets, you may want to use cross-validation instead of a simple train-test split. Cross-validation involves splitting the data into multiple subsets (folds) and training/testing the model multiple times, ensuring that the model's performance is evaluated on different portions of the data. Scikit-learn provides tools like KFold and StratifiedKFold for this purpose.

Test Size: The proportion of data allocated to the test set (e.g., 20% or 30%) depends on the size of the dataset. For larger datasets, smaller test sizes may still yield a representative evaluation, but for smaller datasets, a larger test set might be required to ensure that the model generalizes well.

Splitting the data into training and testing sets is a crucial step in machine learning model development. It allows us to assess how well the model generalizes to new, unseen data and helps avoid overfitting. Scikit-learn's train_test_split() function provides an easy way to split datasets while offering flexibility in handling different data characteristics, including stratification for imbalanced datasets. Proper splitting and validation of your dataset are fundamental to building robust and reliable machine learning models.

4. Linear Models for Regression and Classification

Linear models are the backbone of many machine learning applications. This chapter explores linear regression for predicting numerical values and logistic regression for classification problems. You'll learn how to train, evaluate, and fine-tune these models while understanding key performance metrics.

4.1 Introduction to Linear Models

Linear models are among the simplest and most widely used types of models in machine learning and statistics. They are foundational to understanding machine learning and serve as building blocks for more complex algorithms. Linear models are powerful due to their simplicity, interpretability, and efficiency in many practical problems. They are used for tasks like regression and classification, where the relationship between input features and output predictions is assumed to be linear or close to linear.

In this section, we will explore the core concepts of linear models, their mathematical foundations, their applications, and how they are implemented in Scikit-learn.

4.1.1 What is a Linear Model?

A linear model assumes a linear relationship between the input features (X) and the target variable (y). This means that the target variable can be predicted as a weighted sum of the input features, possibly with an added constant term (intercept).

Mathematically, a linear model is expressed as:

$$y = \beta_0 + \beta_1 x_1 + \beta_2 x_2 + \cdots + \beta_n x_n + \epsilon$$

Where:

- y is the target variable (output),

- $x_1, x_2, \ldots, x_n$ are the input features (independent variables),

- β_0 is the **intercept** (constant term),

- $\beta_1, \beta_2, \ldots, \beta_n$ are the **coefficients** or weights assigned to each feature, and

- ϵ is the error term (or noise), accounting for the difference between the predicted value and the true value.

In a simple linear regression problem, the equation is simplified to:

$$y = \beta_0 + \beta_1 x$$

In this case, β_0 is the intercept and β_1 is the coefficient of the single input feature x.

4.1.2 Types of Linear Models

Linear models can be categorized based on the type of task they are used for. These are the two most common types:

Linear Regression: Linear regression is a technique for predicting a continuous target variable based on one or more input features. The goal is to find the line (or hyperplane, in higher dimensions) that best fits the data, minimizing the difference between the predicted and actual values of the target variable.

Linear regression models are widely used in fields such as economics, engineering, and social sciences. The output is a continuous value, and the relationship between the independent and dependent variables is assumed to be linear.

Example: Predicting house prices based on the size of the house (square footage).

Logistic Regression: Despite its name, logistic regression is actually a classification algorithm used to predict binary outcomes (i.e., two possible classes, such as 0 or 1, true or false, etc.). It is used for classification tasks where the dependent variable is categorical.

Logistic regression models the probability that a given input belongs to a certain class, using the logistic function (also known as the sigmoid function) to transform the output into a probability between 0 and 1.

The equation for logistic regression is:

$$p(y = 1) = \frac{1}{1 + e^{-(\beta_0 + \beta_1 x)}}$$

Where:

- $p(y = 1)$ is the probability of the target variable y being 1 (true),

- β_0 and β_1 are the coefficients,

- x is the input feature, and

- e is the base of the natural logarithm.

Example: Predicting whether a customer will buy a product based on their age and income.

4.1.3 Key Assumptions of Linear Models

Linear models are based on several assumptions. Understanding these assumptions is crucial to making effective use of linear models:

Linearity: There is a linear relationship between the independent variables and the target variable. In the case of linear regression, the model assumes that the target variable is a linear combination of the input features.

Independence of Errors: The residuals (errors) of the model should be independent of each other. In other words, the errors for one observation should not influence the errors for another.

Homoscedasticity: The variance of the errors should be constant across all levels of the independent variables. This means that the spread of the residuals should not change as the value of the predictor variable(s) increases.

Normality of Errors: The residuals should follow a normal distribution, particularly for inference tasks where hypothesis tests are involved.

No Multicollinearity: The independent variables should not be highly correlated with each other. If two or more predictors are highly correlated, it becomes difficult to estimate their individual effects on the target variable, leading to instability in the model's coefficients.

4.1.4 Advantages and Limitations of Linear Models

Advantages:

- **Simplicity**: Linear models are easy to understand and implement, making them a great starting point for predictive modeling.
- **Interpretability**: The coefficients in a linear model indicate the strength and direction of the relationship between each feature and the target variable. This makes linear models highly interpretable.
- **Efficiency**: Linear models tend to be computationally efficient, even with large datasets, making them ideal for situations where speed is important.
- **Well-suited for linearly separable data**: If the data is linearly separable, a linear model can often perform very well.

Limitations:

- **Assumption of Linearity**: Linear models cannot capture non-linear relationships between variables. If the true relationship is non-linear, linear models will not perform well unless the data is transformed.
- **Sensitivity to Outliers**: Linear models are sensitive to outliers, which can skew the results and lead to poor model performance.
- **Multicollinearity**: When the input features are highly correlated, linear models can struggle to determine which feature is most important.
- **Limited to Linearly Separable Problems**: In classification tasks, logistic regression works well for linearly separable problems, but it can fail for more complex, non-linear decision boundaries.

4.1.5 Applications of Linear Models

Despite their simplicity, linear models are widely used in various fields, and they can serve as baseline models for more complex algorithms. Here are a few examples:

Economics: Linear models are often used to understand relationships between different economic variables, such as income and expenditure, or price and demand.

Healthcare: In predicting disease progression, linear regression can be used to model how factors like age, weight, and exercise affect health outcomes.

Marketing: Logistic regression is often used in marketing to predict whether a customer will purchase a product based on demographic information, browsing history, or prior purchases.

Finance: Linear models are used in finance for tasks like stock price prediction, where features like historical prices, volume, and economic indicators can be used to predict future stock prices.

4.1.6 Linear Models in Scikit-learn

Scikit-learn provides efficient implementations of linear models, including Linear Regression and Logistic Regression. Below is an example of how to implement a linear regression model using Scikit-learn:

Example: Linear Regression in Scikit-learn

```python
from sklearn.linear_model import LinearRegression
import numpy as np
import matplotlib.pyplot as plt

# Sample data (features X, target y)
X = np.array([[1], [2], [3], [4], [5]])  # Feature (independent variable)
y = np.array([1, 2, 3, 4, 5])  # Target (dependent variable)

# Create a linear regression model
model = LinearRegression()

# Fit the model to the data
model.fit(X, y)

# Make predictions
y_pred = model.predict(X)

# Plot the results
```

```
plt.scatter(X, y, color='blue', label='Data points')
plt.plot(X, y_pred, color='red', label='Fitted line')
plt.xlabel('X')
plt.ylabel('y')
plt.title('Linear Regression Example')
plt.legend()
plt.show()

# Print the model coefficients
print("Intercept:", model.intercept_)
print("Coefficient:", model.coef_)
```

Explanation:

- In this example, we use LinearRegression from Scikit-learn to fit a model to the data, make predictions, and plot the results.
- The intercept and coefficient of the model are printed out to show the relationship between the input feature and the target variable.

Linear models, including linear regression and logistic regression, are fundamental to machine learning. They provide a simple yet powerful way to understand and predict relationships between variables. While they have their limitations—such as the assumption of linearity and sensitivity to outliers—they remain highly effective for many tasks, especially when the relationship between variables is relatively straightforward. In Scikit-learn, linear models are easy to implement, making them a great starting point for many machine learning projects.

4.2 Linear Regression: Basics and Variations (Ridge, Lasso)

Linear regression is one of the foundational algorithms in machine learning, commonly used for predicting continuous numerical values based on input features. While the basic form of linear regression assumes that the relationship between the features and the target variable is linear, it can face issues such as overfitting, multicollinearity, and sensitivity to outliers, especially when dealing with high-dimensional data. To address these issues, Ridge Regression and Lasso Regression introduce regularization techniques that help to improve model generalization and control complexity.

In this section, we will explore:

- Basic Linear Regression
- Ridge Regression
- Lasso Regression
- Comparison of Ridge and Lasso

4.2.1 Basic Linear Regression

Linear regression seeks to model the relationship between one or more features (independent variables) and a target variable (dependent variable) using a straight line. The objective is to find the best-fitting line that minimizes the residual sum of squares (RSS), the difference between the predicted and actual target values.

The formula for a simple linear regression model with one feature is:

$$y = \beta_0 + \beta_1 x + \epsilon$$

Where:

- y is the target variable,

- x is the feature (input variable),

- β_0 is the intercept,

- β_1 is the coefficient (slope), and

- ϵ represents the error term (residuals).

For multiple features, the model extends to a linear equation involving all the input features:

$$y = \beta_0 + \beta_1 x_1 + \beta_2 x_2 + \cdots + \beta_n x_n + \epsilon$$

The model aims to find the optimal coefficients $(\beta_1, \beta_2, \ldots, \beta_n)$ that minimize the residual sum of squares.

4.2.2 Limitations of Basic Linear Regression

Basic linear regression works well when:

- There is a linear relationship between the independent variables and the target variable.
- The features are not highly correlated (no multicollinearity).
- The model is not too complex (i.e., too many features compared to the number of data points).

However, basic linear regression can be prone to overfitting when:

- There are a large number of features, especially when some features are irrelevant.
- The model becomes overly complex, leading to high variance and poor generalization to unseen data.
- This is where regularization techniques like Ridge Regression and Lasso Regression come into play.

4.2.3 Ridge Regression (L2 Regularization)

Ridge Regression, also known as L2 regularization, introduces a penalty term to the linear regression cost function to control the magnitude of the model coefficients. The idea is to reduce the impact of less important features by shrinking their coefficients, which helps prevent overfitting and enhances the model's ability to generalize.

The cost function for Ridge regression is:

$$J(\beta) = \sum_{i=1}^{m} (y_i - \hat{y}_i)^2 + \lambda \sum_{j=1}^{n} \beta_j^2$$

Where:

- $\sum_{i=1}^{m} (y_i - \hat{y}_i)^2$ is the residual sum of squares (RSS) term (same as in ordinary linear regression),

- λ is the regularization parameter (also known as the ridge penalty),

- $\sum_{j=1}^{n} \beta_j^2$ is the sum of the squared coefficients.

The parameter λ controls the strength of the regularization. A larger value of λ increases the penalty for large coefficients, leading to a simpler model with smaller coefficients, while a smaller value of λ allows the model to fit more closely to the training data.

Ridge regression is particularly useful when:

- The dataset contains many features.
- Multicollinearity is present (i.e., when some features are highly correlated).
- Advantages of Ridge Regression:
- Ridge regression reduces the complexity of the model by shrinking the coefficients, leading to better generalization on unseen data.
- It handles multicollinearity effectively.

Example: Ridge Regression in Scikit-learn

```
from sklearn.linear_model import Ridge
import numpy as np

# Sample data (features X, target y)
X = np.array([[1], [2], [3], [4], [5]])
y = np.array([1, 2, 3, 4, 5])

# Create a Ridge regression model with alpha = 1.0 (regularization strength)
ridge_model = Ridge(alpha=1.0)

# Fit the model to the data
ridge_model.fit(X, y)

# Make predictions
y_pred = ridge_model.predict(X)

# Print model coefficients
print("Intercept:", ridge_model.intercept_)
print("Coefficient:", ridge_model.coef_)
```

4.2.4 Lasso Regression (L1 Regularization)

Lasso Regression, or L1 regularization, introduces a different type of penalty. Instead of squaring the coefficients like Ridge regression, Lasso adds the absolute values of the coefficients to the cost function. This leads to some coefficients being reduced to exactly zero, effectively performing feature selection.

The cost function for Lasso regression is:

$$J(\beta) = \sum_{i=1}^{m} (y_i - \hat{y}_i)^2 + \lambda \sum_{j=1}^{n} |\beta_j|$$

Where:

- The first term is the same as in linear regression (residual sum of squares),
- λ is the regularization parameter (similar to Ridge regression),
- $\sum_{j=1}^{n} |\beta_j|$ is the sum of the absolute values of the coefficients.

The parameter λ controls the strength of the regularization. A larger λ leads to more coefficients being driven to zero, resulting in a sparser model.

Lasso regression is useful when:

- You suspect that many of the features are irrelevant.
- You want to automatically select the most important features for your model.
- Advantages of Lasso Regression:
- Lasso performs feature selection by driving some coefficients to zero, helping with model interpretation and reducing overfitting.
- It works well when there are many features and only a subset of them are relevant to the prediction.

Example: Lasso Regression in Scikit-learn

```
from sklearn.linear_model import Lasso

# Sample data (features X, target y)
X = np.array([[1], [2], [3], [4], [5]])
y = np.array([1, 2, 3, 4, 5])

# Create a Lasso regression model with alpha = 0.1 (regularization strength)
lasso_model = Lasso(alpha=0.1)

# Fit the model to the data
lasso_model.fit(X, y)

# Make predictions
y_pred = lasso_model.predict(X)
```

```
# Print model coefficients
print("Intercept:", lasso_model.intercept_)
print("Coefficient:", lasso_model.coef_)
```

4.2.5 Comparison of Ridge and Lasso

Feature	Ridge Regression (L2)	Lasso Regression (L1)
Penalty term	Square of coefficients (sum of squares)	Absolute values of coefficients (sum of absolute values)
Effect on coefficients	Shrinks coefficients, but does not set them to zero	Can shrink coefficients to exactly zero, performing feature selection
Use case	Effective with multicollinearity and when all features are important	Effective when only a few features are important or for feature selection
Interpretability	All features remain in the model, though some are shrunk	Easier to interpret due to automatic feature selection
Computation	More computationally expensive than Lasso, but less feature elimination	Can result in sparser models, making computation faster when many features are irrelevant

Linear regression forms the basis of many predictive models, and while it is a simple approach, its performance can degrade when dealing with large numbers of features, multicollinearity, or overfitting. Ridge regression and Lasso regression offer powerful extensions to the basic linear regression model by adding regularization terms to control model complexity and improve generalization.

- Ridge Regression is best when we believe all features are useful and want to control their magnitudes.
- Lasso Regression is particularly effective for feature selection when we expect that only a few features are important.

Both models can be easily implemented using Scikit-learn, and they provide a valuable toolset for solving regression problems in a way that is both computationally efficient and interpretable.

4.3 Logistic Regression for Classification

Logistic Regression is one of the most commonly used algorithms in machine learning for binary classification tasks. Despite its name, it is a classification algorithm, not a regression one. Logistic regression is used to predict the probability of a binary outcome, where the target variable is categorical with two possible outcomes (e.g., 0 or 1, true or false, yes or no). It is simple, interpretable, and computationally efficient, which makes it a popular choice for many real-world classification problems.

In this section, we will dive into the basics of logistic regression, how it works, and how to implement it using Scikit-learn.

4.3.1 What is Logistic Regression?

Logistic regression models the probability that a given input point belongs to a particular class. It uses the logistic function (also called the sigmoid function) to map the linear combination of input features to a probability score between 0 and 1. This probability score indicates the likelihood of the data point belonging to a specific class (e.g., class 1)

The logistic regression model is based on the following formula:

$$P(y = 1|X) = \frac{1}{1 + e^{-(\beta_0 + \beta_1 x_1 + \cdots + \beta_n x_n)}}$$

Where:

- $P(y = 1|X)$ is the probability of the target variable y being 1 (the event happening).

- β_0 is the intercept.

- $\beta_1, \ldots, \beta_n$ are the coefficients of the features $x_1, \ldots, x_n$.

- e is the base of the natural logarithm.

- The expression $\beta_0 + \beta_1 x_1 + \cdots + \beta_n x_n$ is the linear combination of the input features.

4.3.2 How Does Logistic Regression Work?

The key difference between linear regression and logistic regression is that the latter applies the sigmoid function (logistic function) to the linear combination of the input features. This function squashes the output of the linear model to a range between 0 and 1, which can be interpreted as the probability that the data point belongs to a certain class.

The sigmoid function is defined as:

$$\sigma(z) = \frac{1}{1 + e^{-z}}$$

Where:

- z is the linear combination of the features, i.e., $z = \beta_0 + \beta_1 x_1 + \cdots + \beta_n x_n$.

.

This function outputs values between 0 and 1, which can be interpreted as probabilities. The threshold value (usually 0.5) is used to convert these probabilities into class labels:

- If $P(y = 1|X) \geq 0.5$, the model predicts class 1.
- If $P(y = 1|X) < 0.5$, the model predicts class 0.

4.3.3 Cost Function and Maximum Likelihood Estimation

To train a logistic regression model, we need to find the best-fitting parameters (i.e., $\beta_0, \beta_1, \ldots, \beta_n$) that minimize the difference between the predicted probabilities and the actual outcomes.

Logistic regression uses the log-likelihood function as the cost function, which is derived from the concept of maximum likelihood estimation (MLE). The goal is to maximize the likelihood of the observed data given the model parameters.

The cost function for logistic regression is given by:

$$J(\beta) = -\frac{1}{m} \sum_{i=1}^{m} [y_i \log(h_\beta(x_i)) + (1 - y_i) \log(1 - h_\beta(x_i))]$$

Where:

- m is the number of training samples,
- y_i is the actual label for the i-th sample (either 0 or 1),
- $h_\beta(x_i)$ is the predicted probability for the i-th sample using the logistic function.

The objective is to minimize this cost function, which corresponds to maximizing the likelihood of the data under the model. This is typically done using optimization algorithms such as Gradient Descent.

4.3.4 Model Interpretation

Once the logistic regression model is trained, the coefficients $\beta_1, \ldots, \beta_n$ provide insight into the relationship between the features and the target variable.

- **Intercept (β_0):** The log-odds of the event happening when all input features are zero.
- **Coefficients ($\beta_1, \ldots, \beta_n$):** The change in the log-odds of the target variable for a one-unit change in the corresponding feature, holding all other features constant.

Since the coefficients are related to the log-odds of the target variable, they can be exponentiated to interpret them in terms of odds ratios:

$$\text{Odds ratio} = e^{\beta_j}$$

For example, if $\beta_1 = 0.5$, the odds of the target event occurring increase by a factor of $e^{0.5} \approx 1.65$ for every one-unit increase in x_1, holding other features constant.

4.3.5 When to Use Logistic Regression

Logistic regression is commonly used when:

- The target variable is binary (i.e., only two possible outcomes, such as "yes/no" or "spam/ham").

- You want a probabilistic interpretation of the outcome (e.g., the likelihood of success or failure).
- Linear decision boundaries are sufficient for the problem at hand (i.e., the data is linearly separable).
- The features are not highly correlated with each other (logistic regression assumes that the features are independent of each other).

It works well in many scenarios such as:

- **Email spam detection**: Predict whether an email is spam or not.
- **Medical diagnoses**: Predict whether a patient has a certain disease based on input features like age, gender, and test results.
- **Customer churn prediction**: Predict whether a customer will leave a service based on their activity.

4.3.6 Logistic Regression in Scikit-learn

In Scikit-learn, logistic regression is implemented using the LogisticRegression class. It provides an easy-to-use interface for training a logistic regression model and making predictions.

Example: Logistic Regression in Scikit-learn

```
from sklearn.linear_model import LogisticRegression
from sklearn.model_selection import train_test_split
from sklearn.datasets import load_iris
from sklearn.metrics import accuracy_score

# Load a sample dataset (Iris dataset)
data = load_iris()
X = data.data
y = (data.target == 0).astype(int)  # Convert to binary classification problem (Setosa vs Non-setosa)

# Split the data into training and testing sets
X_train, X_test, y_train, y_test = train_test_split(X, y, test_size=0.3, random_state=42)

# Create a logistic regression model
model = LogisticRegression(max_iter=200)
```

```
# Train the model
model.fit(X_train, y_train)

# Make predictions
y_pred = model.predict(X_test)

# Evaluate the model
accuracy = accuracy_score(y_test, y_pred)
print(f'Accuracy: {accuracy:.2f}')

# Print model coefficients
print(f'Coefficients: {model.coef_}')
print(f'Intercept: {model.intercept_}')
```

Explanation:

- In this example, we load the Iris dataset and modify it to make it a binary classification task (Setosa vs Non-setosa).
- We split the data into training and testing sets, fit a logistic regression model on the training data, and make predictions on the test data.
- The model's accuracy is evaluated, and the coefficients and intercept are printed for interpretation.

4.3.7 Advantages and Limitations of Logistic Regression

Advantages:

- **Simplicity**: Logistic regression is easy to implement and understand. It's a good starting point for classification problems.
- **Interpretability**: The coefficients in the model provide insight into the relationship between the features and the target variable.
- **Efficiency**: Logistic regression is computationally efficient, especially for small to medium-sized datasets.
- **Probabilistic Output**: It provides probabilities for predictions, which can be useful for certain applications, such as decision-making and risk analysis.

Limitations:

- **Linear Boundaries**: Logistic regression assumes that the data is linearly separable. If the data has non-linear relationships, the model may perform poorly.

- **Sensitive to Outliers**: Logistic regression can be sensitive to outliers, especially when the features are not scaled properly.
- **Assumes Feature Independence**: Logistic regression assumes that the features are independent of each other. If features are highly correlated, the model may struggle (multicollinearity).

Logistic regression is a fundamental and widely used classification algorithm that is simple, interpretable, and effective for binary classification tasks. It works by modeling the probability of an event occurring using the logistic function, which maps the output to a range between 0 and 1. Logistic regression is particularly useful when you need to interpret the relationship between features and the outcome, and when the decision boundaries are linear.

In Scikit-learn, logistic regression is easy to implement, and you can customize various parameters to improve performance, such as the regularization strength and the solver used for optimization. It remains a powerful tool in the machine learning practitioner's toolkit, especially for problems with a relatively simple relationship between input features and the target variable.

4.4 Performance Evaluation Metrics (R^2, MSE, Accuracy, F1-score)

Performance evaluation is a critical aspect of machine learning. It helps to assess how well a model is performing on the task it is designed for, and provides insights into its strengths and weaknesses. In this section, we will explore some of the most commonly used evaluation metrics across regression and classification tasks, namely:

- R^2 (R-squared)
- Mean Squared Error (MSE)
- Accuracy
- F1-score

Each of these metrics offers valuable information about the model's ability to make predictions, but they are suited for different types of problems. Let's dive into each of them.

4.4.1 R^2 (R-squared) - A Metric for Regression

R², or R-squared, is a commonly used evaluation metric for regression models. It measures the proportion of the variance in the dependent variable (the target) that is predictable from the independent variables (features). In other words, it quantifies how well the model is able to fit the data.

Mathematically, R^2 is defined as:

$$R^2 = 1 - \frac{\sum_{i=1}^{n}(y_i - \hat{y}_i)^2}{\sum_{i=1}^{n}(y_i - \bar{y})^2}$$

Where:

- y_i is the actual value of the target variable,

- $\hat{y}_i$ is the predicted value of the target variable,

- $\bar{y}$ is the mean of the actual target values,

- The numerator represents the **residual sum of squares** (RSS), which is the error of the model.

- The denominator represents the **total sum of squares** (TSS), which is the variance in the target variable.

An R^2 value ranges from 0 to 1, where:

- 1 indicates perfect fit (all data points lie on the regression line),

- 0 indicates that the model does not explain any variance in the target variable, and

- A negative value can occur if the model performs worse than a simple mean-based model.

When to Use R²:

- R² is typically used for evaluating the performance of regression models, such as linear regression.
- It is suitable when you want to know how much of the variation in the target variable is explained by the model.

Example: R² in Scikit-learn

from sklearn.metrics import r2_score
import numpy as np

```
# Actual target values
y_actual = np.array([3, -0.5, 2, 7])

# Predicted target values
y_pred = np.array([2.5, 0.0, 2, 8])

# Calculate R-squared
r2 = r2_score(y_actual, y_pred)
print(f"R-squared: {r2:.2f}")
```

4.4.2 Mean Squared Error (MSE) - A Metric for Regression

Mean Squared Error (MSE) is another widely used metric for evaluating regression models. MSE measures the average squared difference between the actual and predicted values. The formula is:

$$MSE = \frac{1}{n} \sum_{i=1}^{n} (y_i - \hat{y}_i)^2$$

Where:

- y_i is the actual value of the target variable,

- $\hat{y}_i$ is the predicted value of the target variable,

- n is the number of samples.

The MSE gives more weight to large errors because it squares the residuals, which makes it more sensitive to outliers. The lower the MSE, the better the model's predictions.

When to Use MSE:

- MSE is used for evaluating regression models where the objective is to minimize the difference between actual and predicted values.
- It's appropriate for models where large errors are particularly undesirable, as it penalizes larger errors more heavily.

Example: MSE in Scikit-learn

```
from sklearn.metrics import mean_squared_error

# Calculate Mean Squared Error
mse = mean_squared_error(y_actual, y_pred)
print(f"Mean Squared Error: {mse:.2f}")
```

4.4.3 Accuracy - A Metric for Classification

Accuracy is one of the most straightforward and widely used metrics for classification models. It measures the proportion of correctly predicted samples to the total number of samples. The formula for accuracy is:

$$\text{Accuracy} = \frac{\text{Number of Correct Predictions}}{\text{Total Number of Predictions}}$$

Accuracy is expressed as a percentage ranging from 0% to 100%. It works well when the classes are balanced and the cost of misclassification is similar for all classes.

When to Use Accuracy:

- Accuracy is suitable for classification problems where the classes are balanced (i.e., the number of samples in each class is approximately the same).
- It is less useful in imbalanced classification problems, where one class may dominate the dataset, as the model can achieve high accuracy simply by predicting the majority class for all samples.

Example: Accuracy in Scikit-learn

```
from sklearn.metrics import accuracy_score

# True labels (actual class)
y_true = [1, 0, 1, 1, 0, 1, 0, 1]

# Predicted labels (model predictions)
y_pred = [1, 0, 0, 1, 0, 1, 1, 1]

# Calculate accuracy
accuracy = accuracy_score(y_true, y_pred)
print(f"Accuracy: {accuracy * 100:.2f}%")
```

4.4.4 F1-score - A Metric for Classification

The F1-score is a metric that is particularly useful for imbalanced classification problems. It is the harmonic mean of precision and recall, and provides a single score that balances both metrics. The F1-score is defined as:

$$F1 = 2 \times \frac{\text{Precision} \times \text{Recall}}{\text{Precision} + \text{Recall}}$$

Where:

- **Precision** is the proportion of positive predictions that are actually correct:

$$\text{Precision} = \frac{TP}{TP + FP}$$

- **Recall** is the proportion of actual positives that are correctly identified:

$$\text{Recall} = \frac{TP}{TP + FN}$$

Where:

- TP is the number of **True Positives** (correct positive predictions),

- FP is the number of **False Positives** (incorrect positive predictions),

- FN is the number of **False Negatives** (incorrect negative predictions).

The F1-score is especially important when:

- There is a class imbalance in the dataset (i.e., one class occurs much more frequently than the other).
- Both precision and recall are important, and we need to balance them.

An F1-score of 1.0 indicates perfect precision and recall, while a score of 0 indicates that the model is failing to correctly classify the positive class.

When to Use F1-score:

- The F1-score is typically used when dealing with imbalanced datasets or when both false positives and false negatives carry significant costs.
- It is often the metric of choice when precision and recall are both crucial.

Example: F1-score in Scikit-learn

from sklearn.metrics import f1_score

 # Calculate F1-score
f1 = f1_score(y_true, y_pred)
print(f"F1-score: {f1:.2f}")

4.4.5 Summary of Evaluation Metrics

Metric	Type	Use Case	Range	Interpretation
R^2 (R-squared)	Regression	Measures how well the model fits the data.	0 to 1	1 means perfect fit, 0 means no fit.
MSE (Mean Squared Error)	Regression	Measures the average squared difference between predicted and actual values.	0 to ∞	Lower values indicate better model performance.
Accuracy	Classification	Measures the proportion of correct predictions.	0% to 100%	Higher values indicate better model performance.
F1-score	Classification	Balances precision and recall, especially for imbalanced datasets.	0 to 1	1 means perfect balance between precision and recall.

Choosing the right performance metric is crucial when evaluating machine learning models, as it influences the interpretation of the model's performance. For regression problems, R^2 and MSE provide valuable insights into the model's ability to predict continuous outcomes. For classification problems, accuracy is a simple and widely used metric, but when dealing with imbalanced classes, the F1-score offers a more balanced measure of performance by considering both precision and recall.

Understanding these metrics helps data scientists and machine learning practitioners make informed decisions about model performance and improvements.

5. Tree-Based Models and Ensemble Learning

Decision trees provide intuitive and powerful methods for classification and regression tasks. This chapter covers decision trees, random forests, and gradient boosting techniques such as XGBoost and LightGBM. You'll discover how ensemble learning methods combine multiple models to improve accuracy and robustness.

5.1 Decision Trees: How They Work and When to Use Them

Decision Trees are one of the most popular and versatile algorithms in machine learning. They are particularly useful for both classification and regression tasks. A decision tree model is intuitive, interpretable, and can handle both categorical and continuous data. This section will explore how decision trees work, their advantages and limitations, and when they are the right choice for a given problem.

5.1.1 What is a Decision Tree?

A decision tree is a tree-like structure in which:

- Each internal node represents a decision based on the value of an input feature (or a set of features),
- Each branch represents the outcome of a decision (a split on the data),
- Each leaf node represents a final predicted output (class label or regression value).

The goal of a decision tree is to split the data into subsets based on feature values, such that each split makes the data in each subset as homogeneous as possible. These splits continue recursively until a stopping criterion is met, such as a maximum tree depth or when further splits do not significantly improve the model's performance.

5.1.2 How Do Decision Trees Work?

A decision tree is built by recursively splitting the dataset based on feature values. The splits are chosen in such a way that the data points in each subset become as similar as possible according to a specific criterion.

The construction process can be broken down into the following steps:

Selecting a Feature and Split Point: The algorithm evaluates each feature and finds the best split based on a certain criterion. For classification tasks, the most common criteria are Gini impurity or Entropy (for information gain). For regression tasks, variance reduction or mean squared error (MSE) can be used as the splitting criterion.

Gini Impurity: Measures the degree of impurity or disorder. A lower Gini impurity indicates that the subset is more homogenous.

$$Gini(t) = 1 - \sum_{i=1}^{K} p_i^2$$

Where p_i is the proportion of class i in node t, and K is the number of classes.

Entropy: Measures the uncertainty or disorder in the dataset. It's often used with the concept of information gain.

$$Entropy(t) = - \sum_{i=1}^{K} p_i \log_2(p_i)$$

Where p_i is the proportion of class i in node t.

Variance: For regression, the algorithm tries to reduce the variance in the data after splitting the dataset.

Splitting the Data: After selecting the best feature and the best split point, the data is divided into two or more subsets. The decision tree recursively splits the data, choosing the best split at each node based on the chosen splitting criterion.

Stopping Criterion: The splitting process continues until one of the following conditions is met:

- The tree reaches a specified maximum depth.
- A node reaches a minimum number of samples.
- Further splits do not improve the model (i.e., when no additional gain can be achieved in classification purity or regression variance).

At this point, each leaf node represents a final decision or prediction.

Prediction: Once the decision tree is trained, predictions for new data are made by traversing the tree, starting at the root node and following the decisions based on the features of the input data until reaching a leaf node. The output at the leaf node is the prediction.

- In classification, the output is the majority class in the leaf node.
- In regression, the output is typically the average value of the target variable in the leaf node.

5.1.3 When to Use Decision Trees

Decision trees can be highly effective in a variety of situations. Here are some scenarios where decision trees shine:

Interpretability and Transparency: One of the biggest advantages of decision trees is their interpretability. Since the decision-making process is represented as a tree, it is easy to follow the logic behind predictions, making decision trees highly transparent. This is especially useful in fields like healthcare, finance, and law, where understanding how decisions are made is critical.

Non-linearity: Decision trees do not assume a linear relationship between the features and the target variable. This makes them suitable for problems where the relationship between features is complex and non-linear.

Handling Mixed Data Types: Decision trees can handle both categorical and numerical data without requiring extensive data preprocessing. They can also naturally handle missing values, which makes them robust for real-world data.

Feature Selection: Decision trees automatically perform feature selection during the splitting process. By evaluating which features contribute most to reducing impurity or variance, they inherently select important features for the model, making them useful when dealing with datasets with many features.

Handling Large Datasets: Decision trees can efficiently handle large datasets and can be parallelized to improve performance on very large datasets. They are also flexible in handling both small and large datasets.

5.1.4 Advantages of Decision Trees

Simple to Understand and Visualize: The model is easy to interpret because decisions are made through a series of simple questions based on feature values. The structure of the tree can be visualized, which helps in understanding how decisions are made.

No Feature Scaling Required: Unlike many other algorithms, decision trees do not require feature scaling or normalization. This simplifies the preprocessing pipeline.

Handles Missing Data: Decision trees can handle missing values by using surrogate splits or by simply choosing the best possible split that does not require a particular feature.

Flexibility: Decision trees can be used for both classification (predicting a category) and regression (predicting a continuous value), making them versatile.

5.1.5 Limitations of Decision Trees

While decision trees have many strengths, they also have several limitations:

Overfitting: Decision trees tend to overfit, especially when they grow deep. They may create overly complex trees that fit the training data very well but perform poorly on unseen data (test set). Pruning (limiting the depth of the tree) or setting a minimum number of samples for each leaf can help mitigate this issue.

Instability: Decision trees are sensitive to small changes in the data. Even a small change in the training set can lead to a completely different tree structure. This is known as variance. Techniques like bagging and boosting (such as Random Forests and Gradient Boosting Machines) can address this instability by combining multiple trees.

Biased Towards Dominant Features: Decision trees may favor features with more categories or continuous variables with more variance. This bias can be reduced by using tree ensembles or using cost complexity pruning.

Limited to Axis-Parallel Decision Boundaries: Decision trees create decision boundaries that are parallel to the axes of the feature space. This can limit their ability to model complex decision boundaries, particularly when features interact in more intricate ways.

Computationally Expensive for Large Datasets: Although decision trees can handle large datasets, they may become computationally expensive if the tree depth is large. As the tree grows deeper, the computational cost of training increases.

5.1.6 When Not to Use Decision Trees

When You Need to Capture Complex Interactions: If the relationships between features are complex and cannot be captured well by axis-parallel splits, decision trees may struggle. In these cases, more advanced models like random forests or gradient boosting may be better choices.

When You Need a Robust Model: While decision trees are flexible, they can overfit on noisy data. If the data has a lot of noise or outliers, decision trees may fail to generalize well. In such cases, a more robust model, like Support Vector Machines (SVM) or Logistic Regression, may be more appropriate.

When You Need Fine Control Over Predictions: While decision trees are easy to interpret, their decision-making process may not provide the precision required for some applications. If you need a high degree of accuracy and predictive power, ensemble methods like Random Forests or XGBoost can be better suited.

Decision trees are a powerful, flexible, and interpretable machine learning algorithm. They are highly effective for both classification and regression tasks, particularly when interpretability and simplicity are essential. However, they are prone to overfitting and can be unstable, which limits their generalization ability in some cases. For such scenarios, techniques like pruning or ensemble methods (e.g., Random Forests or Gradient Boosting) can improve performance and robustness.

In practice, decision trees are widely used due to their intuitive nature, ability to handle diverse data types, and ease of use in both small and large datasets. Understanding when to use them and when to consider alternatives is key to building successful machine learning models.

5.2 Random Forests: Improving Model Stability

Random Forests is one of the most powerful and widely used ensemble learning techniques in machine learning. It is designed to address some of the weaknesses of decision trees, particularly their tendency to overfit and their instability. By combining the predictions of multiple decision trees, Random Forests improve both the accuracy and robustness of models, making them less prone to overfitting and more generalizable to unseen data.

In this section, we will explore how Random Forests work, their advantages, how they improve model stability, and when to use them.

5.2.1 What is a Random Forest?

A Random Forest is an ensemble learning method that builds a collection of decision trees and combines their predictions to produce a more accurate and stable output. The key idea behind Random Forests is to reduce the variance of individual decision trees by averaging multiple models. The ensemble nature of Random Forests ensures that the overall model is less sensitive to small variations in the data, which makes it more robust and stable than a single decision tree.

A Random Forest consists of several decision trees, each of which is trained on a random subset of the training data. The final prediction is made by aggregating the individual predictions of the trees, usually by taking a majority vote for classification tasks or averaging the predictions for regression tasks.

The steps for creating a Random Forest are as follows:

Bootstrap Sampling:

- For each tree, a random subset of the training data is selected through a technique called bootstrap sampling (sampling with replacement). This means that some data points may appear more than once in the subset, while others may be left out entirely.

Random Feature Selection:

- In addition to sampling data, Random Forests also use a random subset of features when splitting each node in the decision trees. Instead of evaluating all features at every split, only a random subset of features is considered, which helps to reduce correlation among the individual trees and improve diversity within the forest.

Tree Construction:

Each tree in the forest is built by recursively splitting the data based on the selected features and data samples. These trees are allowed to grow deep without pruning, which ensures that the individual trees capture complex patterns in the data.

Aggregation:

Once all the trees are built, the predictions from the individual trees are combined. In classification tasks, the prediction is made by taking the majority vote (the class predicted by most trees). In regression tasks, the prediction is made by averaging the predicted values of all the trees.

5.2.2 How Random Forests Improve Model Stability

Random Forests provide several key improvements over individual decision trees, especially in terms of model stability, accuracy, and robustness. Here's how they achieve these improvements:

Reducing Overfitting: One of the main strengths of Random Forests is their ability to reduce overfitting. A single decision tree tends to overfit the data, especially when it is deep and complex. Overfitting occurs when the model captures noise in the data rather than the underlying patterns, leading to poor performance on unseen data. Random Forests mitigate this issue by averaging multiple trees, each trained on a different subset of the data. As a result, the noise and fluctuations in the data are smoothed out, leading to better generalization and less overfitting.

For example, imagine a decision tree that overfits to small fluctuations in the training data. In a Random Forest, the other trees trained on different subsets of the data will not overfit in the same way, and by aggregating their predictions, the model becomes more stable and less likely to overfit.

Reducing Variance: A single decision tree can be highly sensitive to small changes in the data, leading to high variance. In contrast, Random Forests reduce variance by averaging the predictions of multiple trees. This ensemble approach smooths out the impact of any individual tree's errors, resulting in a more stable and robust model. Even if one tree makes a poor prediction due to a noisy subset of the data, the overall prediction is less likely to be affected because other trees will provide more accurate predictions.

Improving Accuracy: Random Forests often achieve better accuracy than individual decision trees. By training multiple trees on different random subsets of the data and using random feature selection, Random Forests can capture a wide range of patterns in the data that might be missed by a single decision tree. The model's diversity comes from the combination of multiple trees trained with different perspectives on the data, which leads to better overall performance.

Handling Imbalanced Data: Random Forests are robust to imbalanced datasets, where one class is significantly more prevalent than the others. In classification problems with imbalanced classes, a single decision tree might become biased toward the majority class, while Random Forests can reduce this bias by considering multiple trees with diverse splits. Moreover, techniques such as class weighting can further improve performance in imbalanced settings.

Reduced Sensitivity to Outliers: Individual decision trees can be sensitive to outliers, especially when the tree grows very deep. Outliers can cause certain branches of the tree to become overfitted to rare cases. In contrast, Random Forests reduce the impact of outliers by averaging the predictions of many trees. While one tree might be influenced by an outlier, the ensemble of trees will usually provide a more balanced prediction.

5.2.3 When to Use Random Forests

Random Forests are a versatile and powerful algorithm that can be used for a wide range of machine learning problems. Here are some scenarios where they are particularly effective:

Classification and Regression: Random Forests can be used for both classification and regression tasks. Whether you're trying to predict a class label or a continuous value, Random Forests can provide accurate and stable predictions. The algorithm is widely used in various domains, including image classification, medical diagnoses, stock market prediction, and more.

When Model Interpretability is Less Important: While individual decision trees are highly interpretable, Random Forests are not as transparent. Since they consist of many decision trees, it can be challenging to interpret the logic behind individual predictions. Therefore, Random Forests are ideal for applications where accuracy and robustness are more important than interpretability.

When You Have Complex, Non-linear Relationships: Random Forests perform well when the data exhibits complex, non-linear relationships. Since each tree in the forest is capable of capturing different aspects of the data, Random Forests can handle intricate interactions between features better than simpler models like linear regression or logistic regression.

When You Need to Avoid Overfitting: Random Forests are particularly useful when the risk of overfitting is high, such as when you have noisy or high-dimensional data. By aggregating the predictions of many decision trees, Random Forests reduce the impact of overfitting and improve generalization.

When Dealing with Missing Data: Random Forests can handle missing data quite well. During the construction of each tree, missing values are dealt with by surrogate splits, which ensure that the tree can still make reasonable decisions even if some features are missing. This is particularly useful in real-world datasets where missing data is common.

5.2.4 Advantages of Random Forests

- **High Accuracy**: Random Forests often achieve superior accuracy compared to individual decision trees and many other machine learning algorithms.
- **Reduced Overfitting**: The ensemble approach helps to prevent overfitting, making Random Forests a reliable choice for many tasks.
- **Handles Large Datasets Well**: Random Forests can handle large datasets with many features and can scale well when trained on more data.
- **Robust to Outliers and Missing Data**: Random Forests are less sensitive to outliers and can handle missing data effectively.
- **Feature Importance**: Random Forests can provide insights into feature importance, helping to identify which features are most influential in making predictions.

5.2.5 Limitations of Random Forests

- **Less Interpretability**: Random Forests sacrifice interpretability for accuracy. The complexity of the model makes it difficult to understand how predictions are made.
- **Computationally Expensive**: While Random Forests are parallelizable, they can be computationally expensive, especially when dealing with large datasets or a high number of trees.

Memory Intensive: Random Forests store many decision trees in memory, which can be resource-intensive for large models.

Random Forests are an incredibly powerful tool in machine learning, offering improved model stability, reduced overfitting, and high accuracy. By combining multiple decision trees and introducing randomness into both the data and feature selection process, Random Forests provide a robust solution for many classification and regression problems. Although they come with some computational overhead and reduced interpretability, their performance makes them a top choice for tasks where accuracy and stability are paramount.

Understanding when to use Random Forests and how they improve upon individual decision trees can help practitioners leverage this algorithm effectively in a wide range of machine learning applications.

5.3 Gradient Boosting & XGBoost for Powerful Predictions

Gradient Boosting and XGBoost are two of the most powerful machine learning algorithms for both classification and regression tasks. They are built on the concept of boosting, which aims to improve the performance of weak models (usually decision trees) by combining them into a strong, accurate predictor. Both algorithms are known for their outstanding predictive power, robustness, and flexibility, and they have become go-to methods for many machine learning practitioners, especially in competitive machine learning scenarios such as Kaggle competitions.

This section will explore the principles of gradient boosting, how it works, and why XGBoost, an optimized version of gradient boosting, is often considered the gold standard in the field.

5.3.1 What is Gradient Boosting?

Gradient Boosting is an ensemble learning technique that builds a model in a stage-wise manner by combining the predictions of multiple weak models (typically decision trees). The core idea is to train each new model to correct the errors made by the previous model, thus "boosting" the overall performance.

In Gradient Boosting, each new model is trained to minimize the residual errors of the ensemble so far. The term "gradient" refers to the fact that the errors are corrected by taking steps in the direction of the negative gradient of the loss function, hence "gradient descent" is used for optimization.

How Gradient Boosting Works:

Initialize the Model: Gradient boosting starts by initializing the model with a simple model, often just the mean or median of the target variable for regression or a constant value for classification. This model serves as the starting point.

Compute Residuals (Errors): After the initial model is trained, the residuals (or errors) are calculated. The residual is the difference between the actual target values and the predicted values from the current model.

Fit a New Model: A new model (usually a shallow decision tree) is trained on the residuals of the previous model. The goal is to learn how to predict the errors made by the previous model.

Update the Model: The predictions from the new model are added to the current model's predictions. The model is updated by adding the predictions of the new tree to the previous ensemble's predictions.

Iterate: This process repeats for a specified number of iterations (or until a stopping criterion is met). With each iteration, the ensemble learns to correct more and more of the residuals, progressively improving the model's accuracy.

Final Model: After several iterations, the final prediction is the combined output of all the individual trees in the ensemble. The final model is typically much more accurate than any individual tree.

Key Components of Gradient Boosting:

Weak Learners: In most cases, the weak learners used are decision trees with a limited depth (shallow trees), typically referred to as stumps. These trees are not complex and are typically overfitting on their own, but when combined, they improve accuracy.

Loss Function: Gradient boosting minimizes the loss function, which is the error between the actual and predicted values. The choice of loss function depends on the problem at hand (e.g., Mean Squared Error for regression or Log Loss for classification).

Learning Rate: The learning rate controls the contribution of each model to the final prediction. A smaller learning rate means that each tree's contribution is smaller, which can help prevent overfitting but may require more trees to achieve the same level of performance.

Number of Estimators (Trees): The number of trees in the ensemble is an important hyperparameter. A higher number of trees generally leads to better performance, but also increases the risk of overfitting.

5.3.2 Advantages of Gradient Boosting:

- **High Predictive Accuracy**: Gradient Boosting is known for producing highly accurate models, especially in complex datasets with non-linear relationships between features.
- **Robust to Overfitting**: By adjusting the learning rate and number of estimators, gradient boosting can strike a balance between bias and variance, making it robust to overfitting in many cases.
- **Works Well with Complex Data**: Gradient Boosting can handle both numerical and categorical data and can model complex patterns and interactions within the features.
- **Flexible**: Gradient Boosting can be used with different types of loss functions, making it versatile for both regression and classification tasks.

5.3.3 Limitations of Gradient Boosting:

- **Computationally Expensive**: Gradient Boosting can be slow to train, especially with a large number of trees and a high learning rate. Training can be computationally expensive.
- **Sensitive to Hyperparameters**: The performance of Gradient Boosting can be sensitive to the choice of hyperparameters, including the learning rate, tree depth, and number of estimators.
- **Prone to Overfitting**: While Gradient Boosting is less likely to overfit than a single decision tree, it is still prone to overfitting if the hyperparameters are not tuned correctly or if there are too many trees.

5.3.4 XGBoost: An Optimized Version of Gradient Boosting

XGBoost (Extreme Gradient Boosting) is an advanced implementation of Gradient Boosting that introduces several improvements to make the algorithm faster, more accurate, and more scalable. XGBoost has become the most popular and widely used library for gradient boosting, especially for large-scale machine learning tasks. It has been the algorithm of choice for many winning solutions in machine learning competitions, including Kaggle.

Key Features of XGBoost:

Regularization: XGBoost introduces regularization terms in both the loss function and the tree construction process. Regularization helps prevent overfitting, which is a common issue with traditional gradient boosting models. The two types of regularization in XGBoost are:

- **L1 Regularization** (Lasso) on the leaf weights.
- **L2 Regularization** (Ridge) on the leaf weights.

This makes XGBoost more robust and better at generalizing to unseen data.

Parallelization: Unlike traditional gradient boosting, which builds trees sequentially, XGBoost can train trees in parallel. This results in faster model training, particularly when dealing with large datasets. The parallelization is achieved through histogram-based methods, where the data is bucketed into discrete bins, making the process of finding the best splits much faster.

Handling Missing Data: XGBoost can automatically handle missing data without requiring imputation. The algorithm learns the optimal way to handle missing values during the training process, making it highly efficient when dealing with datasets with missing entries.

Tree Pruning: XGBoost uses a technique called depth-first pruning, which prunes trees after they are fully grown. This differs from traditional gradient boosting, which prunes trees during construction. The depth-first approach helps the algorithm find the optimal model by pruning the trees based on the maximum benefit rather than just reducing depth.

Optimized for Speed: XGBoost is highly optimized for speed and performance. It supports multi-threading, GPU acceleration, and other advanced techniques that make it one of the fastest gradient boosting implementations available.

Early Stopping: XGBoost includes early stopping, which helps to prevent overfitting by monitoring the performance on a validation set during training. If the performance does not improve after a set number of iterations, the training stops early, saving computational resources and improving generalization.

5.3.5 Advantages of XGBoost:

- **Faster Training**: Thanks to parallelization and optimizations like histogram-based methods, XGBoost trains much faster than traditional gradient boosting algorithms, especially for large datasets.
- **High Accuracy**: XGBoost frequently outperforms other machine learning algorithms in terms of accuracy, especially when fine-tuned.
- **Scalability**: XGBoost is highly scalable and can handle large datasets with ease, making it ideal for industrial-scale machine learning tasks.

- **Handles Missing Data Well**: XGBoost has built-in support for missing values, making it particularly useful when dealing with incomplete datasets.
- **Robust Against Overfitting**: Through regularization and early stopping, XGBoost helps prevent overfitting, ensuring good generalization to unseen data.

5.3.6 Limitations of XGBoost:

- **Complexity**: While XGBoost is highly powerful, it can be complex to tune. There are many hyperparameters to optimize, and finding the best combination can be time-consuming.
- **Memory Consumption**: XGBoost can be memory-intensive, especially when working with large datasets. The algorithm stores additional information for regularization, parallelization, and tree pruning, which increases memory usage.

5.3.7 When to Use Gradient Boosting and XGBoost

Gradient Boosting is ideal when you need a powerful model but do not have concerns about computation time. It is useful for smaller datasets or when interpretability is important. It works well in applications such as customer churn prediction, medical diagnoses, and fraud detection.

XGBoost is preferred when you are working with large datasets or need faster training. It is particularly useful when computational efficiency is critical, and it often performs better on structured data tasks. It is widely used in Kaggle competitions and industries like finance, e-commerce, and marketing.

Both Gradient Boosting and XGBoost are incredibly powerful machine learning algorithms that can significantly improve model performance. Gradient Boosting builds strong predictive models by sequentially correcting errors made by previous models, while XGBoost offers an optimized, faster, and more scalable version of the algorithm with several enhancements such as regularization, parallelization, and better handling of missing data.

For most machine learning tasks, XGBoost is the go-to algorithm due to its speed, scalability, and accuracy. However, if interpretability or simpler models are preferred, traditional gradient boosting might be a better choice. Both algorithms represent cutting-edge techniques in machine learning and have revolutionized the way practitioners approach predictive modeling.

5.4 Hyperparameter Tuning for Tree-Based Models

Hyperparameter tuning is a critical aspect of machine learning model development, as the right set of hyperparameters can significantly improve the performance of a model. Tree-based models, including Decision Trees, Random Forests, Gradient Boosting, and XGBoost, are highly sensitive to their hyperparameters, and tuning them correctly can lead to more accurate, stable, and generalizable models.

In this section, we will explore the most important hyperparameters for tree-based models, techniques for tuning them, and the impact of hyperparameter choices on model performance. We will also discuss tools and strategies for efficient hyperparameter optimization.

5.4.1 Importance of Hyperparameter Tuning

Hyperparameters are parameters that control the training process of a machine learning algorithm and are set before the model starts training. These parameters influence how well the model will perform and can significantly affect both the accuracy and efficiency of the model. For tree-based models, selecting the right hyperparameters can help prevent overfitting or underfitting, improve model stability, and optimize the balance between bias and variance.

Common hyperparameters for tree-based models include parameters controlling tree depth, the number of trees, the learning rate, regularization terms, and more. Proper hyperparameter tuning can lead to a model that performs optimally on both training and test data, thus ensuring good generalization to unseen data.

5.4.2 Key Hyperparameters for Tree-Based Models

While different tree-based models have different sets of hyperparameters, there are some common ones across models like Decision Trees, Random Forests, Gradient Boosting, and XGBoost.

1. Decision Trees:

Decision Trees are relatively simple models with a set of hyperparameters that control the growth of the tree. These hyperparameters include:

- **max_depth**: The maximum depth of the tree. Limiting the depth prevents overfitting by reducing the complexity of the tree.

- **min_samples_split**: The minimum number of samples required to split an internal node. Increasing this value prevents the model from learning overly specific patterns in the data.
- **min_samples_leaf**: The minimum number of samples required to be at a leaf node. Larger values prevent the tree from creating branches that fit noise.
- **max_features**: The number of features to consider when looking for the best split. Reducing the number of features can reduce overfitting and improve generalization.
- **criterion**: The function used to measure the quality of a split (e.g., "gini" for Gini impurity or "entropy" for information gain).

2. Random Forests:

Random Forests use a collection of decision trees, and many of the hyperparameters of individual trees apply to Random Forests as well. Some additional hyperparameters include:

- **n_estimators**: The number of trees in the forest. More trees typically lead to better performance, but they also increase computation time.
- **bootstrap**: Whether to use bootstrap sampling (sampling with replacement) when building trees. Setting this to False would build trees without resampling, but bootstrap sampling often improves generalization.
- **max_samples**: The number of samples to draw from the training set to build each tree. It is used in combination with the bootstrap parameter.

3. Gradient Boosting:

Gradient Boosting builds trees sequentially, where each new tree corrects the residuals of the previous tree. The key hyperparameters for gradient boosting are:

- **n_estimators**: The number of trees in the model. More trees generally improve performance, but they can also lead to overfitting if not tuned properly.
- **learning_rate**: The contribution of each tree to the final model. A smaller learning rate reduces the impact of each individual tree, requiring more trees to achieve the same result. A larger learning rate might lead to faster convergence but risks overfitting.
- **subsample**: The fraction of samples to use for training each tree. Using less than 1.0 introduces randomness and helps to reduce overfitting.
- **max_depth**: Similar to decision trees, this controls the maximum depth of the trees in the boosting process. Shallow trees often prevent overfitting.

- **min_samples_split**: The minimum number of samples required to split an internal node. Like decision trees, higher values help reduce overfitting.

4. XGBoost:

XGBoost is an optimized implementation of gradient boosting, and its hyperparameters offer additional flexibility for tuning. Some important hyperparameters include:

- **learning_rate**: Similar to gradient boosting, this controls the impact of each tree. Lower values help prevent overfitting but require more trees.
- **n_estimators**: The number of boosting rounds or trees. Too many trees may lead to overfitting.
- **max_depth**: Controls the maximum depth of each tree, helping prevent overfitting by restricting the complexity of each individual tree.
- **subsample**: The fraction of training data to use for building each tree. This adds randomness and helps reduce overfitting.
- **colsample_bytree**: The fraction of features to use when building each tree. This controls the feature subset for each tree and can improve model generalization.
- **reg_alpha and reg_lambda**: These parameters control L1 (Lasso) and L2 (Ridge) regularization, respectively, helping to prevent overfitting.

5.4.3 Techniques for Hyperparameter Tuning

Hyperparameter tuning can be done manually or through automated search techniques. The goal is to find the best combination of hyperparameters that maximizes the model's performance. Below are some popular methods for hyperparameter tuning:

1. Grid Search:

Grid search is the most straightforward method for hyperparameter tuning. In grid search, a set of hyperparameters is defined along with a grid of possible values for each parameter. The model is trained and evaluated for all combinations of hyperparameters in the grid, and the best-performing set of hyperparameters is chosen.

Example:

from sklearn.model_selection import GridSearchCV

param_grid = {
    'max_depth': [3, 5, 7, 9],

```
    'min_samples_split': [2, 5, 10],
    'n_estimators': [100, 200, 300]
}

grid_search                =            GridSearchCV(estimator=RandomForestClassifier(),
param_grid=param_grid, cv=5)
grid_search.fit(X_train, y_train)
print("Best parameters:", grid_search.best_params_)
```

2. Random Search:

Unlike grid search, which tries every possible combination of hyperparameters, random search samples random combinations of hyperparameters. This can be much more efficient, especially when the hyperparameter space is large. Random search has been shown to outperform grid search in many cases because it explores the space more broadly.

Example:

```
from sklearn.model_selection import RandomizedSearchCV
from scipy.stats import randint

param_dist = {
    'max_depth': randint(3, 10),
    'min_samples_split': randint(2, 10),
    'n_estimators': randint(50, 300)
}

random_search        =        RandomizedSearchCV(estimator=RandomForestClassifier(),
param_distributions=param_dist, n_iter=100, cv=5)
random_search.fit(X_train, y_train)
print("Best parameters:", random_search.best_params_)
```

3. Bayesian Optimization:

Bayesian optimization is an advanced approach that treats hyperparameter tuning as an optimization problem. It uses probabilistic models to estimate the performance of different hyperparameter configurations and then intelligently chooses the next set of hyperparameters to try based on past results. Libraries like Hyperopt and Optuna are popular for implementing Bayesian optimization.

4. Automated Machine Learning (AutoML):

AutoML tools like TPOT, Auto-sklearn, and H2O.ai can automate the process of model selection and hyperparameter tuning. These tools use advanced techniques like genetic algorithms, reinforcement learning, or hyperparameter optimization to search the hyperparameter space and select the best model configuration.

5.4.4 Impact of Hyperparameter Tuning

Proper hyperparameter tuning can significantly improve the performance of tree-based models. Here's how tuning different hyperparameters impacts model performance:

Tree Depth (max_depth): Controlling the depth of the trees prevents overfitting. Shallow trees tend to have high bias but low variance, whereas deeper trees may overfit the data by capturing too many specific details. Tuning this hyperparameter helps strike a balance between bias and variance.

Number of Estimators (n_estimators): Adding more trees usually improves model performance by reducing bias, but it can lead to overfitting if the model is too complex. Tuning this hyperparameter involves finding the optimal number of trees that maximizes performance without overfitting.

Learning Rate: A smaller learning rate reduces the impact of each tree but requires more trees to achieve the same result. Tuning the learning rate helps optimize training speed and performance.

Regularization (reg_alpha, reg_lambda): Regularization techniques like L1 and L2 penalize overly complex models, helping to prevent overfitting. By adjusting these parameters, you can ensure the model generalizes well to unseen data.

Hyperparameter tuning is a crucial step in building effective tree-based models. The right set of hyperparameters can greatly enhance model performance by improving accuracy, reducing overfitting, and speeding up training. Understanding the impact of key hyperparameters such as tree depth, number of estimators, learning rate, and regularization terms is essential for fine-tuning the models.

Using techniques like grid search, random search, Bayesian optimization, or AutoML, practitioners can efficiently explore the hyperparameter space and identify the optimal configuration for their specific task. By mastering the art of hyperparameter tuning, you can unlock the full potential of tree-based models like Decision Trees, Random Forests, Gradient Boosting, and XGBoost.

6. Support Vector Machines and Kernel Methods

Support Vector Machines (SVMs) are powerful algorithms for classification and regression tasks, especially in high-dimensional spaces. This chapter explains how SVMs work, the importance of kernels, and how to fine-tune hyperparameters to maximize performance on different datasets.

6.1 Understanding Support Vector Machines

Support Vector Machines (SVM) are a powerful and widely used class of supervised learning algorithms for classification, regression, and outlier detection. SVMs are particularly renowned for their ability to classify high-dimensional data with high accuracy, and they have proven to be effective in a variety of fields such as image recognition, bioinformatics, and text classification. In this section, we will explore the fundamental concepts of SVMs, how they work, and when they are useful in machine learning applications.

6.1.1 What is a Support Vector Machine?

A Support Vector Machine (SVM) is a type of supervised learning algorithm that constructs a hyperplane (or a set of hyperplanes) in a high-dimensional space that separates different classes of data. The goal of an SVM is to find the optimal hyperplane that best divides the data into classes. Once the SVM model is trained on the data, it can be used to classify new, unseen data points into the appropriate categories.

In simple terms, SVM seeks to create a decision boundary, called a hyperplane, that best separates the data into distinct classes. What sets SVM apart from other classifiers is its focus on maximizing the margin (distance between the hyperplane and the closest data points from each class), which helps improve the generalization of the model to new data.

6.1.2 Components of SVM

To understand how an SVM works, it's helpful to first break down its core components:

Hyperplane: In a two-dimensional space, a hyperplane is simply a line that separates the data points into two classes. In higher-dimensional spaces (such as 3D or even higher), a hyperplane becomes a plane or a higher-dimensional boundary. The key idea of SVM is to find the hyperplane that best separates the data.

Support Vectors: Support vectors are the data points that are closest to the hyperplane. These points are crucial for defining the margin, and they directly influence the position and orientation of the hyperplane. Only these support vectors contribute to the final decision boundary, making SVM a sparse model that focuses on the critical points.

Margin: The margin is the distance between the hyperplane and the closest data points (support vectors) on either side. SVM aims to maximize this margin, as a larger margin generally leads to better model generalization and performance on unseen data.

Linear vs. Nonlinear Separation: SVM can be used for both linearly separable and non-linearly separable data. If the data is linearly separable, SVM will find a straight line (in 2D) or a hyperplane (in higher dimensions) that separates the classes. When the data is not linearly separable, SVM uses a technique called the kernel trick to map the data into a higher-dimensional space where a linear separation is possible.

6.1.3 How SVM Works: A Step-by-Step Overview

Let's walk through the basic steps of how an SVM works for classification:

Data Representation: The input data is represented as points in an n-dimensional space (where n is the number of features in the dataset). Each point has a label (for supervised learning) that indicates which class the data point belongs to.

Finding the Hyperplane: The SVM algorithm starts by finding the hyperplane that separates the two classes. This hyperplane can be represented by a linear equation in the form:

$$w \cdot x + b = 0$$

Where:

- w is the weight vector, which determines the direction of the hyperplane.

- x is the feature vector of the data point.

- b is the bias term, which shifts the hyperplane.

Maximizing the Margin: The key objective of SVM is to maximize the margin between the hyperplane and the closest data points (support vectors) from each class. This helps to ensure that the classifier will perform well on unseen data. Maximizing the margin leads to better generalization.

Training the Model: The SVM algorithm optimizes the placement of the hyperplane by adjusting the weights and bias in such a way that the margin is as large as possible while keeping the data points correctly classified.

Classification: Once the hyperplane has been found and the model trained, new data points can be classified by determining which side of the hyperplane they lie on. Points on one side are classified as belonging to one class, while points on the other side are classified into the other class.

6.1.4 Linear SVMs

When the data is linearly separable (i.e., the two classes can be separated by a straight line or hyperplane), SVMs work by finding the hyperplane that maximizes the margin between the two classes. The optimal hyperplane is the one that not only separates the classes but also maximizes the distance between the closest data points of each class (the support vectors).

Mathematically, the goal is to find the values of w and b that maximize the margin while minimizing classification errors. The optimization problem that SVM solves can be formulated as:

$$\text{maximize} \quad \frac{2}{\|w\|}$$

subject to the constraint that all data points are correctly classified:

$$y_i(w \cdot x_i + b) \geq 1, \quad \forall i$$

Where y_i represents the label of the data point x_i.

6.1.5 Nonlinear SVMs and the Kernel Trick

When the data is not linearly separable (i.e., the two classes cannot be separated by a straight line or hyperplane), SVMs can still be used by mapping the data into a higher-dimensional space where linear separation is possible. This is done using a technique called the kernel trick.

The kernel trick allows SVM to implicitly map the data into a higher-dimensional space without having to compute the coordinates explicitly. This is achieved by applying a kernel function to the input data, which computes the inner product of the data points in the higher-dimensional space. Some common kernel functions include:

Linear Kernel: No transformation is applied. This kernel is used when the data is already linearly separable.

$$K(x_i, x_j) = x_i \cdot x_j$$

Polynomial Kernel: Transforms the data into a higher-dimensional space where non-linear relationships can be captured.

$$K(x_i, x_j) = (x_i \cdot x_j + 1)^d$$

Where d is the degree of the polynomial.

Radial Basis Function (RBF) Kernel: A popular kernel that maps the data into an infinite-dimensional space, capable of handling complex non-linear relationships.

$$K(x_i, x_j) = e^{-\gamma \|x_i - x_j\|^2}$$

Where γ is a hyperparameter that controls the width of the Gaussian function.

The kernel trick makes SVMs highly powerful because they can handle very complex data patterns by transforming the data into a higher-dimensional space where linear separation is possible, without the need for expensive computations.

6.1.6 Advantages of Support Vector Machines

Effective in High-Dimensional Spaces: SVMs work well in cases where the number of features is large, which is especially useful for text classification and image recognition.

Robust to Overfitting: Especially in high-dimensional spaces, SVMs are less prone to overfitting, particularly when the margin is large.

Works Well with Complex and Nonlinear Data: Through the use of kernel functions, SVMs can handle non-linear relationships between features, making them very flexible.

Memory Efficient: SVMs are memory efficient as they only rely on the support vectors to make predictions, rather than the entire dataset.

6.1.7 Limitations of Support Vector Machines

Training Time: SVMs can be computationally expensive, especially for large datasets, because they involve solving a quadratic optimization problem. The training time increases with the number of data points.

Choice of Kernel: The performance of an SVM depends heavily on the choice of the kernel function and its associated parameters (such as γ in the RBF kernel). Finding the right kernel and tuning the parameters requires experimentation.

Poor Performance on Noisy Data: SVMs may struggle with noisy data (i.e., when there is overlap between the classes). In such cases, the SVM might create an overly complex model that overfits the noise in the data.

6.1.8 When to Use Support Vector Machines

SVMs are particularly useful when:

- The data is high-dimensional, with many features (e.g., text classification, gene expression data).
- The relationship between features and target classes is complex and non-linear.
- You have a small to medium-sized dataset.
- You are dealing with binary classification problems (though SVM can be extended to multi-class classification using techniques like one-vs-one or one-vs-rest).

Support Vector Machines are a powerful class of machine learning algorithms that can handle both linear and nonlinear classification tasks. By constructing a decision boundary (hyperplane) that maximizes the margin between classes, SVMs achieve high accuracy and generalization. The ability to use kernel functions to handle complex data relationships makes SVM a versatile and widely-used tool. However, they may be computationally intensive for large datasets and require careful selection of kernels and hyperparameters. Understanding how SVM works and when to apply it is essential for getting the best performance from this algorithm.

6.2 Hyperparameters in SVMs (C, Kernel, Gamma)

Support Vector Machines (SVMs) are powerful machine learning algorithms that have a wide range of hyperparameters that can significantly affect their performance. These hyperparameters need to be carefully chosen to ensure that the model achieves high accuracy and generalizes well to new, unseen data. Among the key hyperparameters in SVMs, C, kernel, and gamma play particularly important roles in controlling the model's behavior.

In this section, we will dive into each of these hyperparameters, explain their functionality, and discuss how they influence the performance of an SVM model.

6.2.1 The C Parameter (Regularization)

The C parameter is one of the most important hyperparameters in SVM, and it controls the trade-off between maximizing the margin and minimizing the classification error. In other words, it governs the regularization of the model.

Role of C: The C parameter defines the penalty for misclassification. A large value of C allows the model to focus on correctly classifying all the training data points, which leads to a narrow margin and might result in overfitting (too complex a model). Conversely, a smaller value of C results in a wider margin but allows for some misclassifications. This can help prevent overfitting and leads to better generalization.

Mathematically, the SVM optimization problem is formulated to minimize:

$$\frac{1}{2}\|w\|^2 + C\sum_{i=1}^{N} \max(0, 1 - y_i(w \cdot x_i + b))$$

Here, the first term is the margin maximization, and the second term is the penalty for misclassifying data points.

Impact of C:

- **Large C**: The model will try to correctly classify all training points, which could lead to overfitting if the data is noisy or contains outliers. The margin will be smaller, as the SVM tries to minimize misclassification at the cost of generalization.
- **Small C**: A smaller C allows for more misclassifications but results in a larger margin and a simpler model. This can improve the model's ability to generalize to new, unseen data.

Choosing C: The value of C should be chosen through cross-validation or a hyperparameter search process (like grid search or random search). Too small a value of C can lead to underfitting, while too large a value can lead to overfitting. A balance between these extremes is usually desired.

Example:

```
from sklearn.svm import SVC
from sklearn.model_selection import GridSearchCV

# Hyperparameter grid for SVM
param_grid = {'C': [0.1, 1, 10, 100]}

# Performing Grid Search for optimal C value
grid_search = GridSearchCV(SVC(kernel='linear'), param_grid, cv=5)
grid_search.fit(X_train, y_train)

print("Best C value:", grid_search.best_params_['C'])
```

6.2.2 The Kernel Parameter

The kernel parameter defines the function used to transform the input data into a higher-dimensional space. SVM can work with linear data (data that can be separated by a straight line or hyperplane) and nonlinear data (data that cannot be linearly separated). The kernel trick is used to implicitly map the data into a higher-dimensional space, enabling the model to find a linear boundary in that new space even when the original data is not linearly separable.

Role of Kernel: The kernel function enables SVM to perform well on nonlinearly separable data by computing the inner product of data points in a higher-dimensional feature space, without actually computing the mapping explicitly. This allows SVM to classify complex patterns more effectively.

Types of Kernels:

Linear Kernel: The linear kernel is used when the data is linearly separable. It does not transform the data and simply computes the inner product of the feature vectors.

$$K(x_i, x_j) = x_i \cdot x_j$$

Polynomial Kernel: This kernel maps the data into a higher-dimensional space using a polynomial transformation. It allows SVM to capture polynomial relationships between data points.

$$K(x_i, x_j) = (x_i \cdot x_j + 1)^d$$

Here, d is the degree of the polynomial, which controls the complexity of the transformation.

Radial Basis Function (RBF) Kernel: The RBF kernel is a very popular choice because it works well in most cases and can handle complex data. It maps the data into an infinite-dimensional space and is based on the Gaussian function.

$$K(x_i, x_j) = e^{-\gamma \|x_i - x_j\|^2}$$

Where γ is a parameter that controls the width of the Gaussian function. A larger γ means that points closer to each other have more influence, leading to a more flexible decision boundary.

Sigmoid Kernel: The sigmoid kernel is similar to the activation function used in neural networks. It can be useful in some scenarios but is less commonly used in practice.

$$K(x_i, x_j) = \tanh(\alpha x_i \cdot x_j + c)$$

Where α and c are kernel-specific parameters.

Choosing the Kernel: The kernel to use is often chosen based on the problem at hand. If the data is linearly separable, a linear kernel may suffice. If the data has complex, nonlinear relationships, the RBF kernel is often a good choice. Cross-validation or grid search can help determine the best kernel for the data.

Example:

```
from sklearn.svm import SVC

# Define SVM model with RBF kernel
model = SVC(kernel='rbf', C=1, gamma=0.1)
```

```
# Fit model to the training data
model.fit(X_train, y_train)
```

6.2.3 The Gamma Parameter (For Nonlinear Kernels)

The gamma parameter is particularly relevant when using the RBF or polynomial kernels. It determines how much influence a single training example has. The higher the value of gamma, the more influence the data points close to the support vectors have, leading to a more complex decision boundary.

Role of Gamma: The gamma parameter controls the spread of the kernel function. A low value of gamma means that points far away from the support vectors will still have an influence, leading to a smoother decision boundary. A high value of gamma makes the kernel more sensitive to the local data points, which can lead to overfitting if the model becomes too sensitive to noise.

Mathematically, gamma is involved in the RBF kernel function:

$$K(x_i, x_j) = e^{-\gamma \|x_i - x_j\|^2}$$

Where γ controls the width of the Gaussian curve used in the transformation. Larger values of γ result in narrower Gaussian distributions, while smaller values make the Gaussian distribution wider.

Impact of Gamma:

- **Large Gamma**: Leads to a more complex, flexible model with a smaller decision boundary. It may fit noise in the data and result in overfitting.
- **Small Gamma**: Results in a smoother decision boundary, which may not capture the underlying complexity of the data, leading to underfitting.
- **Choosing Gamma**: Like the C parameter, gamma should also be optimized using cross-validation. In general, the optimal value of gamma depends on the scale of the data and the specific problem.

Example:

```
from sklearn.svm import SVC
from sklearn.model_selection import GridSearchCV
```

```
# Hyperparameter grid for SVM with RBF kernel
param_grid = {'gamma': [0.001, 0.01, 0.1, 1, 10]}

# Performing Grid Search for optimal gamma value
grid_search = GridSearchCV(SVC(kernel='rbf', C=1), param_grid, cv=5)
grid_search.fit(X_train, y_train)

print("Best gamma value:", grid_search.best_params_['gamma'])
```

The C, kernel, and gamma parameters are central to the performance of Support Vector Machines. Understanding the roles these hyperparameters play helps in configuring the SVM to achieve optimal results for a given problem:

- C controls the trade-off between achieving a low classification error and maximizing the margin.
- Kernel determines the type of transformation applied to the data, making the SVM capable of handling both linear and nonlinear relationships.
- Gamma (for kernels like RBF) controls how much influence each data point has, affecting the flexibility of the decision boundary.

By carefully tuning these hyperparameters, you can optimize the performance of SVMs, ensuring that the model generalizes well and performs effectively on unseen data. Techniques such as cross-validation, grid search, and random search are commonly used to identify the best values for these hyperparameters.

6.3 Kernel Trick and Its Applications

The kernel trick is one of the most powerful and elegant techniques in machine learning, particularly in the context of Support Vector Machines (SVMs). It allows algorithms, such as SVM, to handle non-linear relationships by transforming data into a higher-dimensional space without explicitly computing the transformation. This enables linear classifiers to perform complex, non-linear classification tasks, which would otherwise be impossible in the original feature space.

In this section, we will explore the kernel trick in detail, explaining how it works, why it is so important, and the various applications of this technique.

6.3.1 What is the Kernel Trick?

At a high level, the kernel trick is a mathematical technique used to compute the inner product of two vectors in a higher-dimensional space without having to explicitly map the data points into that higher-dimensional space. This is especially useful in SVMs, where we need to map non-linearly separable data into a higher-dimensional space to find a linear decision boundary.

The kernel trick is based on **kernel functions**, which compute the inner product of two vectors x and y in a feature space (denoted as $\mathcal{H}$) corresponding to a higher-dimensional transformation $\phi(x)$. Rather than explicitly calculating the transformation $\phi(x)$, the kernel function directly computes the inner product $K(x, y) = \langle \phi(x), \phi(y) \rangle$ in the feature space. This is often computationally more efficient, especially for complex transformations.

- **Key Concept**: The kernel trick avoids the need to compute the actual mapping $\phi(x)$. Instead, it allows SVM and other algorithms to work with the kernel function $K(x, y)$, which gives the same result as computing the inner product of the transformed points in the higher-dimensional space, but in a much more efficient manner.

6.3.2 How Does the Kernel Trick Work?

Consider an example where we have data points that are not linearly separable in their original space. Instead of directly applying a linear classifier, SVM uses the kernel trick to transform the data into a higher-dimensional space where a linear separation is possible.

Let's take a 2D example to illustrate how the kernel trick works. Suppose you have two classes of data points that cannot be separated by a straight line in a 2D space. The kernel trick maps these points into a 3D space, where a flat plane (hyperplane) can separate the two classes.

- **Original Space**: In 2D, the data may be so intertwined that no straight line can separate the classes.
- **Higher-Dimensional Space**: By using a kernel function (such as the polynomial or RBF kernel), we implicitly map the data points into 3D (or higher-dimensional space), where a linear separation is feasible.

Mathematically, the transformation $\phi(x)$ maps the original data point x into a higher-dimensional space, and the kernel function computes the inner product in this space without explicitly computing the transformation.

6.3.3 Types of Kernel Functions

There are several common types of kernel functions used in machine learning, particularly in SVMs. Each kernel function corresponds to a different method of mapping data into higher-dimensional spaces. Here are some of the most widely used kernels:

Linear Kernel:

Formula:

$$K(x, y) = x^T y$$

Description: This is the simplest kernel, and it does not transform the data. It computes the inner product in the original space, so it is used when the data is already linearly separable.

Application: Linear SVMs for linearly separable data.

Polynomial Kernel:

Formula:

$$K(x, y) = (x^T y + c)^d$$

Where c is a constant, and d is the degree of the polynomial.

Description: The polynomial kernel maps the data into a higher-dimensional space using polynomial transformations, allowing SVMs to capture polynomial relationships between data points.

Application: SVMs for classification problems where the relationship between features is polynomial in nature (e.g., capturing interactions between features).

Radial Basis Function (RBF) Kernel (Gaussian Kernel):

Formula:

$$K(x, y) = e^{-\gamma \|x-y\|^2}$$

Where γ is a parameter that controls the spread of the kernel.

Description: The RBF kernel is one of the most popular choices for non-linear SVMs. It maps data points into an infinite-dimensional space using a Gaussian function, and is capable of modeling complex, non-linear relationships.

Application: Commonly used in image recognition, time-series analysis, and other tasks where the data exhibits complex non-linear relationships.

Sigmoid Kernel:

Formula:

$$K(x, y) = \tanh(\alpha x^T y + c)$$

Description: The sigmoid kernel is similar to the activation function in neural networks. It can be used to model the data in a non-linear fashion.

Application: This kernel is less commonly used but might be appropriate in certain cases of non-linear data or when experimenting with neural-like behavior in SVMs.

Gaussian Radial Basis Kernel (Gaussian RBF Kernel):

Formula:

$$K(x, y) = e^{-\|x-y\|^2/(2\sigma^2)}$$

Description: The Gaussian RBF kernel is very similar to the RBF kernel, but it has a different form of Gaussian decay. It is often used for classification problems where the data is not linearly separable.

Application: Image processing and bioinformatics tasks.

6.3.4 Why is the Kernel Trick Useful?

The kernel trick is useful for several reasons:

Handles Non-Linearly Separable Data: It allows SVMs to handle cases where the data is not linearly separable by implicitly transforming the data into a higher-dimensional space where a linear separation is possible.

Computational Efficiency: By using kernel functions to compute the inner products directly, the kernel trick avoids the computational cost of explicitly calculating the transformation of the data into a higher-dimensional space. This is critical when dealing with large datasets and high-dimensional feature spaces.

Flexibility: Different kernels provide different ways to map the data into higher-dimensional spaces, allowing SVMs to be applied to a wide variety of tasks, from simple linear classification to complex image and text recognition problems.

Versatility: The kernel trick can be used not just in classification, but also in regression and other machine learning tasks. This versatility makes it a valuable tool for many applications.

6.3.5 Applications of the Kernel Trick

The kernel trick has found wide application across various domains due to its flexibility and power. Some of the most notable applications include:

Text Classification:

Text classification tasks, such as sentiment analysis or spam detection, often require the use of SVMs with kernel functions. Text data is high-dimensional and sparse, which can benefit from non-linear kernel transformations that capture intricate relationships between words.

Image Recognition:

In image recognition tasks, SVMs with the RBF kernel are commonly used. Images have high-dimensional pixel data, and kernel functions can help map these images into higher-dimensional spaces where classification becomes easier.

Bioinformatics:

In bioinformatics, the kernel trick is used in gene expression analysis, protein classification, and disease prediction. The data in these fields is often non-linearly separable, and SVMs with the RBF kernel help uncover complex patterns in the data.

Financial Forecasting:

In stock market prediction or credit scoring, SVMs with non-linear kernels are employed to model complex, non-linear relationships in historical data.

Time Series Analysis:

SVMs can be applied to time series forecasting problems using kernel functions that can capture time-dependent patterns. This is especially useful in applications such as weather prediction, sales forecasting, and sensor data analysis.

Anomaly Detection:

The kernel trick is also useful in detecting anomalies or outliers in data. By transforming data into higher-dimensional spaces, SVMs can better detect abnormal patterns that may not be visible in the original space.

The kernel trick is a powerful concept that enables Support Vector Machines (SVMs) to handle complex, non-linearly separable data by implicitly mapping it into a higher-dimensional space. The use of kernel functions allows SVMs to capture intricate patterns in the data without the need for explicit transformations, saving computational resources and enabling the model to tackle complex problems efficiently. Various kernel functions, such as linear, polynomial, RBF, and sigmoid, allow for flexibility in modeling different types of data relationships. The kernel trick has a wide range of applications in fields such as text classification, image recognition, bioinformatics, and time series analysis, making it a cornerstone technique in machine learning.

6.4 Tuning and Optimizing SVMs

Support Vector Machines (SVMs) are powerful and versatile machine learning algorithms. However, to achieve optimal performance, it's crucial to carefully tune and optimize their hyperparameters. The right combination of hyperparameters can significantly enhance an SVM's ability to generalize and achieve high accuracy. In this section, we will discuss the main hyperparameters that can be tuned in SVMs, methods for optimizing these parameters, and best practices for model selection.

6.4.1 Key Hyperparameters in SVMs

When working with SVMs, there are several important hyperparameters that influence model performance. These hyperparameters include C, kernel, gamma, and degree (for polynomial kernels). By adjusting these hyperparameters, you can control the model's complexity, flexibility, and ability to handle non-linear relationships in the data.

C (Regularization Parameter)

- **Description**: The C parameter controls the trade-off between achieving a low training error and maintaining a large margin between the support vectors. A high value of C reduces the margin to minimize classification errors, leading to a more complex model that may overfit. A small value of C increases the margin but allows for more misclassifications, leading to a simpler model that may underfit.
- **Tuning**: Choose C values based on cross-validation. Too large a value may lead to overfitting, while too small a value may result in underfitting. A typical approach is to test a range of C values (e.g., 0.1, 1, 10, 100).

Kernel

- **Description**: The kernel parameter defines the function used to map the data into a higher-dimensional space. Common kernels include linear, polynomial, Radial Basis Function (RBF), and sigmoid. Each kernel performs a different type of transformation, and the choice of kernel depends on the data's inherent characteristics.
- **Tuning**: Select the kernel based on the nature of the problem. If the data is linearly separable, use a linear kernel. For non-linearly separable data, the RBF kernel or polynomial kernel might be more appropriate. Cross-validation or model selection strategies can help determine the best kernel.

Gamma (For Non-linear Kernels like RBF and Polynomial)

- **Description**: Gamma is a parameter associated with non-linear kernels, particularly the RBF kernel. It defines the influence of a single training point on the decision boundary. A low gamma results in a smoother decision boundary, while a high gamma leads to a more flexible and complex boundary, increasing the likelihood of overfitting.
- **Tuning**: Gamma values should be tested over a wide range (e.g., 0.001, 0.01, 0.1, 1, 10). In most cases, cross-validation helps to select the optimal value.

Degree (For Polynomial Kernel)

- **Description**: The degree parameter is relevant only for the polynomial kernel. It controls the degree of the polynomial used to map the data into a higher-dimensional space. Higher values of degree result in more complex transformations, while lower values create simpler transformations.
- **Tuning**: If you're using a polynomial kernel, you should test different degrees (e.g., 2, 3, 4) to see how the model performs on your data.

Coef0 (For Polynomial and Sigmoid Kernels)

- **Description**: The coef0 parameter is used in the polynomial and sigmoid kernels to control the influence of higher-degree polynomials or the sigmoid activation function. It adjusts the bias term in the kernel function.
- **Tuning**: Tuning coef0 can be useful when dealing with polynomial or sigmoid kernels, but in practice, it's not as commonly tuned as C, gamma, or kernel choice. Still, it may have an impact on model performance, especially when using polynomial kernels with high degrees.

6.4.2 Methods for Tuning and Optimizing SVM Hyperparameters

There are several approaches to tune and optimize SVM hyperparameters, from manual selection to automated search methods. Below are some common methods:

Grid Search

- **Description**: Grid search is an exhaustive search technique that tests all possible combinations of hyperparameter values in a predefined grid. You specify a set of values for each hyperparameter, and grid search trains the model on each combination to evaluate which configuration performs best.
- **Advantages**: Grid search is simple to implement and guarantees that all combinations of parameters are tested. It can be used with cross-validation to avoid overfitting.
- **Disadvantages**: Grid search can be computationally expensive, especially when the parameter grid is large or the dataset is very large.

Example:

```
from sklearn.model_selection import GridSearchCV
from sklearn.svm import SVC
```

```
# Define parameter grid for SVM
param_grid = {
    'C': [0.1, 1, 10],
    'gamma': [0.001, 0.01, 0.1, 1],
    'kernel': ['linear', 'rbf']
}

# Create a model and perform grid search
grid_search = GridSearchCV(SVC(), param_grid, cv=5)
grid_search.fit(X_train, y_train)

# Print the best hyperparameters
print("Best parameters:", grid_search.best_params_)
```

Randomized Search

- **Description**: Randomized search is a more computationally efficient alternative to grid search. Instead of testing all possible combinations of hyperparameters, it randomly selects a fixed number of combinations from the parameter grid. This method is particularly useful when the hyperparameter space is large.
- **Advantages**: It's faster than grid search, especially when the search space is large. It can potentially find a good combination of hyperparameters even with fewer trials.
- **Disadvantages**: Since it's random, it doesn't guarantee that it will find the optimal combination. However, it often finds good results in fewer iterations.

Example:

```
from sklearn.model_selection import RandomizedSearchCV
from sklearn.svm import SVC
from scipy.stats import uniform

# Define parameter distribution for SVM
param_dist = {
    'C': uniform(0.1, 100),
    'gamma': uniform(0.001, 1),
    'kernel': ['linear', 'rbf']
}
```

```
# Create a model and perform randomized search
randomized_search = RandomizedSearchCV(SVC(), param_dist, n_iter=10, cv=5)
randomized_search.fit(X_train, y_train)

# Print the best hyperparameters
print("Best parameters:", randomized_search.best_params_)
```

Cross-Validation

- **Description**: Cross-validation is a technique used to assess the performance of a model by splitting the data into multiple training and testing subsets. The model is trained on a subset of the data and evaluated on the remaining data. This process is repeated multiple times to ensure that the model's performance is not dependent on the particular split of the data.
- **Advantages**: Cross-validation helps to avoid overfitting and provides a more reliable estimate of model performance by evaluating it on different data subsets.
- **Disadvantages**: It can be computationally expensive, particularly with large datasets or when using expensive models like SVM.

Example:

```
from sklearn.model_selection import cross_val_score
from sklearn.svm import SVC

# Define the SVM model with optimized hyperparameters
model = SVC(C=1, kernel='rbf', gamma=0.01)

# Perform 5-fold cross-validation
cv_scores = cross_val_score(model, X_train, y_train, cv=5)

# Print the mean cross-validation score
print("Mean cross-validation score:", cv_scores.mean())
```

6.4.3 Best Practices for Tuning and Optimizing SVMs

To achieve the best possible performance from your SVM model, follow these best practices:

Start with Default Parameters: Before you begin tuning, start with the default values for the SVM parameters to get a baseline performance. This allows you to understand how the model performs without any hyperparameter tuning.

Use Cross-Validation: When tuning SVM hyperparameters, use cross-validation to evaluate different hyperparameter combinations. This helps ensure that the model generalizes well to new data.

Focus on C and Gamma: C and gamma are two of the most critical hyperparameters in SVMs. Focus on tuning these parameters first, as they have the largest impact on model performance.

Experiment with Different Kernels: If the data is non-linear, experiment with different kernels (e.g., RBF, polynomial). The choice of kernel plays a key role in how well the SVM performs.

Monitor Overfitting and Underfitting: Keep an eye on training and validation performance to ensure that the model is neither overfitting nor underfitting. Adjust C and gamma to balance bias and variance.

Use Grid Search and Randomized Search: Utilize automated search methods like grid search or randomized search to explore hyperparameter spaces efficiently.

Consider Feature Scaling: SVMs are sensitive to the scale of the data, so make sure to apply feature scaling (e.g., StandardScaler or MinMaxScaler) to standardize the input features before training the model.

Tuning and optimizing SVMs is a critical step in building a robust machine learning model. By adjusting hyperparameters such as C, kernel, gamma, and degree, you can control the complexity and flexibility of the model. Techniques like grid search, randomized search, and cross-validation help automate the process of hyperparameter optimization. Following best practices such as focusing on C and gamma, using appropriate kernels, and monitoring overfitting/underfitting will improve the chances of achieving an optimal model. SVMs, with their powerful kernel trick and optimization strategies, can handle a wide variety of classification and regression problems effectively when tuned properly.

7. Clustering and Unsupervised Learning

Unsupervised learning enables us to find hidden patterns in data without labeled outputs. This chapter introduces clustering techniques like K-Means, DBSCAN, and hierarchical clustering, along with dimensionality reduction techniques like PCA. You'll learn when and how to apply these methods to real-world data.

7.1 Introduction to Clustering Methods

Clustering is a fundamental concept in unsupervised machine learning, where the goal is to group similar data points together into clusters. Unlike supervised learning, where labeled data is used to train a model, clustering methods work on unlabeled data to discover inherent structures or patterns within the data. It is an essential technique for exploring and understanding datasets, especially when there is no prior knowledge about the data.

In this section, we will provide an introduction to clustering methods, explaining what clustering is, why it's useful, the different types of clustering, and some of the most commonly used clustering algorithms.

7.1.1 What is Clustering?

Clustering refers to the task of grouping a set of objects in such a way that objects in the same group (cluster) are more similar to each other than to those in other groups. The measure of similarity (or dissimilarity) can vary depending on the type of data and the specific application. In clustering, the algorithm automatically finds these patterns based on the data's features.

For example, in customer segmentation, a clustering algorithm might group customers based on their purchasing behavior, such that customers with similar buying patterns are clustered together. In image recognition, clustering can be used to group similar images, helping with tasks like image categorization.

The primary goal of clustering is to explore the underlying structure of the data and reveal hidden patterns, outliers, or trends. It can also serve as a preprocessing step for other machine learning tasks, such as classification or anomaly detection.

7.1.2 Types of Clustering

Clustering algorithms can be broadly classified into several categories, each with its characteristics and use cases:

Centroid-based Clustering:

- In centroid-based clustering, the objective is to partition the data into clusters where each cluster is represented by a central point, called the centroid. The algorithm assigns each data point to the cluster whose centroid is closest.
- The most popular example of centroid-based clustering is K-Means clustering, which tries to minimize the variance within each cluster by adjusting the centroids.
- **Example**: K-Means, K-Medoids.

Density-based Clustering:

- Density-based clustering focuses on identifying regions of high data density and forming clusters based on these regions. These algorithms can discover clusters of arbitrary shape and are particularly useful when the data contains noise or outliers.
- A key advantage of density-based methods is that they do not require specifying the number of clusters beforehand.
- **Example**: DBSCAN (Density-Based Spatial Clustering of Applications with Noise), OPTICS (Ordering Points to Identify Clustering Structure).

Hierarchical Clustering:

Hierarchical clustering builds a tree-like structure (dendrogram) that represents the nested grouping of data points. There are two types of hierarchical clustering:

- **Agglomerative (bottom-up):** Starts with each data point as its own cluster and merges the closest clusters iteratively.
- **Divisive (top-down):** Starts with all data points in one cluster and recursively divides the clusters into smaller ones.
- Hierarchical clustering does not require the number of clusters to be specified in advance.
- **Example**: Agglomerative hierarchical clustering, Divisive hierarchical clustering.

Model-based Clustering:

- Model-based clustering methods assume that the data is generated from a mixture of underlying probability distributions. These models fit the data to identify clusters, usually by estimating parameters like the mean and covariance of the distributions.
- One of the most commonly used model-based clustering algorithms is Gaussian Mixture Models (GMMs), which assume that the data points are drawn from a mixture of Gaussian distributions.
- **Example**: Gaussian Mixture Models (GMM), Expectation-Maximization (EM) algorithm.

Graph-based Clustering:

- Graph-based clustering algorithms treat data as a graph, where each data point is a node, and edges represent relationships or similarities between data points. The algorithm finds clusters by detecting connected components or partitions within the graph.
- These algorithms are particularly useful in cases where data has a natural graph-like structure (e.g., social networks, web pages).
- **Example**: Spectral clustering, Community detection algorithms in networks.

7.1.3 Commonly Used Clustering Algorithms

Several clustering algorithms are widely used in practice, each with its strengths, weaknesses, and ideal use cases. Here are some of the most commonly used clustering algorithms:

K-Means Clustering:

- **Description**: K-Means is one of the simplest and most popular clustering algorithms. It partitions the data into a predefined number of clusters (K) and assigns each data point to the nearest cluster centroid. The algorithm iteratively refines the centroids by minimizing the within-cluster sum of squared distances (also known as inertia).
- **Strengths**: Fast and efficient, particularly for large datasets. It works well when the clusters are spherical and evenly sized.
- **Limitations**: Sensitive to the initial choice of centroids and the value of K. It struggles with non-spherical clusters and outliers.

DBSCAN (Density-Based Spatial Clustering of Applications with Noise):

- **Description**: DBSCAN is a density-based clustering algorithm that identifies clusters as dense regions of points. It does not require the number of clusters to be specified in advance and can handle noise (outliers). DBSCAN works by expanding clusters from core points that have a minimum number of neighbors within a specified radius.
- **Strengths**: Can discover arbitrarily shaped clusters and is robust to outliers.
- **Limitations**: The performance can be sensitive to the choice of parameters (e.g., the radius of neighborhood points). It may struggle when clusters vary widely in density.

Agglomerative Hierarchical Clustering:

- **Description**: Agglomerative hierarchical clustering starts by treating each data point as its own cluster and then iteratively merges the closest clusters until a stopping criterion (e.g., a desired number of clusters) is met. The process can be visualized using a dendrogram, which shows the hierarchy of cluster merges.
- **Strengths**: Does not require the number of clusters to be specified in advance and produces a hierarchical structure that can be useful for visualizing relationships between data points.
- **Limitations**: Computationally expensive for large datasets (with time complexity $O(n^2)$), and it may not perform well with large amounts of noise.

Gaussian Mixture Models (GMM):

- **Description**: GMM is a probabilistic model-based clustering method that assumes that the data is generated from a mixture of several Gaussian distributions. Each cluster is modeled by a Gaussian distribution with its own mean and covariance. The Expectation-Maximization (EM) algorithm is typically used to estimate the parameters of the GMM.
- **Strengths**: Can handle clusters with different shapes and sizes. Provides soft assignments, meaning each data point can belong to multiple clusters with different probabilities.
- **Limitations**: Assumes the data follows a Gaussian distribution, which may not always be the case. It also requires specifying the number of clusters and can be sensitive to the initial conditions.

Spectral Clustering:

- **Description**: Spectral clustering is based on the eigenvalues of a similarity matrix derived from the data points. The algorithm uses these eigenvalues to reduce the dimensionality of the data and performs clustering on the reduced space. Spectral clustering is particularly effective for clustering data that is connected in a graph-like structure.

- **Strengths**: Can identify clusters that are not necessarily spherical and works well with graph-based data.
- **Limitations**: Computationally expensive, especially for large datasets, as it involves computing the eigenvalues of the similarity matrix.

7.1.4 Applications of Clustering

Clustering has a wide range of applications across various fields. Some notable applications include:

Customer Segmentation: In marketing, clustering is used to segment customers based on purchasing behavior, demographics, or preferences. This helps businesses tailor marketing strategies to specific customer groups.

Image Compression: Clustering can be used to group similar pixels in an image, reducing the amount of data needed to represent the image and enabling compression.

Anomaly Detection: Clustering algorithms can identify outliers or anomalies in data. For example, in network security, clustering can help detect unusual behavior that may indicate a security breach.

Document Clustering: In natural language processing (NLP), clustering is used to group similar documents or web pages based on content. This can be useful for tasks like topic modeling or search engine optimization.

Genomics: Clustering is applied in bioinformatics to group genes, proteins, or other biological data based on similarity. This can help identify patterns in gene expression or protein interactions.

Social Network Analysis: In social network analysis, clustering is used to identify communities of people or groups based on social interactions or other features.

Clustering methods are essential tools in unsupervised machine learning, enabling the discovery of inherent patterns and structures within unlabeled data. By grouping similar data points together, clustering helps uncover relationships, identify outliers, and gain insights from complex datasets. There are various types of clustering algorithms, such as centroid-based, density-based, hierarchical, model-based, and graph-based, each suited for different kinds of data and tasks. Understanding the characteristics of each algorithm and selecting the right one for the task at hand is crucial for achieving meaningful clustering results.

7.2 K-Means and Its Variants

K-Means is one of the most widely used and well-known clustering algorithms in machine learning. It is a centroid-based, unsupervised learning algorithm that partitions data into a predefined number of clusters, K, based on similarity. The algorithm's simplicity and efficiency make it an attractive choice for a variety of clustering tasks. In this section, we will explore how the K-Means algorithm works, its limitations, and some popular variants of K-Means that address specific challenges or enhance its performance.

7.2.1 How K-Means Works

K-Means is a relatively simple algorithm that works in the following steps:

Initialization:

- Choose the number of clusters, K, which defines how many groups the algorithm should partition the data into.
- Randomly initialize K centroids (the center points for each cluster). These can either be selected randomly from the data points or randomly positioned in the feature space.

Assignment:

Assign each data point to the nearest centroid based on a distance metric (typically Euclidean distance). Each data point is placed in the cluster whose centroid is closest to it.

Update:

Once all the data points have been assigned to clusters, recalculate the centroids by computing the mean of all data points in each cluster.

Repeat:

Repeat the Assignment and Update steps until the centroids no longer change significantly or until a maximum number of iterations is reached. This means that the algorithm has converged, and the clustering is complete.

The objective of K-Means is to minimize the within-cluster sum of squared distances (also known as inertia) between the data points and their respective centroids. The algorithm tries to find centroids that minimize this objective function, essentially grouping similar data points together.

7.2.2 Advantages of K-Means

- **Simplicity and Efficiency**: K-Means is easy to understand and implement. It is computationally efficient, making it suitable for large datasets.
- **Scalability**: K-Means can handle a large number of data points, especially when using efficient implementations like the MiniBatch K-Means algorithm.
- **Interpretability**: The resulting clusters are easy to interpret, as each cluster is represented by its centroid, which can be understood as the "average" data point of that cluster.

7.2.3 Limitations of K-Means

Despite its simplicity and efficiency, K-Means has several limitations that can affect its performance, especially on certain types of data:

Choosing the Right K: The algorithm requires the user to specify the number of clusters, K, beforehand. In practice, it is difficult to know the ideal K without experimentation or domain knowledge. Methods like the Elbow Method and Silhouette Score can help, but they are not always foolproof.

Sensitivity to Initialization: The initial choice of centroids can significantly impact the final clusters. If the centroids are chosen poorly, K-Means can converge to a local minimum, leading to suboptimal clustering results.

Assumption of Spherical Clusters: K-Means assumes that the clusters are spherical (i.e., each cluster has roughly the same shape and size). It may struggle to correctly cluster data with non-spherical or elongated clusters.

Sensitivity to Outliers: Outliers can significantly affect the centroid positions, leading to poor clustering. Since K-Means minimizes the mean distance between points and centroids, outliers can distort the cluster boundaries.

Requires Numeric Data: K-Means uses Euclidean distance, which requires the data to be numeric. It does not work well with categorical data unless it is transformed into a numeric format (e.g., using one-hot encoding).

7.2.4 Variants of K-Means

There are several variants of the basic K-Means algorithm designed to address some of its limitations or improve its performance. Below are some of the most popular variants:

K-Means++:

- **Description**: K-Means++ is an enhanced version of the traditional K-Means algorithm designed to improve the initialization of centroids. In standard K-Means, centroids are randomly chosen, which can lead to poor initial cluster assignments. K-Means++ addresses this by choosing the initial centroids more strategically.
- **How It Works**: K-Means++ selects the first centroid randomly and then chooses each subsequent centroid with probability proportional to its distance from the nearest already chosen centroid. This initialization strategy helps ensure that the centroids are spread out, which increases the likelihood of better convergence and reduces the chance of converging to a poor local minimum.
- **Advantages**: K-Means++ leads to faster convergence and typically results in better clustering performance compared to traditional K-Means.
- **Example**: The KMeans class in Scikit-Learn allows you to specify the initialization method as k-means++ to use this variant.

MiniBatch K-Means:

- **Description**: MiniBatch K-Means is a variant designed for scalability and speed when dealing with large datasets. Instead of using the entire dataset to update the centroids in each iteration, MiniBatch K-Means uses small random subsets (mini-batches) of data to update the centroids.
- **How It Works**: At each iteration, a small batch of random data points is selected, and the centroids are updated based on this subset rather than the entire dataset. This significantly reduces the computational cost, especially for large datasets.
- **Advantages**: MiniBatch K-Means is faster and more efficient than traditional K-Means for large datasets, while still maintaining reasonable clustering performance.

- **Limitations**: While it can speed up the process, MiniBatch K-Means may not always produce clusters as accurate as the standard K-Means algorithm, especially if the batch size is too small.

Example:

from sklearn.cluster import MiniBatchKMeans
minibatch_kmeans = MiniBatchKMeans(n_clusters=3, batch_size=100)
minibatch_kmeans.fit(X_train)

K-Medoids (Partitioning Around Medoids):

- **Description**: K-Medoids is a variant of K-Means that replaces the centroid with a real data point (a medoid) as the center of each cluster. The medoid is the point in the cluster that minimizes the sum of dissimilarities to all other points in the cluster. K-Medoids is more robust to outliers compared to K-Means because it uses actual data points instead of the mean.
- **How It Works**: Instead of minimizing squared Euclidean distance (as in K-Means), K-Medoids minimizes the dissimilarity measure (e.g., Manhattan distance, Euclidean distance, or any other suitable metric) between data points.
- **Advantages**: K-Medoids is more robust to noise and outliers than K-Means, as the medoid is less sensitive to extreme values.
- **Limitations**: K-Medoids can be computationally more expensive than K-Means, especially for large datasets, since it involves computing the pairwise dissimilarities between data points.

Bisecting K-Means:

- **Description**: Bisecting K-Means is a hybrid clustering algorithm that combines the benefits of hierarchical clustering and K-Means. It starts with all data points in a single cluster and iteratively splits the data into two clusters using K-Means, selecting the cluster to split based on the sum of squared errors.
- **How It Works**: At each step, Bisecting K-Means performs K-Means with K=2 on the chosen cluster and replaces that cluster with the resulting two clusters. The process is repeated until the desired number of clusters is obtained.
- **Advantages**: Bisecting K-Means can produce better results compared to standard K-Means in some cases, particularly when dealing with clusters of varying sizes and densities. It also tends to be more stable because of the hierarchical approach to splitting clusters.

- **Limitations**: Bisecting K-Means can be more computationally expensive than K-Means due to its iterative splitting process.

Fuzzy C-Means:

- **Description**: Fuzzy C-Means (FCM) is a variation of K-Means that allows data points to belong to multiple clusters with varying degrees of membership, rather than assigning each data point to exactly one cluster. Each point is assigned a degree of membership (a probability) for each cluster.
- **How It Works**: FCM minimizes the weighted sum of squared distances from the points to the cluster centers, with each point's contribution weighted by its degree of membership to the clusters.
- **Advantages**: Fuzzy C-Means is more flexible than K-Means and can handle situations where data points lie near the boundaries between clusters.
- **Limitations**: Fuzzy C-Means can be computationally expensive and may be slower than K-Means.

K-Means is a powerful and efficient clustering algorithm that is widely used in practice, but it comes with some limitations, such as sensitivity to initialization, the requirement to specify the number of clusters, and its assumption of spherical clusters. Variants like K-Means++, MiniBatch K-Means, K-Medoids, Bisecting K-Means, and Fuzzy C-Means address some of these challenges and offer more flexibility and robustness for specific clustering tasks. By understanding the strengths and weaknesses of each variant, practitioners can choose the most appropriate clustering method based on the data characteristics and the specific problem they are trying to solve.

7.3 Density-Based Clustering (DBSCAN)

Density-Based Spatial Clustering of Applications with Noise (DBSCAN) is one of the most popular and widely used clustering algorithms in machine learning, particularly for datasets with noise, outliers, and clusters of arbitrary shapes. Unlike traditional clustering algorithms such as K-Means, which assume that clusters are spherical and of roughly equal size, DBSCAN focuses on identifying dense regions of data, making it a powerful tool for more complex datasets.

In this section, we will explore the DBSCAN algorithm in detail, explain how it works, its key parameters, its advantages and limitations, and real-world applications where DBSCAN can be used effectively.

7.3.1 What is DBSCAN?

DBSCAN is a density-based clustering algorithm that groups data points based on their proximity to each other. The fundamental idea behind DBSCAN is that clusters are regions of high data density, and points in low-density regions are considered outliers or noise.

Unlike K-Means, which requires the number of clusters (K) to be specified in advance, DBSCAN automatically determines the number of clusters and can find clusters of arbitrary shapes. The algorithm also has the advantage of being able to identify noise—points that do not belong to any cluster.

The core concept behind DBSCAN is the definition of core points, border points, and noise points:

- **Core Point**: A point is considered a core point if it has at least a specified number of neighbors (minPts) within a given radius (epsilon, ε). These neighbors are points within the ε distance from the core point.
- **Border Point**: A border point has fewer than minPts neighbors within ε but is within the ε distance of a core point.
- **Noise Point**: A point is considered noise if it is neither a core point nor a border point. It is located in a sparse region where no other points are close enough.

DBSCAN has two main parameters:

- **Epsilon (ε):** The maximum distance between two points to be considered neighbors.
- **MinPts**: The minimum number of points required to form a dense region (i.e., the minimum number of neighbors a point must have to be classified as a core point).

7.3.2 How DBSCAN Works

The DBSCAN algorithm works through the following steps:

- **Choose an unvisited point**: Start with an arbitrary unvisited point in the dataset.
- **Find neighbors**: Identify all points within the ε radius from the current point. If the point has at least MinPts neighbors, it is classified as a core point, and a new cluster is formed.
- **Expand the cluster**: If a point is a core point, all its neighbors are added to the same cluster. Then, the algorithm recursively checks each of the neighboring

points. If any of these neighboring points is also a core point, its neighbors are added to the cluster as well.

- **Mark as visited**: Once the algorithm has finished processing the core point and its neighbors, mark them as visited and move on to the next unvisited point in the dataset.
- **Repeat the process**: Repeat the process until all points in the dataset have been visited and assigned to a cluster or labeled as noise.

DBSCAN does not require the user to specify the number of clusters beforehand, which is an advantage over algorithms like K-Means. It can also identify clusters of varying shapes and sizes and is more robust to outliers.

7.3.3 Advantages of DBSCAN

DBSCAN offers several key advantages over traditional clustering methods like K-Means and hierarchical clustering:

No Need to Specify the Number of Clusters: Unlike K-Means, DBSCAN automatically determines the number of clusters. This is particularly useful when the number of clusters is not known in advance or varies depending on the data.

Ability to Find Arbitrary Shaped Clusters: DBSCAN can discover clusters of arbitrary shapes, as it is based on density rather than distance. This makes it suitable for datasets where clusters are not spherical or linear.

Noise and Outlier Detection: DBSCAN can naturally detect and handle noise. Points that do not meet the density requirements (i.e., points that do not belong to any cluster) are labeled as noise points, which can be useful for data preprocessing or anomaly detection.

Efficient for Large Datasets: When implemented with efficient spatial indexing structures such as k-d trees or R-trees, DBSCAN can scale to large datasets, making it suitable for clustering tasks involving millions of data points.

Works Well with Non-linearly Separable Data: DBSCAN does not make assumptions about the data being linearly separable, which allows it to perform well on complex datasets that may have irregular boundaries.

7.3.4 Limitations of DBSCAN

Despite its strengths, DBSCAN has several limitations that can affect its performance, especially in certain types of data:

Sensitivity to Parameters: DBSCAN's performance depends heavily on the values of ε (epsilon) and MinPts. If ε is too small, DBSCAN may fail to detect clusters, while if it is too large, the algorithm may merge distinct clusters. Similarly, setting MinPts too high may cause the algorithm to fail in identifying meaningful clusters. Choosing the optimal values for these parameters is often challenging and requires experimentation or domain knowledge.

Difficulty with Varying Densities: DBSCAN assumes that all clusters have a similar density. In cases where clusters have vastly different densities, DBSCAN may struggle to identify clusters correctly. For instance, it may classify low-density regions of a high-density cluster as noise.

High Computational Complexity: Although DBSCAN can be efficient with spatial indexing structures, the algorithm has a time complexity of $O(n \log n)$ when spatial indexing is used, and $O(n^2)$ in the worst case if no indexing is applied. This can make it computationally expensive for very large datasets with millions of data points.

Handling of High-Dimensional Data: DBSCAN may not perform well on high-dimensional datasets because the concept of "density" becomes less meaningful in high-dimensional spaces, a phenomenon known as the curse of dimensionality. The distance between points tends to become similar as the dimensionality increases, making it harder for DBSCAN to distinguish between dense and sparse regions.

7.3.5 Applications of DBSCAN

DBSCAN is widely used in a variety of applications due to its ability to handle noise and detect clusters of arbitrary shapes. Some of the key applications of DBSCAN include:

Geospatial Data Analysis: DBSCAN is commonly used in applications like geographic data analysis, where clusters might represent geographic regions with high-density activity, such as areas of high population density or clusters of similar geographic features (e.g., traffic accidents, earthquakes).

Anomaly Detection: Since DBSCAN can identify noise points, it is particularly useful in anomaly detection tasks, where outliers (or anomalous behavior) need to be detected and separated from normal data. This can be applied in areas such as fraud detection, network intrusion detection, or defect detection in manufacturing.

Image Segmentation: In computer vision and image processing, DBSCAN can be used to segment an image into regions based on pixel intensity or color. It can identify regions of high intensity (clusters of similar pixels) and separate them from background noise or other objects.

Social Network Analysis: In social network analysis, DBSCAN can help identify groups or communities within a network of interconnected individuals. It can be used to detect tightly-knit groups, like friends or collaborators, and separate isolated nodes or outliers.

Bioinformatics: In bioinformatics, DBSCAN can be used to group similar gene expression data points, identify patterns in biological data, or classify cells with similar characteristics in cellular analysis.

Recommendation Systems: DBSCAN can be applied to recommendation systems to group users or products based on similarities in behavior, preferences, or ratings. It is particularly useful in detecting subgroups of users with similar interests or behaviors.

DBSCAN is a powerful and flexible clustering algorithm that excels in situations where the number of clusters is not known in advance and when the data contains noise or irregularly shaped clusters. Its density-based approach allows it to identify complex patterns in data and handle outliers effectively. However, choosing the appropriate values for the ε and MinPts parameters can be challenging, and DBSCAN may struggle with datasets containing clusters of varying densities or high-dimensional data. Despite these limitations, DBSCAN is a highly valuable tool in a wide range of applications, from geospatial analysis and anomaly detection to image segmentation and bioinformatics.

7.4 Hierarchical Clustering and Dendrograms

Hierarchical clustering is a powerful unsupervised machine learning algorithm used to group similar objects into clusters. It builds a hierarchy of clusters that can be visualized as a tree structure, commonly referred to as a dendrogram. This approach contrasts with methods like K-Means, which require the number of clusters to be specified in advance. Hierarchical clustering, on the other hand, allows for an exploratory analysis, giving the user the flexibility to choose the number of clusters after inspecting the dendrogram.

In this section, we will explore how hierarchical clustering works, the two main types of hierarchical clustering, the concept of a dendrogram, and its advantages and limitations.

7.4.1 What is Hierarchical Clustering?

Hierarchical clustering is a method of cluster analysis that seeks to build a hierarchy of clusters. The result is typically represented as a tree-like diagram known as a dendrogram, which illustrates the nested grouping of objects and the sequence of merging (in agglomerative clustering) or splitting (in divisive clustering).

There are two main types of hierarchical clustering:

Agglomerative Hierarchical Clustering (Bottom-up approach): This is the most common approach. The algorithm begins with each data point as its own cluster and then iteratively merges the two closest clusters until all points belong to a single cluster or until a stopping criterion is met (such as a pre-specified number of clusters).

Divisive Hierarchical Clustering (Top-down approach): This method starts with all the data points in a single cluster and then recursively splits the most dissimilar cluster into smaller clusters until each data point is in its own cluster.

Among these, agglomerative hierarchical clustering is more widely used due to its simplicity and efficiency in practice.

7.4.2 How Agglomerative Hierarchical Clustering Works

The agglomerative hierarchical clustering algorithm proceeds as follows:

- **Initialization**: Each data point is initially treated as a separate cluster.
- **Calculate Proximity**: At each step, the algorithm calculates the similarity (or dissimilarity) between every pair of clusters. The similarity measure typically used is Euclidean distance for continuous data, but other distance metrics such as Manhattan distance, Cosine similarity, or Pearson correlation can also be used.
- **Merge Closest Clusters**: Identify the two clusters that are the closest to each other (based on the chosen distance metric) and merge them into a single cluster.
- **Update the Distance Matrix**: After merging the clusters, update the distance matrix to reflect the distances between the new cluster and the remaining clusters.
- **Repeat the Process**: Repeat the process of calculating distances and merging clusters until all the data points are in a single cluster or until the desired number of clusters is reached.

The output of agglomerative hierarchical clustering is a hierarchical structure of clusters, which is typically visualized as a dendrogram.

7.4.3 Types of Linkage Criteria

The way in which the distance between two clusters is defined during the merging step is known as the linkage criteria. Different linkage methods can result in different clusterings, and the choice of linkage criteria depends on the structure of the data and the desired clustering properties. The most common linkage methods are:

Single Linkage (Nearest Point Linkage):

- The distance between two clusters is defined as the shortest distance between any single pair of points from the two clusters.
- This method tends to create long, "chain-like" clusters. It is more sensitive to noise and outliers.

Complete Linkage (Farthest Point Linkage):

- The distance between two clusters is defined as the longest distance between any pair of points from the two clusters.
- Complete linkage produces more compact clusters, and it is less sensitive to outliers compared to single linkage.

Average Linkage:

- The distance between two clusters is defined as the average of all pairwise distances between points in the two clusters.
- Average linkage strikes a balance between single and complete linkage, producing clusters that are neither too tight nor too elongated.

Ward's Linkage (Minimum Variance):

- The distance between two clusters is defined by the increase in variance when two clusters are merged. Specifically, Ward's method minimizes the total within-cluster variance at each step.
- This approach tends to produce clusters of equal size and is often preferred when dealing with continuous data.

7.4.4 Dendrogram: Visualizing the Hierarchy

A dendrogram is a tree-like diagram that illustrates the arrangement of clusters produced by hierarchical clustering. The dendrogram is a critical tool for understanding the relationships between clusters and helps the user decide on the optimal number of clusters.

Key features of a dendrogram:

- **Leaves**: The leaves (or the tips) of the tree represent individual data points.
- Branches: The branches of the tree represent clusters formed by merging (or splitting) clusters.
- **Height**: The height of a branch in the dendrogram indicates the distance or dissimilarity between the two clusters being merged. The higher the branch, the greater the dissimilarity between the clusters being merged.

Cutting the Dendrogram: By "cutting" the dendrogram at a certain height (i.e., choosing a threshold for the merging process), you can decide the number of clusters. The height at which you cut corresponds to the maximum dissimilarity allowed between clusters, and the number of resulting clusters is determined by how many branches remain above the cut.

Example: Using hierarchical clustering in Scikit-Learn, we can generate a dendrogram like this:

```
from sklearn.cluster import AgglomerativeClustering
import scipy.cluster.hierarchy as sch
import matplotlib.pyplot as plt

# Create the data points
X = [[1, 2], [1.5, 1.8], [5, 8], [8, 8], [1, 0.6], [9, 11]]

# Perform hierarchical clustering
model = AgglomerativeClustering(distance_threshold=0, n_clusters=None)
model = model.fit(X)

# Create the linkage matrix
linkage_matrix = sch.linkage(X, method='ward')

# Plot the dendrogram
sch.dendrogram(linkage_matrix)
plt.show()
```

In the dendrogram above, the height of each merge indicates the distance at which clusters were merged. By visually inspecting the dendrogram, we can decide on the number of clusters to retain.

7.4.5 Advantages of Hierarchical Clustering

No Need to Predefine the Number of Clusters: Hierarchical clustering does not require the user to specify the number of clusters in advance, making it particularly useful for exploratory analysis when the number of clusters is unknown.

Flexible with Cluster Shapes: Hierarchical clustering is capable of discovering clusters of arbitrary shapes. This makes it suitable for complex datasets that may not conform to the spherical clusters assumed by algorithms like K-Means.

Produces a Hierarchical Structure: The dendrogram provides a rich representation of the data, showing how clusters are nested and the relationships between different clusters at different levels of granularity.

Works Well with Small to Medium-Sized Datasets: Hierarchical clustering is computationally feasible for small to medium-sized datasets and provides a good clustering solution without making assumptions about the number of clusters.

7.4.6 Limitations of Hierarchical Clustering

Computational Complexity: Hierarchical clustering has a time complexity of $O(n^2)$ for agglomerative clustering, making it less efficient for very large datasets. In practice, this can limit its application to smaller datasets, though approximate methods and optimizations like the BIRCH algorithm can help scale it up.

Sensitivity to Noise and Outliers: Hierarchical clustering is more sensitive to noise and outliers compared to other clustering algorithms like DBSCAN. Outliers may cause incorrect merges and influence the final structure of the dendrogram.

Choice of Linkage Method: The choice of the linkage method can significantly influence the resulting clusters. For example, single linkage may produce elongated or chain-like clusters, while complete linkage may result in compact but potentially fragmented clusters. Selecting the appropriate linkage method requires experimentation or domain knowledge.

Difficult with Large Datasets: For very large datasets, the memory and time complexity can become prohibitive, especially when dealing with a high number of data points. However, methods like BIRCH (Balanced Iterative Reducing and Clustering using Hierarchies) can help handle large-scale hierarchical clustering more efficiently.

7.4.7 Applications of Hierarchical Clustering

Hierarchical clustering is widely used in various fields due to its versatility and intuitive results. Some common applications include:

Bioinformatics and Genomics: Hierarchical clustering is extensively used for grouping similar genes or samples based on gene expression data. It helps in identifying patterns in biological data, such as identifying gene families or grouping similar species.

Image Analysis: In image segmentation, hierarchical clustering can group similar pixels or regions of an image, leading to the identification of distinct objects or regions within an image.

Customer Segmentation: In marketing, hierarchical clustering can be used to segment customers based on their purchasing behavior, demographics, or preferences. The dendrogram helps visualize and decide the optimal number of customer segments.

Text Mining: Hierarchical clustering can be used for document clustering or topic modeling, where documents are grouped based on their content, helping to uncover latent topics or themes in large text corpora.

Hierarchical clustering is a versatile and intuitive clustering method that is ideal for situations where the number of clusters is not known in advance. By constructing a dendrogram, hierarchical clustering provides a clear view of the relationships between data points and clusters, allowing for flexible analysis of the data at multiple levels of granularity. While hierarchical clustering has its limitations, particularly in terms of computational efficiency for large datasets, it remains a valuable tool for many clustering tasks, especially when cluster shape and structure are complex.

7.5 Dimensionality Reduction (PCA, t-SNE, UMAP)

Dimensionality reduction is a crucial step in the preprocessing and analysis of high-dimensional data. It refers to the process of reducing the number of features or dimensions of a dataset while preserving as much of the relevant information as possible.

High-dimensional data, often referred to as "curse of dimensionality," can be challenging to visualize, interpret, and analyze. By reducing the dimensionality of data, we can mitigate these challenges and uncover underlying patterns in the data that may not be apparent in the original high-dimensional space.

In this section, we will focus on three popular dimensionality reduction techniques: Principal Component Analysis (PCA), t-Distributed Stochastic Neighbor Embedding (t-SNE), and Uniform Manifold Approximation and Projection (UMAP). Each technique has its strengths and applications, and understanding when and how to use them is crucial for effective analysis of complex data.

7.5.1 Principal Component Analysis (PCA)

Principal Component Analysis (PCA) is one of the most widely used linear dimensionality reduction techniques. PCA transforms the data into a new set of orthogonal features called principal components, which are ordered by the amount of variance they explain in the data. The first principal component captures the most variance, the second captures the second most variance, and so on.

How PCA Works:

Standardize the Data: PCA requires the data to be standardized (mean of 0, variance of 1) before applying the transformation. This ensures that all features contribute equally to the analysis, regardless of their original scales.

Calculate the Covariance Matrix: The covariance matrix is computed to determine the relationships between the features (i.e., how the features vary together). If two features have a high covariance, they are highly correlated.

Eigenvalues and Eigenvectors: PCA computes the eigenvalues and eigenvectors of the covariance matrix. The eigenvectors represent the directions (principal components), and the eigenvalues indicate the magnitude of variance along those directions.

Project the Data: The data is projected onto the first few principal components (the ones with the largest eigenvalues) to reduce the number of dimensions.

Advantages of PCA:

- **Simplicity**: PCA is relatively simple to implement and computationally efficient, especially when using optimized libraries like Scikit-Learn.

- **Variance Preservation**: PCA aims to retain as much variance as possible, meaning that the resulting lower-dimensional space still captures much of the original information.
- **Noise Reduction**: By reducing the dimensionality, PCA can help filter out noise and irrelevant features that contribute little to the variance in the data.

Limitations of PCA:

- **Linear Assumption**: PCA is a linear technique, which means it may not capture complex, non-linear relationships in the data.
- **Interpretability**: The transformed principal components are combinations of the original features, which can sometimes be difficult to interpret directly.

Applications of PCA:

- **Data Visualization**: PCA is widely used to reduce the dimensionality of data for visualization in 2D or 3D spaces. It helps in visualizing high-dimensional data, such as images or gene expression data.
- **Noise Reduction**: PCA can be used as a preprocessing step to remove noisy features and retain the most informative features in the dataset.
- **Feature Selection**: PCA can help in identifying the most important features in a dataset by analyzing the explained variance of each principal component.

7.5.2 t-Distributed Stochastic Neighbor Embedding (t-SNE)

t-Distributed Stochastic Neighbor Embedding (t-SNE) is a non-linear dimensionality reduction technique primarily used for the visualization of high-dimensional data. Unlike PCA, which focuses on linear relationships, t-SNE is particularly effective for preserving local structure, meaning that similar data points will be grouped together in the lower-dimensional space.

How t-SNE Works:

Pairwise Similarities: t-SNE starts by calculating pairwise similarities between all data points in the high-dimensional space using a probability distribution, typically based on Gaussian distributions.

Optimization: It then attempts to find a low-dimensional representation of the data that minimizes the divergence between the original high-dimensional pairwise probabilities and the corresponding low-dimensional probabilities. This is done using gradient descent.

Preserving Local Structure: t-SNE focuses on preserving the relative distances between nearby points. It does not prioritize global structure, making it particularly effective for clustering and identifying patterns in complex datasets.

Advantages of t-SNE:

- **Effective for Visualization**: t-SNE is especially useful for visualizing high-dimensional data in 2D or 3D space, particularly when dealing with data that has complex non-linear relationships.
- **Clustering and Pattern Recognition**: t-SNE is excellent at revealing clusters or groups in the data, which may not be immediately obvious in high-dimensional space.

Limitations of t-SNE:

- **Computationally Expensive**: t-SNE can be computationally expensive for large datasets, as it requires pairwise distance calculations between all data points.
- **Does Not Preserve Global Structure**: t-SNE emphasizes local relationships over global structure, which can lead to distortions when trying to understand the overall structure of the data.
- **Non-Deterministic**: t-SNE uses random initialization, which means that the resulting 2D or 3D embeddings may vary across different runs.

Applications of t-SNE:

- **Data Visualization**: t-SNE is frequently used to visualize complex datasets like images, text, and high-dimensional feature vectors in machine learning models.
- **Exploratory Data Analysis**: t-SNE can help explore high-dimensional datasets, reveal hidden patterns, and identify outliers or clusters that might warrant further investigation.

7.5.3 Uniform Manifold Approximation and Projection (UMAP)

Uniform Manifold Approximation and Projection (UMAP) is a modern, non-linear dimensionality reduction technique that is similar to t-SNE but with several advantages. UMAP is based on manifold learning and focuses on preserving both local and global structure in the data.

How UMAP Works:

Graph Construction: UMAP first constructs a weighted graph based on pairwise similarities between data points. This graph is constructed in the high-dimensional space using a measure of local neighborhood relationships, such as the nearest neighbors.

Optimization: UMAP then optimizes the graph to find a low-dimensional representation that best preserves both local and global structures. It uses a combination of manifold learning and stochastic gradient descent to minimize the distance between data points in the lower-dimensional space.

Embedding: The result is a low-dimensional embedding that can be used for visualization or further analysis. Unlike t-SNE, UMAP tends to preserve more of the global structure of the data, making it useful for tasks that require an understanding of both local and global relationships.

Advantages of UMAP:

- **Speed**: UMAP is computationally efficient and scales well to large datasets, making it a popular choice for dimensionality reduction on big data.
- **Preservation of Global and Local Structure**: UMAP is effective at preserving both local and global structures in the data, making it more reliable than t-SNE for some tasks.
- **Flexibility**: UMAP allows for a high degree of flexibility, such as specifying the number of neighbors to consider or adjusting the optimization process to suit specific needs.

Limitations of UMAP:

- **Parameter Sensitivity**: UMAP's performance depends on the selection of hyperparameters, such as the number of neighbors or the minimum distance between points in the low-dimensional space. The optimal settings can vary based on the dataset.
- **Interpretability**: Like t-SNE, UMAP's transformation is non-linear, and the transformed data may not have an easily interpretable relationship with the original features.

Applications of UMAP:

- **Data Visualization**: UMAP is widely used for visualizing complex datasets, especially those in fields like genomics, neuroscience, and natural language processing.
- **Clustering**: UMAP can help reveal underlying clusters or structures within the data, making it a valuable tool for exploratory analysis and feature engineering.
- **Anomaly Detection**: By visualizing data in a lower-dimensional space, UMAP can help identify outliers or anomalous data points in high-dimensional datasets.

7.5.4 Comparing PCA, t-SNE, and UMAP

Aspect	PCA	t-SNE	UMAP
Type of Transformation	Linear	Non-linear	Non-linear
Preserves Local Structure	No	Yes	Yes
Preserves Global Structure	Yes	No	Yes
Speed	Fast ($O(n^2)$)	Slow ($O(n^2)$)	Fast ($O(n \log n)$)
Scalability	High (large datasets)	Low (large datasets)	High (large datasets)
Interpretability	High (linear components)	Low (non-linear embedding)	Low (non-linear embedding)
Use Cases	Noise reduction, feature selection	Visualization, clustering	Visualization, clustering, anomaly detection

Dimensionality reduction techniques like PCA, t-SNE, and UMAP are essential tools in data science and machine learning, helping to simplify high-dimensional datasets and reveal hidden patterns. PCA is ideal for linear data and when computational efficiency is a priority. t-SNE excels at capturing local structures and is widely used for visualization, while UMAP offers a balance between speed and accuracy, preserving both local and global data relationships. By choosing the right technique based on the specific characteristics of the data and the goals of the analysis, dimensionality reduction can significantly enhance data understanding and downstream modeling tasks.

8. Feature Engineering and Selection

The quality of your features often determines the success of your ML model. This chapter dives into feature extraction, transformation, and selection techniques such as Recursive Feature Elimination (RFE) and Principal Component Analysis (PCA). You'll learn how to craft and select the best features to enhance model performance.

8.1 What is Feature Engineering?

Feature engineering is a crucial step in the machine learning pipeline that involves transforming raw data into meaningful features that improve the performance of machine learning models. In simple terms, it is the process of selecting, modifying, and creating new input variables (features) from raw data to better represent the underlying patterns of the problem at hand. Feature engineering is often considered more of an art than a science because it requires a deep understanding of both the data and the problem domain.

Effective feature engineering can significantly enhance the predictive power of a machine learning model, making it one of the most important aspects of a data science workflow. While modern machine learning algorithms, such as deep learning models, can automate some of the feature extraction processes, traditional algorithms still rely heavily on well-engineered features for optimal performance. This section will explain the importance of feature engineering, the process involved, and some key techniques used to engineer features effectively.

8.1.1 Importance of Feature Engineering

The importance of feature engineering lies in its ability to enhance the performance of machine learning models by providing them with more relevant, informative, and usable data. Poor feature selection or ineffective feature engineering can lead to:

Underfitting: When features are not well-engineered, the model may not capture the underlying patterns in the data, leading to poor performance on both the training and test datasets.

Overfitting: On the flip side, if irrelevant or too many features are included, the model might overfit the training data, performing well on it but failing to generalize to unseen data.

Increased Model Complexity: Irrelevant or noisy features can complicate the model, making it harder to interpret and less efficient.

Data Utilization: Raw data is often in a form that is not directly usable for machine learning models. Feature engineering helps to transform this data into formats that the model can understand and learn from.

Thus, effective feature engineering leads to improved model accuracy, reduced complexity, and better generalization to unseen data.

8.1.2 The Feature Engineering Process

Feature engineering is typically an iterative and experimental process that involves several key steps. Below are the common stages of feature engineering:

Understanding the Data:

- The first step in feature engineering is to explore the dataset and understand its characteristics. This includes understanding the distribution of features, identifying missing values, understanding the relationships between variables, and determining if there are any obvious patterns or trends that need to be captured.
- Common techniques for this step include summary statistics, correlation matrices, and visualization tools like histograms, boxplots, or scatter plots.

Data Cleaning:

- Data cleaning is a fundamental part of feature engineering, as raw data is often messy and contains errors, missing values, or outliers that can distort the model.
- Data cleaning involves handling missing values (imputing, removing, or replacing), dealing with outliers (either by removing or capping them), and ensuring that the data is in a consistent format (for example, ensuring that numerical data does not contain non-numeric characters).

Feature Selection:

- In feature selection, you choose which features to keep, discard, or transform. Not all features contribute equally to the model's performance, and irrelevant or redundant features can harm the model's ability to generalize.

- There are different techniques for feature selection, such as filter methods (e.g., correlation analysis), wrapper methods (e.g., recursive feature elimination), and embedded methods (e.g., Lasso regression, decision trees).

Feature Transformation:

- Sometimes the features need to be transformed or created in new ways to better represent the underlying patterns in the data. This could involve scaling or normalizing features, encoding categorical variables, or creating new features by combining existing ones.
- Common transformations include applying logarithms, square roots, or polynomial features to make the data more linear or capturing more complex relationships.

Feature Creation:

- Feature creation refers to the process of generating new features from the existing ones, often by applying domain knowledge. This can involve creating interaction terms, aggregating features, or deriving new features based on business logic or context.
- For example, if a dataset includes a timestamp column, new features like "day of the week," "hour of the day," or "month" can be created to capture seasonal patterns or time-related trends.

Feature Encoding:

- For categorical data, the features need to be encoded into a numerical format that can be understood by machine learning models. Common encoding techniques include one-hot encoding, label encoding, and ordinal encoding.
- One-hot encoding creates binary columns for each category, while label encoding assigns an integer value to each category. Ordinal encoding is used when the categories have a meaningful order.

Feature Scaling:

- Feature scaling is the process of standardizing or normalizing features so that they all have the same scale. This is particularly important for algorithms that rely on distance metrics (e.g., K-Nearest Neighbors, Support Vector Machines) or gradient-based optimization (e.g., linear regression, neural networks).

- Common scaling techniques include min-max scaling (scaling the values between 0 and 1) and standardization (scaling to have a mean of 0 and a standard deviation of 1).

Evaluating and Iterating:

After transforming and selecting features, it is crucial to evaluate the model's performance and iterate. Sometimes, it's necessary to revisit earlier steps, test new transformations, or remove redundant features. Continuous testing and improvement are central to successful feature engineering.

8.1.3 Techniques for Feature Engineering

Below are some commonly used techniques for feature engineering:

Handling Missing Data:

- **Imputation**: Impute missing values using the mean, median, or mode of the respective feature or use advanced techniques like K-Nearest Neighbors imputation or regression-based imputation.
- **Removing Missing Data**: In some cases, rows or columns with missing data might be dropped if they constitute a small portion of the dataset and do not contribute meaningfully to the analysis.

One-Hot Encoding:

- One-hot encoding is commonly used for transforming categorical variables into a numerical format. It creates a new binary column for each possible category value, where "1" indicates the presence of the category and "0" indicates the absence.
- **Example**: For a "Color" column with values ["Red", "Green", "Blue"], one-hot encoding would create three columns: "Color_Red," "Color_Green," and "Color_Blue."

Label Encoding:

- Label encoding assigns a unique integer to each category in a categorical feature. While it is more compact than one-hot encoding, it may introduce unintended ordinal relationships if the categorical variable has no inherent order.
- **Example**: For a "Size" column with values ["Small", "Medium", "Large"], label encoding might convert these values to integers like [0, 1, 2].

Feature Scaling (Normalization/Standardization):

- **Normalization (Min-Max Scaling):** Scales the feature values to a fixed range, typically between 0 and 1.
- **Standardization (Z-score Normalization):** Scales the data so that it has a mean of 0 and a standard deviation of 1.

Polynomial Features:

Polynomial features are new features created by raising existing features to a higher power. This can help capture non-linear relationships between features and improve model performance, especially for algorithms like linear regression.

Binning:

- Binning is a technique used to group continuous variables into discrete intervals. This can help reduce the effect of minor observation errors or outliers and is particularly useful when data is skewed.
- **Example**: A "Age" column with values ranging from 0 to 100 can be binned into categories like [0-18], [19-35], [36-55], [56+].

Date/Time Feature Extraction:

When working with timestamp features, it's often useful to extract components like the day of the week, the month, the year, or even the time of day. These new features can reveal patterns related to specific time periods.

Interaction Features:

Interaction features are created by combining two or more features to capture relationships that might not be apparent in individual features alone. For example, multiplying "Age" and "Income" might create an interaction feature that better represents purchasing power.

Text Feature Engineering:

For text data, feature extraction techniques such as bag of words, TF-IDF (Term Frequency-Inverse Document Frequency), and word embeddings (such as Word2Vec or

GloVe) can be used to convert text into numerical features that can be processed by machine learning algorithms.

Dimensionality Reduction:

Techniques like PCA (Principal Component Analysis) or t-SNE (t-Distributed Stochastic Neighbor Embedding) can be used for reducing the number of features, especially when working with high-dimensional datasets like images, text, or genomics data.

Feature engineering is an essential skill in data science and machine learning, as it can greatly influence the performance of the model. By understanding the data, cleaning and transforming it appropriately, and selecting the most informative features, you can ensure that your machine learning model has the best chance of success. While feature engineering can be a time-consuming and iterative process, its impact on model accuracy and generalization makes it one of the most important steps in building machine learning systems.

8.2 Feature Extraction Techniques

Feature extraction is a critical aspect of machine learning that involves transforming raw data into a set of features that can be used to train predictive models. It is particularly important when working with unstructured data such as text, images, and audio, where raw inputs may not directly correspond to usable features. Unlike feature engineering, which involves creating and selecting features based on domain knowledge, feature extraction is more about transforming raw data into a format that can be processed by machine learning algorithms.

This section will explore several common feature extraction techniques used across different types of data, including text, image, and audio. Each technique helps in converting unstructured data into a structured format, making it more manageable and insightful for the model.

8.2.1 Feature Extraction from Text Data

Text data is inherently unstructured, making it one of the most challenging data types to work with. To transform text into usable features, a variety of techniques are employed to capture the underlying meaning or patterns in the data. Below are the most common methods used for text feature extraction:

1. Bag of Words (BoW)

The Bag of Words (BoW) model is one of the simplest and most widely used methods for text feature extraction. It represents text as a collection of words or phrases while disregarding grammar and word order.

How it works:

- Each unique word in the corpus becomes a feature, and the frequency or presence of each word is recorded.
- The result is a vector (or matrix for multiple texts) representing the frequency of each word in the text.

Example:

Text 1: "I love machine learning."
Text 2: "Machine learning is fun."
The vocabulary: ["I", "love", "machine", "learning", "is", "fun"]
Text 1: [1, 1, 1, 1, 0, 0]
Text 2: [0, 0, 1, 1, 1, 1]

Pros:

- Simple and easy to implement.
- Effective for capturing the frequency of words in small or medium-sized datasets.

Cons:

- Ignores word order and context.
- The resulting feature space can become very large (high-dimensional) and sparse, especially for large corpora.

2. TF-IDF (Term Frequency-Inverse Document Frequency)

The TF-IDF technique is an improvement on BoW and aims to evaluate the importance of a word within a document relative to its frequency across a corpus.

How it works:

- Term Frequency (TF) measures how frequently a word appears in a document.

- Inverse Document Frequency (IDF) measures the importance of the word based on how frequently it appears across all documents.
- The TF-IDF score is the product of these two measures, where higher values indicate more important words within a document.

Formula:

$$\text{TF-IDF}(w) = \text{TF}(w) \times \log\left(\frac{N}{\text{DF}(w)}\right)$$

Where:

- w is the word,
- N is the total number of documents,
- $\text{DF}(w)$ is the number of documents containing the word w.

Example:

If the word "machine" appears frequently in one document but is rare across the corpus, its TF-IDF score will be higher for that document.

Pros:

- Helps in identifying words that are important in a document but less common across all documents.
- Reduces the impact of commonly used words like "the", "a", "of".

Cons:

- Still ignores word order and context.
- May be computationally expensive for large datasets.

3. Word Embeddings (Word2Vec, GloVe)

Word embeddings are a more advanced technique for capturing semantic meaning in text. These methods represent words as dense vectors of continuous numbers, capturing not only the frequency but also the contextual relationships between words.

How it works:

- Words with similar meanings are mapped to similar vector representations in a lower-dimensional space.
- Word2Vec and GloVe are popular algorithms for generating word embeddings. Word2Vec uses a shallow neural network to learn word associations based on context, while GloVe performs factorization on a word co-occurrence matrix.

Example:

The word "king" might be represented as a vector [0.23, 0.56, 0.12], and "queen" might be represented as a vector [0.21, 0.59, 0.14], with both vectors being close in Euclidean space.

Pros:

- Captures semantic relationships, such as synonyms or antonyms.
- Produces compact, dense vector representations.

Cons:

- Requires significant computational resources for training.
- Pretrained embeddings might not fully capture domain-specific meanings unless fine-tuned.

4. Doc2Vec

Doc2Vec extends the Word2Vec approach by generating vector representations for entire documents, rather than just individual words. This method is particularly useful for capturing the context of the entire text, making it more suitable for tasks like document classification.

How it works:

Doc2Vec learns a vector representation for each document based on the context of words in the document, similar to how Word2Vec learns word embeddings.

Pros:

- Suitable for document-level classification tasks.

- Captures both local word relationships and global document context.

Cons:

- Requires a large amount of data for effective training.

8.2.2 Feature Extraction from Image Data

Images are another type of unstructured data that require feature extraction before they can be processed by machine learning models. Various techniques are employed to extract meaningful features from images:

1. Histogram of Oriented Gradients (HOG)

Histogram of Oriented Gradients (HOG) is a popular feature extraction technique used in object detection. It captures the structure and appearance of objects by looking at the distribution of gradients or edge directions in localized regions of an image.

How it works:

- The image is divided into small cells, and the gradient orientation and magnitude are computed for each cell.
- The histogram of gradient directions is then computed for each cell and used to describe the appearance of objects in the image.

Pros:

- Good at capturing object shapes and structures.
- Widely used in applications like face detection and pedestrian detection.

Cons:

- Not very effective for handling varying lighting conditions, rotations, or scales.

2. Scale-Invariant Feature Transform (SIFT)

SIFT is an algorithm used to detect and describe local features in images. It extracts key points in an image that are invariant to scale, rotation, and affine transformations.

How it works:

- SIFT detects key points based on local image properties (such as corners or edges) and describes them using descriptors that are invariant to scale and orientation.

Pros:

- Effective for object recognition and image matching, even in varying conditions.
- Provides robustness to transformations.

Cons:

- Computationally expensive.
- Some versions of the algorithm are patented and may require licensing.

3. Convolutional Neural Networks (CNNs)

Convolutional Neural Networks (CNNs) are a deep learning technique widely used for feature extraction from images. CNNs automatically learn hierarchical features, starting from low-level features like edges and corners to high-level features like textures and shapes.

How it works:

- CNNs consist of convolutional layers that apply filters to image data, extracting features at various levels of abstraction.
- These learned features can then be used for tasks such as image classification, object detection, and segmentation.

Pros:

- Automatically learns hierarchical features from raw image data.
- Effective for complex image tasks like classification, object detection, and segmentation.

Cons:

- Requires large amounts of labeled data for training.
- Computationally intensive, requiring specialized hardware (e.g., GPUs).

8.2.3 Feature Extraction from Audio Data

Audio data is often used in speech recognition, music classification, and other domains. Feature extraction from audio typically involves transforming the raw audio waveform into a set of numerical features that capture the relevant characteristics of the sound.

1. Mel-frequency Cepstral Coefficients (MFCCs)

MFCCs are widely used in speech and audio signal processing. They represent the short-term power spectrum of an audio signal and are particularly effective in capturing the timbral texture of speech or music.

How it works:

- The audio signal is first transformed into the frequency domain using techniques like Short-Time Fourier Transform (STFT).
- MFCCs are then computed by taking the logarithm of the power spectrum, applying a Mel scale filter bank, and performing a discrete cosine transform (DCT).

Pros:

- Effective for speech and audio classification tasks.
- Compact representation of audio features.

Cons:

- Assumes stationary signals, which may not work well for non-stationary sounds.

2. Chroma Features

Chroma features represent the 12 different pitch classes in music, making them particularly useful for music and genre classification.

How it works:

- Chroma features are derived from the spectrogram of an audio signal, focusing on the harmonic content and pitch.

Pros:

- Effective for music classification and analysis.
- Captures harmonic content and musical structure.

Cons:

- Less effective for non-musical audio or speech.

Feature extraction plays a critical role in transforming raw, unstructured data (such as text, images, and audio) into usable features that can be processed by machine learning models. Whether through traditional techniques like BoW and HOG or more advanced methods like word embeddings and CNNs, the choice of feature extraction method depends on the type of data and the task at hand. Effective feature extraction can significantly enhance the performance of machine learning models, making it a key component of any successful data science or machine learning project.

8.3 Feature Importance in Tree-Based Models

Feature importance is a critical concept in machine learning that helps in identifying which features (or variables) are most influential in predicting the target variable. In tree-based models, such as Decision Trees, Random Forests, and Gradient Boosting Machines (GBMs), feature importance is particularly useful for understanding the internal workings of the model and for improving model interpretability. Tree-based models work by recursively splitting the data into subsets based on feature values, and these splits are what give us an insight into which features are most relevant.

This section will explain how feature importance is computed in tree-based models, the different methods for evaluating it, and how it can be used to optimize model performance and interpretability.

8.3.1 How Tree-Based Models Work

To understand feature importance, it's essential to have a basic understanding of how tree-based models work. A decision tree is a hierarchical model that recursively splits data based on feature values, aiming to reduce impurity at each node. The goal of these splits is to create pure child nodes that closely resemble the target variable, with little variation within each group.

For instance, in a binary classification problem, a decision tree might split data based on a feature like "age" and then continue to split the data at each subsequent node based on other features. The process continues until the tree reaches its maximum depth or a stopping criterion is met.

Tree-based models like Random Forests and Gradient Boosting Machines aggregate the outputs of multiple decision trees to improve model performance. In these models, feature importance reflects how frequently and how significantly each feature is used across all the trees to make splits.

8.3.2 Calculating Feature Importance

In decision trees, the importance of a feature can be derived by evaluating how much each feature contributes to reducing a measure of impurity, such as Gini impurity (used in classification tasks) or Mean Squared Error (MSE) (used in regression tasks), at each split. The basic idea is that features that reduce impurity the most across all splits in the tree are deemed more important.

There are two primary methods to calculate feature importance in tree-based models:

Gini Impurity (Classification) / MSE Reduction (Regression)

- For classification tasks, Gini impurity measures the degree of impurity in a node. A lower Gini score indicates a more "pure" node, where most of the samples belong to one class. The feature that results in the largest reduction in Gini impurity after a split is considered more important.
- For regression tasks, the reduction in Mean Squared Error (MSE) is used to calculate feature importance. A feature that reduces MSE more significantly during splits is considered more influential in making predictions.

Formula for Gini Impurity:

$$Gini(t) = 1 - \sum_{i=1}^{k} p_i^2$$

where p_i is the probability of class i in node t, and k is the number of classes. A lower Gini score suggests better splits, and thus a higher feature importance.

Formula for MSE:

$$MSE = \frac{1}{n} \sum_{i=1}^{n} (y_i - \hat{y}_i)^2$$

where y_i is the true value and $\hat{y}_i$ is the predicted value. A large reduction in MSE indicates that a feature contributes significantly to the model's predictive power.

Mean Decrease Impurity (MDI)

- This method calculates feature importance based on how often a feature is used to split the data across all the trees in the model. The more a feature is used to reduce impurity in various nodes, the more important it is considered.
- MDI is computed as the sum of the reduction in impurity (e.g., Gini impurity) for each node where a feature is used for splitting. The feature importance is proportional to the total reduction in impurity across all nodes where that feature is used.

Formula for MDI:

$$Importance(f) = \sum_{t \in T} \Delta \text{Impurity}_{f,t}$$

where T is the set of all trees, f is a feature, and $\Delta\text{Impurity}_{f,t}$ is the reduction in impurity when feature f is used in tree t.

Mean Decrease Accuracy (MDA) / Permutation Importance

- The Mean Decrease Accuracy (MDA) or permutation importance method evaluates feature importance by assessing the decrease in model accuracy when the values of a given feature are randomly shuffled.
- The intuition behind this method is simple: if a feature is important for making accurate predictions, shuffling its values will cause a significant drop in the model's accuracy. Conversely, if the feature is not important, shuffling its values will have little to no effect on performance.
- In this method, the feature importance is calculated by comparing the model's performance (e.g., accuracy, R^2, or MSE) before and after permuting the values of each feature.

Steps for MDA:

- Calculate the baseline performance of the model on the test set.
- Shuffle the values of the feature under consideration.
- Recalculate the performance metric (e.g., accuracy, MSE).
- The decrease in performance indicates the importance of that feature.
- This method can be applied to any type of model, not just tree-based models, making it more flexible.

8.3.3 Feature Importance in Random Forests and Gradient Boosting Machines

Feature importance in ensemble methods like Random Forests and Gradient Boosting Machines (GBM) is typically calculated by aggregating the feature importances from individual trees.

Random Forests: A random forest is an ensemble of decision trees, where each tree is trained on a random subset of the data and a random subset of features. Feature importance is computed by averaging the feature importance scores across all the trees. The more a feature contributes to reducing impurity across the trees, the higher its importance score will be.

Gradient Boosting Machines (GBMs): Similar to random forests, GBMs also consist of an ensemble of decision trees. However, in GBMs, trees are built sequentially, with each tree trying to correct the errors made by the previous tree. Feature importance in GBMs is computed by summing up the feature importance scores across all the trees in the ensemble.

In both methods, the feature importance scores reflect the contribution of each feature to the overall model performance, based on how often it is used in the tree splits and how much it reduces impurity.

8.3.4 Visualizing Feature Importance

Visualizing feature importance is a powerful way to understand the relevance of each feature in a tree-based model. Some common methods for visualizing feature importance include:

Bar Charts: A simple bar chart can display the importance of each feature in descending order, providing a clear view of which features are most influential.

Tree Plots: Decision tree plots often highlight which features are used for splitting and how the splits impact the target variable. These plots can give a deeper understanding of the role of individual features.

Partial Dependence Plots (PDP): PDPs show the relationship between a feature and the target variable while averaging out the effects of all other features. These plots can help visualize how the importance of a feature affects model predictions across its range.

8.3.5 Using Feature Importance to Improve Models

Feature importance is not just a tool for model interpretability; it can also be used to improve model performance. Here are some ways to leverage feature importance:

Feature Selection:

By identifying the most important features, you can remove less relevant features, simplifying the model and reducing the risk of overfitting. This can also help speed up training times by reducing the number of features the model needs to process.

Model Optimization:

Knowing which features are the most important can help you tune hyperparameters, such as the maximum depth of the tree, the number of trees in an ensemble, or the minimum samples required to split a node. This can improve model accuracy and prevent overfitting.

Domain Insights:

Feature importance can provide valuable insights into the underlying data and problem domain. Understanding which features are driving predictions can help inform business decisions, guide further data collection, or suggest areas for improvement.

Handling Multicollinearity:

If features are highly correlated with one another, the model may be assigning similar importance to them. By removing or combining highly correlated features, you can reduce multicollinearity and make the model more interpretable.

Feature importance in tree-based models is a valuable tool for understanding how the model makes decisions and for improving model performance. By calculating feature importance through methods like Gini impurity reduction, mean decrease accuracy, or permutation importance, you can identify the most influential features, optimize your model, and gain insights into the underlying data. Visualizing feature importance further enhances the interpretability of the model, making it easier to explain the model's predictions to stakeholders. In practice, understanding feature importance helps in building more efficient, accurate, and interpretable machine learning models.

8.4 Selecting the Best Features Using Recursive Feature Elimination

Feature selection is a crucial step in the machine learning pipeline. By selecting only the most relevant features, you can improve model performance, reduce overfitting, and speed up computation. One of the most effective techniques for feature selection is Recursive Feature Elimination (RFE). RFE works by iteratively constructing models and selecting the best-performing subset of features by eliminating the least important ones.

In this section, we will dive into the concept of RFE, how it works, its advantages and limitations, and how to implement it effectively.

8.4.1 What is Recursive Feature Elimination (RFE)?

Recursive Feature Elimination (RFE) is a feature selection technique that recursively removes the least important features based on model performance. The process continues until the desired number of features remains. RFE is particularly useful when you have a large set of features and need to identify the most informative ones for your machine learning model.

The general idea behind RFE is as follows:

- **Train the model**: Fit the model using all the features.
- **Rank features**: Evaluate the importance of each feature based on the model's performance. This is typically done using feature importance scores, such as those calculated in tree-based models, or by looking at the weight of the features in linear models.
- **Eliminate the least important feature**: Remove the feature that contributes the least to model performance.
- **Repeat the process**: Re-train the model with the remaining features and repeat steps 2-3 until only the most important features are left.

- **Stop when a stopping criterion is met**: This could be a predefined number of features, or when performance no longer improves with further elimination.

RFE helps you identify the best subset of features that optimally improves the predictive performance of the model, while simultaneously reducing the model's complexity.

8.4.2 How Does RFE Work?

The key to understanding how RFE works lies in its iterative nature. The algorithm essentially eliminates features one by one in a recursive fashion, and after each elimination, the model is re-trained, and the importance of the remaining features is re-evaluated. Below are the main steps involved in applying RFE:

Model Training: First, a machine learning model is trained on the complete dataset with all available features. The model could be a decision tree, support vector machine, or any other model that allows you to measure feature importance (such as coefficients in linear models or feature importances in tree-based models).

Ranking Features: After training, RFE ranks the features based on their importance. For example:

In decision trees, the importance of features is determined by how much each feature reduces impurity (e.g., Gini impurity or MSE).

In linear models like Logistic Regression, feature importance is determined by the magnitude of the coefficients (the larger the coefficient, the more important the feature).

Elimination: The least important feature (i.e., the one with the lowest importance score) is removed from the feature set. The model is then retrained using the remaining features.

Repetition: The above process is repeated until the desired number of features is left. At each iteration, fewer features are used, and the model's performance is continually assessed to ensure that the most important features remain.

Stopping Criteria: The process stops when a predefined number of features are left or when removing additional features no longer improves model performance.

8.4.3 RFE with Cross-Validation

In many cases, we want to ensure that feature elimination does not lead to overfitting or underfitting. To handle this, RFE with cross-validation (RFECV) is often used. Cross-validation helps to assess the model's performance by splitting the dataset into multiple training and testing sets, thus providing a more reliable estimate of how well the model will generalize to new, unseen data.

In RFECV, the RFE process is combined with cross-validation to evaluate the performance of the model at each iteration. This method selects the optimal number of features by evaluating the model's performance across multiple splits of the data. It helps prevent the model from being biased by a specific train-test split and ensures that the selected features generalize well across the entire dataset.

8.4.4 Advantages of RFE

RFE offers several advantages when selecting the most relevant features for machine learning models:

Reduces Overfitting:

By eliminating irrelevant features, RFE helps to simplify the model and reduces the risk of overfitting, particularly when dealing with high-dimensional datasets.

Improves Model Interpretability:

Selecting a smaller number of features makes the model more interpretable, as it is easier to understand the impact of a few important features compared to a large set of features.

Handles Multicollinearity:

RFE can help remove features that are highly correlated with one another. By doing so, it reduces multicollinearity, which can degrade the performance of some models (e.g., linear regression).

Model Agnostic:

RFE can be applied to a wide range of machine learning models, from decision trees and support vector machines to linear models and ensemble methods. It is not restricted to any particular type of model, making it a versatile feature selection technique.

Improves Computational Efficiency:

Reducing the number of features leads to faster training times and reduced computational requirements, especially when working with large datasets.

8.4.5 Limitations of RFE

While RFE is a powerful tool for feature selection, it also has some limitations:

Computationally Expensive:

RFE requires training the model multiple times, once for each feature elimination. This can be computationally expensive, especially when the number of features is large, or when using complex models like support vector machines or gradient boosting models.

Sensitive to Model Selection:

The effectiveness of RFE depends on the model used to rank feature importance. For instance, if you use a linear model, it may not perform as well if the relationship between features and the target is highly non-linear. Similarly, tree-based models may not always provide the most stable feature importance scores when features are highly correlated.

Not Ideal for Non-linear Models:

RFE works best with models where feature importance is directly measurable (e.g., linear models, decision trees). For non-linear models like neural networks, where feature importance isn't as transparent, RFE may not always provide meaningful results.

Risk of Over-elimination:

RFE may remove features that could have contributed to model performance in interaction with other features. While RFE looks at individual feature importance, it does not always account for the potential importance of feature combinations.

8.4.6 Implementing RFE in Python with Scikit-learn

Scikit-learn provides a built-in implementation of RFE through the RFE class. Here's an example of how to implement RFE using a Support Vector Machine (SVM) model:

```
from sklearn.feature_selection import RFE
from sklearn.svm import SVC
```

```python
from sklearn.datasets import load_iris

# Load dataset
data = load_iris()
X, y = data.data, data.target

# Initialize SVM model
model = SVC(kernel="linear")

# Initialize RFE with the model and number of features to select
rfe = RFE(estimator=model, n_features_to_select=2)

# Fit the RFE model
rfe.fit(X, y)

# Print selected features
print(f"Selected features: {rfe.support_}")
print(f"Feature ranking: {rfe.ranking_}")
```

In this example:

- We load the Iris dataset and use an SVM model with a linear kernel.
- We specify that we want to select the top 2 features using n_features_to_select=2.
- rfe.support_ gives us a Boolean array indicating which features are selected, and rfe.ranking_ gives the ranking of each feature, with 1 indicating the most important feature.

If we want to incorporate cross-validation into the feature selection process, we can use RFECV:

```python
from sklearn.feature_selection import RFECV
from sklearn.model_selection import StratifiedKFold

# Initialize RFECV with the model and cross-validation
rfecv = RFECV(estimator=model, step=1, cv=StratifiedKFold(5))

# Fit the RFECV model
rfecv.fit(X, y)

# Print optimal number of features
```

```
print(f"Optimal number of features: {rfecv.n_features_}")
print(f"Best features: {rfecv.support_}")
```

Here, RFECV automatically selects the optimal number of features based on cross-validation performance, allowing you to choose the number of features that results in the best model performance.

Recursive Feature Elimination (RFE) is a powerful feature selection technique that helps to identify the most relevant features in a dataset by recursively eliminating the least important ones. This process leads to more efficient models that are easier to interpret, less prone to overfitting, and computationally less expensive. While RFE is highly effective, it can be computationally demanding, especially with large datasets or complex models. However, with techniques like RFECV, RFE can be used in combination with cross-validation to ensure optimal model performance and generalization.

9. Hyperparameter Tuning and Model Selection

Machine learning models require fine-tuning to perform optimally. This chapter explores hyperparameter optimization techniques like GridSearchCV and RandomizedSearchCV, as well as Bayesian optimization. You'll also learn how to select the best model for your dataset using cross-validation strategies.

9.1 Understanding Hyperparameters in Machine Learning

In machine learning, hyperparameters play a crucial role in shaping the behavior and performance of a model. While model parameters (such as the weights in a neural network or the coefficients in a linear regression) are learned directly from the training data, hyperparameters are external configurations that need to be set before the training process begins. These values govern the learning process and have a significant impact on the accuracy, efficiency, and generalization ability of a model. Understanding and tuning hyperparameters is essential for building effective machine learning models.

This section explores what hyperparameters are, their types, how they affect model performance, and how they can be optimized for the best results.

9.1.1 What Are Hyperparameters?

Hyperparameters are configuration settings that determine how a machine learning model is trained. These values control aspects such as how fast the model learns, how complex the model can be, and how the training process evolves. Unlike model parameters, which are learned during the training process, hyperparameters are pre-set by the practitioner and typically require experimentation to find the best values.

Hyperparameters are essential because they influence the optimization of the model, its accuracy, and its ability to generalize well to new, unseen data. In the context of machine learning, hyperparameters can vary from simple values like the number of iterations to more complex settings such as the learning rate, regularization strength, and model architecture.

9.1.2 Types of Hyperparameters

There are two main types of hyperparameters in machine learning: model hyperparameters and algorithm hyperparameters. Both influence the learning process but in different ways.

Model Hyperparameters: These are hyperparameters that define the structure and behavior of a model. They dictate the capacity of the model and how it will interpret the data.

- **Example 1**: In decision trees, the maximum depth of the tree is a hyperparameter. A deeper tree might capture more complex patterns but could lead to overfitting.
- **Example 2**: In neural networks, the number of layers and the number of neurons in each layer are hyperparameters. A larger network can capture more intricate patterns, but it also requires more data to avoid overfitting.
- **Example 3:** For support vector machines (SVM), the choice of kernel function (linear, polynomial, radial basis function (RBF), etc.) and the value of the C parameter, which controls the trade-off between maximizing the margin and minimizing classification errors, are important model hyperparameters.

Algorithm Hyperparameters: These are hyperparameters related to the learning process, such as how the model is trained, how the optimization process works, and how quickly the model converges.

- **Learning Rate**: Controls the step size in the optimization algorithm (e.g., gradient descent). A higher learning rate might cause the model to converge faster, but it could also overshoot the optimal solution. A lower learning rate provides finer control over optimization but can slow down the convergence.
- **Batch Size**: In deep learning, the batch size controls how many training samples are used in each iteration of the optimization process. Smaller batches can lead to noisier updates and more frequent adjustments, while larger batches provide more stable estimates of the gradient.
- **Number of Epochs**: Refers to the number of times the entire training dataset is passed through the model during training. More epochs typically lead to better training but can also increase the risk of overfitting.

9.1.3 Why Hyperparameters Matter

Hyperparameters have a significant impact on how well a model performs, and their correct setting can mean the difference between a model that generalizes well and one that overfits or underperforms. Here are some of the key reasons why hyperparameters matter:

Model Performance: The choice of hyperparameters directly affects the accuracy and robustness of the machine learning model. For example:

- A model with a poorly chosen learning rate might either converge too slowly or fail to converge at all.
- Regularization hyperparameters help prevent overfitting by penalizing overly complex models.
- Hyperparameters like the number of hidden layers in a neural network or the depth of a decision tree can make the model too simple or too complex for the given task.

Overfitting and Underfitting: Incorrectly set hyperparameters can lead to overfitting (where the model learns to fit the training data too well, capturing noise as patterns) or underfitting (where the model fails to capture the underlying structure of the data).

- Overfitting can be mitigated by adjusting regularization hyperparameters or reducing the complexity of the model (e.g., fewer layers in a neural network or shallower decision trees).
- Underfitting can be addressed by increasing model complexity or allowing the model to train for more epochs.

Training Efficiency: Hyperparameters also impact the efficiency of the training process, both in terms of speed and the amount of computational resources required. For instance:

- A smaller batch size can result in slower training times but can also provide better generalization.
- Setting an optimal learning rate ensures that the model converges quickly without wasting computational resources.

Generalization Ability: Properly tuned hyperparameters help the model generalize better to unseen data, which is the ultimate goal in machine learning. Hyperparameters like the number of trees in a random forest or the dropout rate in a neural network can directly influence how well the model performs on new, unseen examples.

9.1.4 Common Hyperparameters Across Different Models

Different machine learning models come with their own sets of hyperparameters. Below are some common hyperparameters found across various models:

Linear Models (e.g., Linear Regression, Logistic Regression):

- **Regularization (L1, L2):** Controls the penalty applied to the model's coefficients to prevent overfitting.
- **Learning Rate:** For optimization algorithms like gradient descent.
- **Solver:** Determines the algorithm used to fit the model (e.g., 'liblinear' or 'saga').

Decision Trees and Random Forests:

- **Max Depth:** Limits the depth of the tree, preventing it from growing too deep and overfitting.
- **Min Samples Split:** Specifies the minimum number of samples required to split an internal node.
- **Max Features:** Limits the number of features to consider when looking for the best split.
- **Number of Trees (for Random Forests):** Determines how many trees are used in the ensemble.

Support Vector Machines (SVM):

- **C:** Controls the trade-off between maximizing the margin and minimizing classification errors.
- **Kernel:** Defines the function used to transform data into a higher-dimensional space (linear, polynomial, RBF, etc.).
- **Gamma:** Defines the influence of a single training example on the decision boundary.

Neural Networks:

- **Number of Layers and Units per Layer:** Defines the architecture of the network.
- **Learning Rate:** Affects how much the weights are adjusted with each training step.
- **Dropout Rate:** A regularization technique to prevent overfitting by randomly setting some neurons to zero during training.
- **Batch Size:** Defines how many samples are processed before the model is updated.
- **Activation Function:** Defines the function applied to each neuron (e.g., ReLU, sigmoid, tanh).

Gradient Boosting Models (e.g., XGBoost, LightGBM):

- **Learning Rate:** Determines the step size for each iteration of boosting.

- **Number of Estimators (Trees):** The total number of trees in the boosting model.
- **Max Depth**: Limits the depth of individual trees.
- **Subsample**: Fraction of samples used to train each tree to prevent overfitting.

9.1.5 Tuning Hyperparameters

Hyperparameter tuning is the process of finding the optimal values for these parameters in order to maximize model performance. There are several approaches to hyperparameter optimization:

Manual Search:

Manually adjusting hyperparameters by trial and error can be useful for small models or for understanding the impact of specific parameters.

Grid Search:

Grid search is an exhaustive search method that evaluates all combinations of hyperparameters from a predefined set of values. While thorough, it can be computationally expensive and time-consuming.

Random Search:

Instead of exhaustively searching through all possible hyperparameter combinations, random search samples combinations randomly from a predefined search space. This method is often faster and can still yield good results, especially when the search space is large.

Bayesian Optimization:

Bayesian optimization uses probabilistic models to estimate the best hyperparameters. This technique tries to intelligently explore the hyperparameter space, making it more efficient than grid search or random search.

Hyperband and Genetic Algorithms:

These methods combine ideas from random search, early stopping, and optimization to explore hyperparameter spaces more efficiently.

Hyperparameters are a key element in the machine learning pipeline. They control the learning process and significantly influence model performance, training efficiency, and generalization ability. Understanding the different types of hyperparameters and their impact on model training is crucial for building effective and robust models. While selecting optimal hyperparameters requires experimentation and computational resources, techniques like grid search, random search, and Bayesian optimization can help automate the process. Ultimately, carefully tuning hyperparameters leads to more accurate, efficient, and interpretable models.

9.2 Using GridSearchCV for Hyperparameter Tuning

Hyperparameter tuning is a critical step in optimizing machine learning models to achieve better performance. While choosing the right hyperparameters is essential for building robust and accurate models, doing this manually through trial and error can be time-consuming and inefficient. One of the most effective methods for systematically tuning hyperparameters is using GridSearchCV.

In this section, we will explore what GridSearchCV is, how it works, its benefits, and how to use it for hyperparameter tuning with examples.

9.2.1 What is GridSearchCV?

GridSearchCV is an exhaustive search technique provided by Scikit-learn to perform hyperparameter tuning. It is designed to evaluate all possible combinations of a set of hyperparameters for a given model and determine the best combination based on model performance. GridSearchCV essentially automates the process of finding the optimal hyperparameters by iterating over a predefined hyperparameter grid and evaluating each configuration using cross-validation.

How it works:

- **Hyperparameter Grid**: You define a range of hyperparameter values that you want to test. This range is typically specified as a dictionary, where the keys represent hyperparameters and the values are lists or ranges of possible values.
- **Cross-Validation**: GridSearchCV uses cross-validation to evaluate the model for each combination of hyperparameters. This means the dataset is split into multiple folds, and the model is trained and tested on different subsets of the data, ensuring more reliable estimates of model performance.

- **Model Evaluation**: GridSearchCV computes performance metrics (such as accuracy, mean squared error, etc.) for each hyperparameter combination using cross-validation. It then selects the best-performing combination of hyperparameters.

The "CV" in GridSearchCV stands for cross-validation, indicating that GridSearchCV performs cross-validation on each combination of hyperparameters to assess their effectiveness.

9.2.2 The Structure of GridSearchCV

Here's a brief overview of how GridSearchCV is structured:

- **Parameter Grid**: The set of hyperparameters that you want to test. This is provided as a dictionary or a list of values for each hyperparameter.
- **Estimator**: The machine learning model or algorithm to be used (e.g., Logistic Regression, Decision Trees, SVM, etc.).
- **Scoring**: The performance metric used to evaluate the models (e.g., accuracy, precision, recall, etc.).
- **Cross-Validation**: The number of folds used in the cross-validation process to evaluate each model configuration.

9.2.3 Steps to Perform Hyperparameter Tuning with GridSearchCV

Here are the general steps to use GridSearchCV for hyperparameter tuning:

Define the Hyperparameter Grid: The first step is to define a grid of hyperparameter values to search through. The grid is a dictionary, where the keys are the hyperparameters, and the values are the lists or ranges of possible values.

Example:

```
param_grid = {
    'C': [0.1, 1, 10],  # Regularization strength for SVM
    'kernel': ['linear', 'rbf'],  # Type of kernel for SVM
    'gamma': [0.1, 1, 'scale']  # Kernel coefficient
}
```

Instantiate the Model: Select the model that you want to tune. For instance, you may choose an SVM model, Random Forest, Logistic Regression, or any other model available in Scikit-learn.

Example:

from sklearn.svm import SVC
model = SVC()

Create the GridSearchCV Object: Instantiate the GridSearchCV object, passing the model, the parameter grid, the cross-validation settings, and the scoring metric (optional). By default, GridSearchCV will use accuracy as the scoring metric for classification tasks.

Example:

from sklearn.model_selection import GridSearchCV

grid_search = GridSearchCV(estimator=model, param_grid=param_grid, cv=5, scoring='accuracy')

- **estimator=model**: The model you want to tune.
- **param_grid=param_grid**: The hyperparameter grid you want to explore.
- **cv=5**: The number of cross-validation folds to use.
- **scoring='accuracy'**: The metric used to evaluate the models. For classification, accuracy is commonly used, but you can also choose metrics like precision, recall, F1-score, etc.

Fit the Model: Once you have defined the GridSearchCV object, the next step is to fit the model to the training data. GridSearchCV will train and evaluate the model for each hyperparameter combination and return the best-performing set of hyperparameters.

Example:

grid_search.fit(X_train, y_train)

Extract the Best Model: After fitting the model, you can access the best-performing model by using the best_estimator_ attribute. This gives you the model with the optimal set of hyperparameters.

Example:

```
best_model = grid_search.best_estimator_
print(f"Best Hyperparameters: {grid_search.best_params_}")
```

Evaluate the Best Model: Once you've found the best hyperparameters, you can evaluate the best model on your test data or use it for prediction.

Example:

```
y_pred = best_model.predict(X_test)
```

View the Results: You can view the performance results of all the hyperparameter combinations evaluated by GridSearchCV. The cv_results_ attribute stores detailed information about each combination's performance.

Example:

```
print(f"All Results: {grid_search.cv_results_}")
```

9.2.4 Example: Hyperparameter Tuning with GridSearchCV

Here's a complete example of hyperparameter tuning using GridSearchCV for an SVM model:

```
from sklearn.svm import SVC
from sklearn.model_selection import GridSearchCV
from sklearn.datasets import load_iris
from sklearn.model_selection import train_test_split

# Load dataset
data = load_iris()
X = data.data
y = data.target

# Split dataset into training and test sets
X_train, X_test, y_train, y_test = train_test_split(X, y, test_size=0.3, random_state=42)

# Define parameter grid for SVM
param_grid = {
    'C': [0.1, 1, 10],
```

```
    'kernel': ['linear', 'rbf'],
    'gamma': [0.1, 1, 'scale']
}

# Initialize SVM model
model = SVC()

# Set up GridSearchCV
grid_search = GridSearchCV(estimator=model, param_grid=param_grid, cv=5,
scoring='accuracy')

# Fit the model
grid_search.fit(X_train, y_train)

# Get the best model
best_model = grid_search.best_estimator_

# Print best hyperparameters
print(f"Best Hyperparameters: {grid_search.best_params_}")

# Evaluate the best model on the test set
y_pred = best_model.predict(X_test)

# Calculate accuracy
accuracy = (y_pred == y_test).mean()
print(f"Test Set Accuracy: {accuracy:.4f}")
```

9.2.5 Evaluating Results with GridSearchCV

After performing GridSearchCV, you can evaluate the performance of the model using different attributes:

- **best_params_**: Displays the combination of hyperparameters that gave the best performance.
- **best_score_**: Shows the best cross-validation score achieved by the model.
- **cv_results_**: Provides detailed results of all hyperparameter combinations and their respective scores.

Example:

```
print(f"Best Parameters: {grid_search.best_params_}")
print(f"Best Cross-Validation Score: {grid_search.best_score_}")
```

9.2.6 Benefits of GridSearchCV

GridSearchCV offers several advantages:

- **Exhaustive Search**: GridSearchCV searches through all possible combinations of the specified hyperparameters, ensuring that you explore every option.
- **Cross-Validation**: By using cross-validation, GridSearchCV provides a more reliable estimate of model performance than a single train-test split.
- **Ease of Use**: GridSearchCV is easy to use and integrates seamlessly with Scikit-learn models.

9.2.7 Limitations of GridSearchCV

While GridSearchCV is powerful, it does have some limitations:

- **Computational Cost**: Grid search can be computationally expensive, especially if the hyperparameter grid is large or if the model is complex. Each combination requires training the model multiple times.
- **Grid Search Limitations**: Grid search evaluates every combination exhaustively, which can be inefficient if the hyperparameter space is vast. Random search or more advanced optimization techniques can sometimes be more efficient.

GridSearchCV is an essential tool for hyperparameter tuning in machine learning. By systematically searching through a range of hyperparameters and evaluating each combination using cross-validation, it helps identify the optimal model configuration. While it is computationally expensive, it remains one of the most effective methods for improving model performance. For large-scale hyperparameter spaces, alternative techniques like random search or Bayesian optimization may be worth considering. Regardless, GridSearchCV provides a simple and powerful way to tune hyperparameters and improve your machine learning models.

9.3 RandomizedSearchCV vs. GridSearchCV

Hyperparameter tuning is an essential step in optimizing machine learning models, and both GridSearchCV and RandomizedSearchCV are widely used techniques to perform this task. Both methods help in searching for the best hyperparameter configuration, but they differ in the approach, computational efficiency, and effectiveness. In this section, we'll compare RandomizedSearchCV and GridSearchCV, outlining their similarities, differences, and when to use each technique.

9.3.1 What is GridSearchCV?

GridSearchCV (Grid Search with Cross-Validation) is an exhaustive search method that evaluates all possible combinations of a predefined set of hyperparameters. The method systematically trains and tests the model for every combination of the hyperparameters provided in the parameter grid and selects the best combination based on a predefined performance metric (e.g., accuracy, F1-score).

Key Characteristics of GridSearchCV:

- **Exhaustive Search**: GridSearchCV evaluates all possible combinations of the hyperparameter values provided in the parameter grid.
- **Cross-Validation**: It performs cross-validation to assess the model's performance for each combination of hyperparameters, which helps in estimating how well the model will generalize to unseen data.
- **Computational Cost**: Since GridSearchCV evaluates all combinations exhaustively, it can become computationally expensive, especially if the hyperparameter grid is large.

9.3.2 What is RandomizedSearchCV?

RandomizedSearchCV is a stochastic alternative to GridSearchCV. Instead of trying every combination of hyperparameters in the specified grid, RandomizedSearchCV randomly samples from the hyperparameter space and evaluates a fixed number of randomly selected combinations. This method is especially useful when the hyperparameter space is large, and performing an exhaustive search is computationally expensive.

Key Characteristics of RandomizedSearchCV:

- **Randomized Search**: RandomizedSearchCV randomly selects hyperparameter combinations from the parameter grid and evaluates them.
- **Cross-Validation**: Like GridSearchCV, RandomizedSearchCV uses cross-validation to estimate model performance for each combination of hyperparameters.

- **Computational Efficiency**: It can be computationally cheaper than GridSearchCV, especially when the hyperparameter space is large, as it evaluates fewer combinations.

9.3.3 Key Differences Between GridSearchCV and RandomizedSearchCV

While both GridSearchCV and RandomizedSearchCV serve the same purpose of hyperparameter tuning, they differ in several important aspects:

Aspect	GridSearchCV	RandomizedSearchCV
Search Method	Exhaustive search over all hyperparameter combinations	Randomly samples hyperparameter combinations
Computation Cost	High, especially when the hyperparameter grid is large	Generally lower, as it evaluates fewer combinations
Efficiency	Can be slow and inefficient with a large search space	More efficient with large search spaces
Search Coverage	Guaranteed to explore all possible combinations	Only explores a subset of combinations, may miss the optimal combination
Parameter Grid	Requires a predefined grid of values to search	Can sample from a broader range of values, including distributions
Flexibility	Less flexible; can be computationally expensive for large grids	More flexible, allowing exploration of larger spaces within limited resources
Performance Guarantee	Guarantees to find the optimal solution (within the grid)	Does not guarantee the optimal solution but finds a good solution faster

9.3.4 When to Use GridSearchCV

GridSearchCV is ideal in the following scenarios:

Small Search Space: When the hyperparameter space is small, exhaustive search can be computationally feasible and guarantees finding the best combination of parameters.

Example: If you are tuning just two or three hyperparameters with a limited set of values, GridSearchCV can explore all combinations quickly.

Highly Deterministic Results: If you need to ensure that you explore all possibilities and leave no stone unturned, GridSearchCV is the right choice. It will test every single combination and return the optimal one.

Well-Defined Hyperparameter Ranges: When the range of hyperparameters to be tested is well-defined and not too large, GridSearchCV ensures that all options are evaluated.

9.3.5 When to Use RandomizedSearchCV

RandomizedSearchCV is preferred in the following cases:

Large Search Space: When the hyperparameter space is large, RandomizedSearchCV can efficiently explore a subset of the space without the computational cost of an exhaustive search. It is particularly useful for models with many hyperparameters or wide ranges of possible values.

Example: If you are tuning a deep learning model with multiple layers and each layer has a large number of neurons, the search space grows exponentially, and GridSearchCV becomes impractical.

Limited Computational Resources: If you have limited computational resources and time, RandomizedSearchCV can still provide a good solution by sampling from the hyperparameter space and evaluating only a fixed number of combinations.

Exploratory Tuning: When you're unsure of the exact hyperparameter values that might work best and want to quickly explore a broad set of possibilities, RandomizedSearchCV can help you identify a good combination of hyperparameters before fine-tuning further.

Faster Results with Good Performance: If you're looking for good results in a shorter amount of time, RandomizedSearchCV is more likely to give you a strong model faster by evaluating fewer combinations than GridSearchCV.

9.3.6 Example Comparison

Here's an example comparing how to use GridSearchCV and RandomizedSearchCV for tuning a Support Vector Machine (SVM).

GridSearchCV Example:

```python
from sklearn.svm import SVC
from sklearn.model_selection import GridSearchCV
from sklearn.datasets import load_iris
from sklearn.model_selection import train_test_split

# Load dataset
data = load_iris()
X = data.data
y = data.target

# Split dataset into training and test sets
X_train, X_test, y_train, y_test = train_test_split(X, y, test_size=0.3, random_state=42)

# Define the parameter grid
param_grid = {
    'C': [0.1, 1, 10, 100],
    'kernel': ['linear', 'rbf'],
    'gamma': ['scale', 'auto']
}

# Create the SVM model
model = SVC()

# Create the GridSearchCV object
grid_search = GridSearchCV(estimator=model, param_grid=param_grid, cv=5,
scoring='accuracy')

# Fit the grid search
grid_search.fit(X_train, y_train)

# Output best parameters and results
print(f"Best Parameters: {grid_search.best_params_}")
print(f"Best Score: {grid_search.best_score_}")
```

RandomizedSearchCV Example:

```python
from sklearn.svm import SVC
from sklearn.model_selection import RandomizedSearchCV
from sklearn.datasets import load_iris
from sklearn.model_selection import train_test_split
```

```python
import numpy as np

# Load dataset
data = load_iris()
X = data.data
y = data.target

# Split dataset into training and test sets
X_train, X_test, y_train, y_test = train_test_split(X, y, test_size=0.3, random_state=42)

# Define the parameter distribution
param_dist = {
    'C': np.logspace(-3, 3, 7),  # Log scale from 0.001 to 1000
    'kernel': ['linear', 'rbf'],
    'gamma': ['scale', 'auto']
}

# Create the SVM model
model = SVC()

# Create the RandomizedSearchCV object
random_search = RandomizedSearchCV(estimator=model,
param_distributions=param_dist, n_iter=10, cv=5, scoring='accuracy',
random_state=42)

# Fit the random search
random_search.fit(X_train, y_train)

# Output best parameters and results
print(f"Best Parameters: {random_search.best_params_}")
print(f"Best Score: {random_search.best_score_}")
```

Both GridSearchCV and RandomizedSearchCV are valuable tools for hyperparameter tuning, but they have different strengths depending on the task at hand:

- GridSearchCV is the best option when you have a small hyperparameter space and require exhaustive, deterministic search.
- RandomizedSearchCV is the more efficient choice when you have a large hyperparameter space, limited computational resources, or when you're looking for a good solution faster without needing to explore every possible combination.

In practice, RandomizedSearchCV is often used when dealing with complex models or when time and computational resources are constrained, while GridSearchCV remains a powerful choice for smaller, more manageable search spaces.

9.4 Advanced Optimization with Bayesian Search

Hyperparameter optimization plays a crucial role in improving the performance of machine learning models. Traditional techniques like GridSearchCV and RandomizedSearchCV are widely used for hyperparameter tuning, but they come with certain limitations, particularly when dealing with large search spaces or complex models. These methods exhaustively search through the space, which can be computationally expensive and inefficient.

A more sophisticated approach to hyperparameter tuning is Bayesian optimization, which uses probabilistic models to intelligently explore the hyperparameter space. Bayesian Search, or Bayesian Optimization, offers a more efficient method for optimizing hyperparameters by focusing on the most promising regions of the search space, rather than blindly exploring all combinations.

In this section, we will explore what Bayesian optimization is, how it works, its advantages over traditional search methods, and how to implement it in Scikit-learn using libraries like Optuna and Scikit-Optimize.

9.4.1 What is Bayesian Optimization?

Bayesian Optimization is an advanced optimization technique that models the objective function (the function we want to optimize, e.g., model performance) using a probabilistic model, typically a Gaussian Process (GP). The core idea is to model the objective function as a distribution over possible functions and use this model to decide where to sample next. Instead of testing all possible combinations of hyperparameters, Bayesian optimization intelligently selects the most promising hyperparameters to evaluate, reducing the number of evaluations needed to find the optimal solution.

Key Concepts:

- **Probabilistic Modeling**: Bayesian optimization uses a probabilistic model to estimate the performance of the objective function across the hyperparameter space. The model is updated with each evaluation to improve predictions.

- **Acquisition Function**: An acquisition function decides where to sample next by balancing exploration (trying new, uncertain areas of the space) and exploitation (focusing on areas that are likely to yield the best results). Common acquisition functions include Expected Improvement (EI), Probability of Improvement (PI), and Upper Confidence Bound (UCB).
- **Gaussian Process (GP):** The Gaussian Process is the most commonly used model in Bayesian optimization. It models the relationship between hyperparameters and model performance based on prior observations.

By using the Gaussian process and acquisition function, Bayesian optimization can efficiently narrow down the search space, resulting in fewer evaluations to find the optimal set of hyperparameters.

9.4.2 Advantages of Bayesian Optimization

Bayesian optimization has several advantages over traditional search methods such as GridSearchCV and RandomizedSearchCV:

- **Efficient Search**: Unlike GridSearchCV, which explores the hyperparameter space exhaustively, Bayesian optimization intelligently explores the space by focusing on promising regions. This makes it far more efficient, especially when the search space is large.
- **Less Computational Cost**: Bayesian optimization requires fewer evaluations to converge to an optimal solution. This is particularly useful for complex models that take a long time to train.
- **Better Handling of Expensive Evaluations**: When the objective function (model performance) is expensive to compute, such as when training deep learning models or large ensembles, Bayesian optimization can minimize the number of evaluations needed.
- **Works Well with Limited Resources**: Since Bayesian optimization focuses on the most promising hyperparameters, it is ideal when you have limited computational resources or time.

9.4.3 How Bayesian Optimization Works

Bayesian optimization proceeds in an iterative fashion:

- **Start with Prior Knowledge**: Initially, a probabilistic model is constructed based on prior knowledge (which could be uniform or informed guesses about the search space). This prior model is updated as new evaluations are made.

- **Evaluate the Objective Function**: The acquisition function is used to decide which combination of hyperparameters to evaluate next. This is done based on the current model's predictions and the uncertainty about the performance of different hyperparameter combinations.
- **Update the Model**: After evaluating a set of hyperparameters, the model is updated with the new result.
- **Repeat**: The process continues iteratively until a stopping criterion is met, such as a maximum number of iterations or convergence to the optimal solution.

Each iteration of Bayesian optimization focuses on a promising region of the hyperparameter space, gradually refining the model and reducing the number of required evaluations.

9.4.4 Implementing Bayesian Optimization in Python

There are several libraries in Python that implement Bayesian optimization for hyperparameter tuning. Some popular options include Optuna, Scikit-Optimize, and Spearmint. Here, we'll cover how to use Optuna and Scikit-Optimize to implement Bayesian optimization for hyperparameter tuning.

Example Using Optuna

Optuna is a powerful and flexible library for hyperparameter optimization that supports Bayesian optimization. It provides easy integration with machine learning models and can be used for optimizing any type of objective function.

Install Optuna: If you don't have Optuna installed, you can install it using pip:

pip install optuna

Optuna Example: In this example, we will use Optuna to perform Bayesian optimization for hyperparameter tuning of a Support Vector Machine (SVM).

```
import optuna
from sklearn.svm import SVC
from sklearn.datasets import load_iris
from sklearn.model_selection import train_test_split
from sklearn.metrics import accuracy_score

# Load dataset
```

```
data = load_iris()
X = data.data
y = data.target

# Split dataset into training and test sets
X_train, X_test, y_train, y_test = train_test_split(X, y, test_size=0.3, random_state=42)

# Define the objective function for Optuna
def objective(trial):
    # Define hyperparameter search space
    C = trial.suggest_loguniform('C', 1e-5, 1e5)  # Regularization parameter
    gamma = trial.suggest_categorical('gamma', ['scale', 'auto'])  # Kernel coefficient
    kernel = trial.suggest_categorical('kernel', ['linear', 'rbf'])  # Type of kernel

    # Create and train the SVM model
    model = SVC(C=C, gamma=gamma, kernel=kernel)
    model.fit(X_train, y_train)

    # Predict and evaluate the model
    y_pred = model.predict(X_test)
    return accuracy_score(y_test, y_pred)

# Create a study object and start the optimization
study = optuna.create_study(direction='maximize')  # Maximize accuracy
study.optimize(objective, n_trials=50)

# Output the best hyperparameters and result
print(f"Best Hyperparameters: {study.best_params}")
print(f"Best Accuracy: {study.best_value:.4f}")
```

- trial.suggest_loguniform allows us to sample the C hyperparameter on a logarithmic scale, while trial.suggest_categorical selects from discrete values for gamma and kernel.
- The objective function trains the model, predicts on the test set, and returns the accuracy score. Optuna will optimize this objective function.

Example Using Scikit-Optimize

Scikit-Optimize is another popular library for Bayesian optimization, which is built on top of Scikit-learn. It provides an easy-to-use interface for hyperparameter tuning using Gaussian Process-based optimization.

Install Scikit-Optimize: You can install Scikit-Optimize via pip:

pip install scikit-optimize

Scikit-Optimize Example: Here's an example of using Scikit-Optimize to perform Bayesian optimization for an SVM model.

```
from skopt import BayesSearchCV
from sklearn.svm import SVC
from sklearn.datasets import load_iris
from sklearn.model_selection import train_test_split

# Load dataset
data = load_iris()
X = data.data
y = data.target

# Split dataset into training and test sets
X_train, X_test, y_train, y_test = train_test_split(X, y, test_size=0.3, random_state=42)

# Define the search space for hyperparameters
search_space = {
    'C': (1e-5, 1e5, 'log-uniform'),  # Regularization parameter
    'gamma': ['scale', 'auto'],       # Kernel coefficient
    'kernel': ['linear', 'rbf']       # Type of kernel
}

# Create the SVM model
model = SVC()

# Perform Bayesian optimization
bayes_search = BayesSearchCV(model, search_space, n_iter=50, cv=5)
bayes_search.fit(X_train, y_train)

# Output the best hyperparameters and results
print(f"Best Hyperparameters: {bayes_search.best_params_}")
```

print(f"Best Accuracy: {bayes_search.best_score_:.4f}")

- Scikit-Optimize uses BayesSearchCV to perform Bayesian optimization, where we define the search space for each hyperparameter.
- The optimization process is similar to Optuna's, and the best hyperparameters are printed once the optimization process is complete.

Bayesian optimization is a powerful technique for hyperparameter tuning that offers significant improvements over traditional methods like GridSearchCV and RandomizedSearchCV, particularly when dealing with complex models and large search spaces. By using probabilistic models, Bayesian optimization intelligently navigates the hyperparameter space and minimizes the number of evaluations needed to find the optimal hyperparameters.

Using libraries like Optuna and Scikit-Optimize, you can efficiently perform Bayesian optimization and dramatically improve your machine learning model's performance while saving computational resources. Whether you're dealing with machine learning models, deep learning networks, or complex ensemble methods, Bayesian optimization is a valuable tool for any data scientist or machine learning practitioner.

10. Handling Imbalanced Data and Anomaly Detection

Real-world datasets often suffer from class imbalance, leading to biased models. This chapter introduces techniques such as SMOTE for balancing datasets, as well as anomaly detection methods like Isolation Forests and One-Class SVMs to identify rare or fraudulent patterns in data.

10.1 Understanding Class Imbalance in Datasets

Class imbalance is a common problem in machine learning, particularly when working with classification tasks. It refers to a situation where the distribution of classes within the dataset is skewed, meaning one class significantly outnumbers the other. For example, in a binary classification task like fraud detection, the number of legitimate transactions may far exceed fraudulent ones, leading to an imbalanced dataset.

Class imbalance can negatively impact the performance of machine learning models, especially when the model has to predict the minority class accurately. In this section, we will explore what class imbalance is, why it is a problem, and how it can affect model performance. Additionally, we will look into techniques for dealing with class imbalance in datasets.

10.1.1 What is Class Imbalance?

Class imbalance occurs when one class in a dataset is represented much more frequently than the other(s). In a binary classification scenario, class imbalance typically involves a large majority class and a small minority class. In a multi-class classification scenario, class imbalance can involve one or more classes that are underrepresented relative to the others.

For example, consider a medical dataset used to predict the presence of a disease (positive class) versus the absence of the disease (negative class). If the majority of patients in the dataset do not have the disease, the dataset will be imbalanced, with the negative class being more prevalent.

Example of an Imbalanced Dataset:

Class Count
Positive   100
Negative   1,000

In this scenario, the Negative class is overrepresented, while the Positive class is underrepresented. This imbalance could make it difficult for a model to effectively learn to identify the minority class (the positive class).

10.1.2 Why is Class Imbalance a Problem?

Class imbalance poses several challenges during machine learning model training and evaluation:

Bias Toward the Majority Class: Most machine learning algorithms aim to minimize overall error. When one class dominates the dataset, the model may learn to predict the majority class with high accuracy, ignoring the minority class. This leads to high accuracy in predicting the majority class but poor performance on the minority class.

For example, in a fraud detection model where fraudulent transactions are only 1% of the total, a model predicting only "non-fraud" transactions will achieve an accuracy of 99%. However, this model is ineffective because it fails to identify fraudulent transactions, which are the more important class.

Inaccurate Performance Metrics: Common performance metrics like accuracy, precision, recall, and F1-score may be misleading when there is a class imbalance. For example, accuracy can be high even if the model performs poorly on the minority class. In such cases, it is essential to focus on other metrics like precision, recall, F1-score, and AUC-ROC to evaluate the model performance properly.

Model Overfitting or Underfitting: When the model is biased toward the majority class, it might end up overfitting the majority class, leading to a lack of generalization to new, unseen data, especially for the minority class. Conversely, underfitting can also occur if the minority class is underrepresented, preventing the model from learning important features of the minority class.

Difficulty in Model Evaluation: Due to the imbalance, the evaluation of model performance becomes tricky. Focusing on overall accuracy does not provide a clear picture of the model's ability to generalize to both classes. Special attention needs to be given to the correct identification of the minority class.

10.1.3 How Class Imbalance Affects Common Algorithms

Several machine learning algorithms behave differently when dealing with imbalanced datasets. The most common algorithms include decision trees, support vector machines, k-nearest neighbors, and logistic regression. Let's explore how they typically perform when faced with class imbalance:

Decision Trees: Decision trees can overfit the majority class if the data is highly imbalanced. Because they split the data at each node to minimize error, they will often favor the majority class if it is more prevalent. This can lead to deep trees that fail to generalize to the minority class.

Logistic Regression: In imbalanced datasets, logistic regression may predict the majority class with high accuracy, but it could ignore the minority class. This is especially true if the regularization is not tuned properly.

K-Nearest Neighbors (KNN): KNN tends to favor the majority class because it classifies based on proximity to the nearest data points. In an imbalanced dataset, the majority class will dominate the neighborhood, causing KNN to perform poorly on the minority class.

Support Vector Machines (SVMs): SVMs can also be affected by class imbalance, especially if the cost of misclassification is not adjusted. Without proper tuning, the model may prioritize the majority class and ignore the minority class, leading to poor performance.

10.1.4 Measuring Performance on Imbalanced Datasets

When dealing with class imbalance, accuracy is not a reliable measure of model performance, as it might be misleading. A model predicting only the majority class might achieve a high accuracy score but perform poorly in identifying the minority class. Instead, consider the following performance metrics for evaluating models on imbalanced datasets:

Precision: Precision is the fraction of relevant instances among the retrieved instances (i.e., how many of the predicted positive cases are actually positive). It is crucial for scenarios where false positives are costly.

$$\text{Precision} = \frac{TP}{TP + FP}$$

Where:

- TP = True Positives (correctly predicted positives)

- FP = False Positives (incorrectly predicted positives)

Recall (Sensitivity): Recall is the fraction of relevant instances that have been retrieved over the total amount of relevant instances. It is essential for scenarios where false negatives are costly.

$$\text{Recall} = \frac{TP}{TP + FN}$$

Where:

- FN = False Negatives (missed positive cases)

F1-Score: The F1-score is the harmonic mean of precision and recall and provides a balance between the two. It is useful when you need to strike a balance between precision and recall.

$$\text{F1-score} = 2 \times \frac{\text{Precision} \times \text{Recall}}{\text{Precision} + \text{Recall}}$$

Area Under the Receiver Operating Characteristic Curve (AUC-ROC): AUC-ROC is a performance measurement for classification problems at various threshold settings. It tells you how well the model can distinguish between the classes.

Confusion Matrix: A confusion matrix provides a comprehensive view of model performance, showing the number of true positives, false positives, true negatives, and false negatives.

10.1.5 Techniques for Handling Class Imbalance

There are several strategies to deal with class imbalance:

Resampling Techniques: Resampling methods are commonly used to adjust the class distribution by either increasing the minority class (oversampling) or decreasing the majority class (undersampling).

- **Oversampling the Minority Class**: This involves replicating samples from the minority class to balance the dataset.
- **SMOTE (Synthetic Minority Over-sampling Technique):** A more advanced oversampling technique that creates synthetic samples for the minority class by interpolating between existing samples.
- **Undersampling the Majority Class**: This involves reducing the number of instances in the majority class to balance the dataset. However, it may result in losing useful information.

Class Weighting: Some algorithms, such as Logistic Regression, Support Vector Machines, and Random Forests, allow for assigning weights to classes. By increasing the weight for the minority class, the model will penalize misclassifications of the minority class more heavily, encouraging the model to focus on learning the minority class.

Anomaly Detection: In some cases, especially when the imbalance is severe, the problem can be treated as an anomaly detection problem, where the minority class is considered as an anomaly or outlier.

Ensemble Methods: Ensemble techniques such as Balanced Random Forests and EasyEnsemble are designed to handle imbalanced datasets by creating multiple balanced subsets of the data and combining the results.

Cost-Sensitive Learning: In this approach, you modify the learning algorithm to consider the cost of misclassifying the minority class. This can be done by adding penalties to the objective function based on class frequencies.

Data Augmentation: Similar to oversampling, this technique involves creating new data points by applying transformations or adding noise to the existing minority class data, which helps to increase the representation of the minority class.

Class imbalance is a significant challenge in machine learning and can lead to biased models that fail to predict the minority class accurately. Understanding the problem and using appropriate techniques such as resampling, class weighting, and performance metrics like precision, recall, and F1-score can help mitigate its impact. By adopting these strategies, machine learning practitioners can improve the performance of models on imbalanced datasets and ensure more reliable predictions, especially for critical applications like fraud detection, medical diagnostics, and rare event prediction.

10.2 Techniques to Handle Imbalanced Data (SMOTE, Weighting Classes)

Class imbalance is a common problem in machine learning, especially in real-world datasets, where one class is underrepresented compared to the other. It can significantly affect the performance of machine learning models, leading them to focus on the majority class and neglect the minority class. To address this issue, various techniques can be employed to ensure that models perform well even in the presence of imbalance. In this section, we will discuss two key techniques to handle imbalanced data: SMOTE (Synthetic Minority Over-sampling Technique) and class weighting.

10.2.1 SMOTE (Synthetic Minority Over-sampling Technique)

SMOTE is one of the most popular techniques for dealing with class imbalance, especially when the dataset contains a very small number of instances in the minority class. SMOTE works by creating synthetic examples rather than duplicating existing minority class examples.

How SMOTE Works:

Select a Minority Class Instance: For each instance in the minority class, SMOTE identifies its k-nearest neighbors (typically k = 5).

Create Synthetic Samples: For each selected minority class instance, SMOTE generates synthetic samples by taking the differences between the selected instance and its neighbors, multiplying these differences by a random number between 0 and 1, and then adding this to the original instance. This creates new, synthetic instances that lie along the line between the original instance and its neighbors.

Repeat for All Minority Instances: The synthetic samples are generated for all instances in the minority class, resulting in a more balanced dataset.

Advantages of SMOTE:

- **Avoids Overfitting**: By generating synthetic data points instead of duplicating existing ones, SMOTE prevents the model from overfitting to repeated instances.
- **Increases Diversity**: Since synthetic samples are created by combining information from the original instances and their neighbors, the method helps to add variety to the minority class, potentially improving generalization.
- **Helps Model Learn More Complex Patterns**: SMOTE allows models to learn patterns from synthetic samples that are not confined to the existing minority class examples.

Disadvantages of SMOTE:

- **Overlapping Classes**: If the data contains noise or the minority class is sparse, SMOTE might generate synthetic samples in areas where they do not represent the true distribution of the minority class, leading to misclassifications.
- **Outlier Sensitivity**: SMOTE can amplify the effect of outliers because it creates synthetic data based on the nearest neighbors, which may include outliers.
- **Computational Complexity**: SMOTE can be computationally expensive when working with large datasets or when using a large value for k.

Implementation of SMOTE in Python:

You can easily implement SMOTE using the imbalanced-learn library, which provides an implementation of SMOTE.

pip install imbalanced-learn

Here is an example of how to apply SMOTE to a dataset:

```
from imblearn.over_sampling import SMOTE
from sklearn.datasets import make_classification
from sklearn.model_selection import train_test_split

# Create an imbalanced dataset
X, y = make_classification(n_samples=1000, n_features=20, n_classes=2,
            n_clusters_per_class=1, weights=[0.95, 0.05], random_state=42)

# Split the dataset into training and testing sets
X_train, X_test, y_train, y_test = train_test_split(X, y, test_size=0.3, random_state=42)

# Apply SMOTE to the training data
```

```
smote = SMOTE(sampling_strategy='auto', random_state=42)
X_resampled, y_resampled = smote.fit_resample(X_train, y_train)

print(f"Original dataset shape: {y_train.value_counts()}")
print(f"Resampled dataset shape: {y_resampled.value_counts()}")
```

In this code:

- sampling_strategy='auto' ensures that the minority class is oversampled to match the majority class size.
- fit_resample() applies SMOTE and returns the resampled dataset with synthetic minority class examples.

10.2.2 Weighting Classes

Another effective approach to handle imbalanced datasets is class weighting, where the model is penalized more for misclassifying the minority class. Many machine learning algorithms, including logistic regression, support vector machines (SVM), and decision trees, provide an option to assign class weights.

How Class Weighting Works:

In the case of imbalanced classes, models that assign equal importance to both classes may end up ignoring the minority class because it occurs less frequently. By assigning higher weights to the minority class, the model is incentivized to pay more attention to correctly classifying instances from the minority class.

Higher Weights for Minority Class: In an imbalanced dataset, the minority class will be assigned a higher weight so that the model will incur a greater penalty for misclassifying instances from the minority class. This makes the model more likely to correctly classify instances from the minority class.

Balanced Loss Function: The weighted loss function is used to ensure that the model considers both classes equally during training, thereby preventing the model from being biased toward the majority class.

Advantages of Class Weighting:

- **No Data Duplication**: Unlike SMOTE, class weighting does not require generating synthetic samples, meaning that there is no risk of introducing noise or outliers into the dataset.
- **Simplicity**: Class weighting is straightforward to implement and can often be added to existing models without requiring significant changes to the dataset.
- **Effective for Small Datasets**: For smaller datasets where SMOTE may generate noisy or unrealistic synthetic samples, class weighting can help the model focus more on the minority class without creating synthetic data.

Disadvantages of Class Weighting:

Hyperparameter Tuning: Finding the optimal class weight is often a matter of trial and error and requires tuning the weight hyperparameters to achieve the best performance. Sensitive to Extreme Imbalance: In cases of extreme imbalance (e.g., when one class constitutes less than 1% of the total dataset), class weighting may still lead to poor model performance, as the model may still struggle to identify the minority class effectively.

Implementation of Class Weighting in Python:

Many algorithms in Scikit-learn, such as Logistic Regression, Random Forests, SVM, and others, allow you to specify class weights.

Here's an example of using class weights in Logistic Regression:

```
from sklearn.linear_model import LogisticRegression
from sklearn.datasets import make_classification
from sklearn.model_selection import train_test_split
from sklearn.metrics import classification_report

# Create an imbalanced dataset
X, y = make_classification(n_samples=1000, n_features=20, n_classes=2,
            n_clusters_per_class=1, weights=[0.95, 0.05], random_state=42)

# Split the dataset into training and testing sets
X_train, X_test, y_train, y_test = train_test_split(X, y, test_size=0.3, random_state=42)

# Create the logistic regression model with class weights
model = LogisticRegression(class_weight='balanced', random_state=42)

# Fit the model to the training data
```

```
model.fit(X_train, y_train)

# Evaluate the model
y_pred = model.predict(X_test)
print(classification_report(y_test, y_pred))
```

In this example:

- class_weight='balanced' automatically adjusts the weights inversely proportional to class frequencies in the training data. This means the minority class will be given a higher weight.
- classification_report() provides a detailed performance evaluation using precision, recall, and F1-score, which are more meaningful when handling imbalanced datasets.

10.2.3 Combining SMOTE and Class Weighting

In some cases, it may be beneficial to combine both SMOTE and class weighting. SMOTE can be used to balance the class distribution by generating synthetic samples, while class weighting ensures that the model pays more attention to the minority class during training.

This combination can be useful in situations where the imbalance is extreme and synthetic samples help the model generalize better, while class weights guide the model's focus on the minority class.

Handling class imbalance is essential for building accurate and reliable machine learning models, especially when the minority class is of high importance, such as in fraud detection, medical diagnostics, and rare event prediction. SMOTE and class weighting are two effective techniques for addressing this issue:

- SMOTE generates synthetic data points to balance the dataset, preventing overfitting and improving the model's ability to generalize.
- Class Weighting adjusts the loss function to penalize the misclassification of the minority class, guiding the model to focus more on it without altering the data distribution.

Depending on the dataset and the specific problem, you may choose to apply one or both techniques to improve model performance on imbalanced datasets.

10.3 Detecting Anomalies with Isolation Forests

Anomaly detection is an essential task in various machine learning applications, particularly when identifying rare events or unusual patterns within a dataset. Anomalies, or outliers, are data points that deviate significantly from the general distribution of the data. Detecting anomalies is critical in fields like fraud detection, network security, defect detection in manufacturing, and medical diagnoses, among others.

In this section, we will discuss the Isolation Forest algorithm, which is a powerful and efficient method for anomaly detection. We will explore how it works, why it is well-suited for anomaly detection, and how to implement it in Python using Scikit-learn.

10.3.1 What is Isolation Forest?

Isolation Forest (iForest) is an algorithm specifically designed for anomaly detection in high-dimensional datasets. It works by isolating observations that are different from the majority of the data. The basic idea is that anomalies are easier to isolate than normal points because they are rare and significantly different from other data points.

Unlike traditional anomaly detection methods like k-Nearest Neighbors (k-NN) or Gaussian Mixture Models (GMM), which focus on measuring distances between data points or fitting the data to a distribution, Isolation Forest takes a different approach by randomly partitioning the feature space and isolating observations.

10.3.2 How Isolation Forest Works

The working principle behind Isolation Forest is based on the concept of isolation. The idea is that the algorithm isolates anomalies by creating random splits in the feature space. Since anomalies are different from the majority of the data, they are easier to isolate with fewer partitions. Normal points, on the other hand, are more similar to each other and require more splits to be isolated.

The steps of the Isolation Forest algorithm can be described as follows:

Random Partitioning: The algorithm creates multiple random trees (known as decision trees or isolation trees) by randomly selecting a feature and then randomly selecting a value within the range of that feature. The data points are then split into two parts based on the chosen feature and value.

Isolation: Each tree attempts to isolate the data points by recursively splitting the data along randomly chosen feature values. The number of splits required to isolate a data point is a measure of its "anomaly score." Data points that are isolated quickly (with fewer splits) are likely anomalies, while data points that take many splits to isolate are considered normal.

Anomaly Score: The isolation score is calculated based on the average path length required to isolate a point across all trees in the forest. The shorter the path length, the more anomalous the point is considered to be. Anomaly scores closer to 1 indicate that a point is more likely to be an anomaly, while scores closer to 0 indicate normal points.

Decision Making: Based on the anomaly scores, the algorithm assigns a label (anomaly or normal) to each data point. Points with high anomaly scores are classified as anomalies.

The key advantage of Isolation Forest lies in its ability to scale efficiently with high-dimensional data. This is because it does not rely on distance metrics or density-based methods, which can become computationally expensive as the number of features increases.

10.3.3 Advantages of Isolation Forest

Efficiency and Scalability: Isolation Forest is computationally efficient, even for large datasets with high dimensionality. Unlike traditional anomaly detection methods, which may suffer from the curse of dimensionality, Isolation Forest can handle high-dimensional data without excessive computational cost.

Works Well with High-Dimensional Data: Isolation Forest performs well in scenarios where other anomaly detection methods, such as k-NN or GMM, may struggle due to the sparsity or complexity of high-dimensional spaces.

No Assumption of Distribution: Unlike statistical methods that assume the data follows a specific distribution (e.g., Gaussian), Isolation Forest makes no such assumption, making it more flexible and suitable for a wide variety of anomaly detection tasks.

Non-Linear Decision Boundaries: The method does not rely on linear decision boundaries, allowing it to capture more complex patterns in the data that may be indicative of anomalies.

Less Sensitivity to Outliers: Isolation Forest can detect anomalies even in the presence of other outliers, as it focuses on isolating points that are distinctly different from the rest of the data.

10.3.4 Disadvantages of Isolation Forest

Interpretability: While Isolation Forest can be effective in detecting anomalies, the model is not as interpretable as some other methods, such as decision trees or rule-based models. It is difficult to understand the exact decision-making process for each individual anomaly detection.

Choosing the Number of Trees: The algorithm requires setting the number of trees in the forest. Choosing an insufficient number of trees may result in inaccurate anomaly detection, while too many trees can lead to increased computational cost.

Sensitivity to Hyperparameters: The performance of the algorithm depends on the settings of its hyperparameters, such as the number of trees, the subsample size, and the contamination factor (the expected proportion of anomalies in the data).

10.3.5 Implementing Isolation Forest in Python

The IsolationForest algorithm is available in the Scikit-learn library, making it easy to implement in Python. Below is an example of how to use Isolation Forest for anomaly detection.

```
pip install scikit-learn
```

Here is an example using the IsolationForest class from Scikit-learn:

```
from sklearn.ensemble import IsolationForest
from sklearn.datasets import make_classification
import numpy as np
import matplotlib.pyplot as plt

# Create a synthetic imbalanced dataset
X, _ = make_classification(n_samples=1000, n_features=2, n_informative=2,
            n_clusters_per_class=1, weights=[0.98, 0.02], random_state=42)

# Add some anomalies to the dataset
X_with_anomalies = np.vstack([X, np.random.uniform(low=-6, high=6, size=(10, 2))])
```

```
# Initialize the Isolation Forest model
model = IsolationForest(contamination=0.02, random_state=42)

# Fit the model to the data
model.fit(X_with_anomalies)

# Predict anomalies in the data
y_pred = model.predict(X_with_anomalies)

# Convert predictions (-1 for anomalies, 1 for normal)
anomalies = X_with_anomalies[y_pred == -1]
normal = X_with_anomalies[y_pred == 1]

# Plot the results
plt.scatter(normal[:, 0], normal[:, 1], c='blue', label='Normal')
plt.scatter(anomalies[:, 0], anomalies[:, 1], c='red', label='Anomalies')
plt.legend()
plt.title("Anomaly Detection with Isolation Forest")
plt.show()
```

In this example:

- We create a synthetic dataset with a significant class imbalance using make_classification.
- Anomalies are added to the dataset manually by generating random data points.
- The IsolationForest model is initialized with the contamination parameter set to 0.02, meaning we expect 2% of the data to be anomalies.
- The model is trained using fit(), and anomalies are detected using the predict() method, where anomalies are labeled as -1 and normal points are labeled as 1.
- The results are plotted to show how anomalies are detected (red points) compared to normal data points (blue points).

10.3.6 Hyperparameters of Isolation Forest

The performance of the Isolation Forest algorithm can be controlled through several key hyperparameters:

n_estimators: The number of trees in the forest. More trees can lead to better performance but may increase computational cost. Default is 100.

max_samples: The number of samples to draw from the data to train each tree. This can be a fraction (e.g., 0.8) or an integer. Lower values make the algorithm faster but might reduce accuracy.

contamination: The proportion of anomalies in the dataset. This parameter is important as it tells the model how many anomalies to expect. If you don't know the exact proportion of anomalies, you may need to experiment with this value.

bootstrap: Whether to use bootstrap sampling when building trees. This can help improve the performance of the model when using smaller datasets.

random_state: Controls the randomness of the algorithm for reproducibility.

Isolation Forest is an efficient and effective algorithm for detecting anomalies in datasets, especially in high-dimensional spaces. Unlike traditional anomaly detection methods that rely on distance metrics or distribution assumptions, Isolation Forest focuses on isolating anomalies by partitioning the feature space. It is computationally efficient, works well with large and high-dimensional datasets, and does not require explicit knowledge of the distribution of data.

By implementing and tuning Isolation Forest, you can detect outliers or rare events in a variety of applications, including fraud detection, network security, and predictive maintenance.

10.4 One-Class SVM for Outlier Detection

Outlier detection, or anomaly detection, plays a critical role in identifying rare events or unusual data points in a dataset that significantly differ from the rest of the data. These outliers might represent important information such as fraudulent transactions, defective products, or system faults, depending on the context. One of the popular methods for outlier detection is the One-Class Support Vector Machine (One-Class SVM), which is particularly effective when the data consists mostly of one class (normal data), and we want to identify points that deviate significantly from this class.

In this section, we will explore the One-Class SVM algorithm, how it works, its advantages and limitations, and how to implement it for outlier detection using Scikit-learn.

10.4.1 What is One-Class SVM?

One-Class SVM is a variation of the Support Vector Machine (SVM) designed specifically for anomaly detection. Unlike the standard SVM, which is used for classification, the One-Class SVM algorithm focuses on learning a boundary that encapsulates the majority of the data, classifying everything outside this boundary as an anomaly or outlier.

In a typical classification problem, we aim to separate two classes (positive and negative) by finding a hyperplane that maximizes the margin between the classes. However, in one-class SVM, the goal is to learn a hyperplane (or a set of hyperplanes in higher-dimensional spaces) that best represents the normal class and then classify data points that fall outside this boundary as outliers.

The basic idea behind One-Class SVM is:

- **Normal Data Points**: These are points that are similar to the majority of the data, and the model attempts to fit the hyperplane so that these points are within the learned boundary.
- **Outliers**: These are points that do not fit the pattern of normal data and are located outside the learned boundary. The One-Class SVM will classify these points as anomalies.

10.4.2 How One-Class SVM Works

One-Class SVM relies on the concept of a decision function to classify data points. The decision function is trained on data that represents the normal behavior (in a one-class scenario, this could be data containing only the normal class). The steps involved in One-Class SVM are as follows:

Training: The One-Class SVM is trained on the dataset containing only "normal" points. The algorithm learns a decision boundary that encloses the majority of the data. This decision boundary is typically a high-dimensional boundary in feature space.

Boundary Definition: The algorithm attempts to fit the boundary (usually a hyperplane or a non-linear boundary) that encompasses the majority of the data points. Data points near the boundary are considered normal, while those far from the boundary are classified as outliers.

Outlier Detection: When the model is trained, it can be used to predict new points. If a point lies inside the boundary (i.e., close to the learned decision function), it is classified as normal; if it lies outside the boundary, it is considered an outlier.

Decision Function: The decision function of a One-Class SVM outputs a score indicating how well a data point fits the normal pattern. Data points that are classified as outliers are those that have a negative decision function value (indicating that they lie outside the learned boundary).

10.4.3 Hyperparameters of One-Class SVM

One-Class SVM has several key hyperparameters that can be adjusted to improve its performance, depending on the specific dataset and task:

kernel: Specifies the type of kernel to use for transforming the data into a higher-dimensional space. Common choices include:

- 'linear': A linear kernel, which works well if the data is linearly separable.
- 'rbf': A radial basis function (RBF) kernel, which is useful for non-linear data.
- 'poly': A polynomial kernel.
- 'sigmoid': A sigmoid kernel.

nu: This parameter controls the number of outliers or anomalies the model can tolerate. It is the upper bound on the fraction of margin errors (outliers) in the dataset. The value of nu must lie between 0 and 1. A smaller value indicates that fewer points are considered outliers, while a larger value allows more points to be considered anomalies.

gamma: This parameter is used when the kernel is RBF, polynomial, or sigmoid. It controls the curvature of the decision boundary. A high value of gamma can make the decision boundary very tight, which may lead to overfitting, while a lower value results in a smoother boundary that might be more generalizable.

coef0: This is a parameter used in the polynomial and sigmoid kernels. It controls the trade-off between the kernel's higher-order and lower-order terms. It is not relevant for the linear kernel.

degree: This is the degree of the polynomial kernel. It controls the complexity of the decision boundary for the polynomial kernel type.

10.4.4 Advantages of One-Class SVM

Effective in High Dimensions: One-Class SVM works well even with high-dimensional data where traditional outlier detection methods might struggle. This makes it suitable for anomaly detection in complex datasets.

No Need for Labeled Data: Unlike supervised learning methods, One-Class SVM does not require labeled data. It learns solely from the normal data and identifies outliers based on their deviation from this learned model.

Non-Linear Boundaries: By using kernels (such as the RBF kernel), One-Class SVM can model complex non-linear boundaries, making it a versatile algorithm for various types of data.

Flexibility: It can be applied to various domains such as fraud detection, image processing, and network security, among others.

10.4.5 Disadvantages of One-Class SVM

Sensitive to Hyperparameters: The performance of One-Class SVM can be sensitive to the choice of hyperparameters, such as nu and gamma. Tuning these parameters can be computationally expensive and may require cross-validation or grid search.

Memory Consumption: One-Class SVM may require substantial memory when dealing with large datasets, particularly when using non-linear kernels like RBF.

Interpretability: Like most kernel-based methods, One-Class SVM models are often harder to interpret compared to simpler models such as decision trees or linear regression. It may be challenging to understand the reasons why a particular point is considered an outlier.

10.4.6 Implementing One-Class SVM in Python

In Python, One-Class SVM can be implemented using the OneClassSVM class from Scikit-learn. Below is an example of how to use One-Class SVM for anomaly detection.

pip install scikit-learn

Here is an example using One-Class SVM for outlier detection:

from sklearn.svm import OneClassSVM
import numpy as np

```python
import matplotlib.pyplot as plt

# Create synthetic data (normal data)
X_normal = np.random.randn(100, 2)

# Add some outliers
X_outliers = np.random.uniform(low=-6, high=6, size=(10, 2))

# Combine normal data with outliers
X_combined = np.vstack([X_normal, X_outliers])

# Initialize the One-Class SVM model
model = OneClassSVM(kernel='rbf', nu=0.1, gamma='scale')

# Fit the model on the normal data
model.fit(X_normal)

# Predict anomalies on the combined data
y_pred = model.predict(X_combined)

# Convert predictions (-1 for outliers, 1 for normal)
normal = X_combined[y_pred == 1]
outliers = X_combined[y_pred == -1]

# Plot the results
plt.scatter(normal[:, 0], normal[:, 1], c='blue', label='Normal')
plt.scatter(outliers[:, 0], outliers[:, 1], c='red', label='Outliers')
plt.legend()
plt.title("Outlier Detection with One-Class SVM")
plt.show()
```

In this example:

- We generate synthetic data with normal points drawn from a standard normal distribution and outliers from a uniform distribution.
- We train the One-Class SVM model using only the normal data (X_normal).
- We then predict anomalies in the combined dataset (X_combined) and classify points as either normal or outliers.
- Finally, the results are visualized, with normal data points shown in blue and outliers shown in red.

One-Class SVM is a powerful and flexible algorithm for detecting outliers and anomalies in datasets, particularly in situations where the dataset consists mostly of normal data, and we need to identify rare or unusual points. It works well with high-dimensional data and does not require labeled data, making it a valuable tool in various fields such as fraud detection, fault detection, and cybersecurity.

While One-Class SVM has several advantages, such as its ability to learn non-linear decision boundaries and its efficiency with high-dimensional data, it also has limitations, including sensitivity to hyperparameter tuning and potential memory consumption for large datasets. However, with the right parameter settings, One-Class SVM can be an effective anomaly detection tool for many real-world applications.

11. Pipelines and Model Deployment

Building machine learning models is only part of the journey—deploying them efficiently is just as critical. This chapter covers how to automate preprocessing and modeling steps using Scikit-Learn pipelines, and how to save, load, and deploy models using Flask and FastAPI for real-world applications.

11.1 Automating Machine Learning Workflows with Pipelines

In machine learning, one of the most important aspects of building effective models is the process of transforming raw data into useful features, training the model, and deploying it for predictions. This process, often referred to as the machine learning workflow, typically involves a series of steps, such as data preprocessing, feature engineering, model selection, training, evaluation, and prediction. Each of these steps requires specific tasks to be performed sequentially or in combination. While this process is fundamental to machine learning, it can be repetitive, error-prone, and time-consuming when done manually.

This is where pipelines come in. A pipeline is a way to automate, organize, and streamline the entire machine learning workflow, ensuring that the steps are executed consistently and efficiently. Pipelines allow you to encapsulate all the steps of the process into a single object, making it easier to maintain, reproduce, and scale machine learning tasks. In this section, we will explore what pipelines are, how they help automate machine learning workflows, and how to implement them using Scikit-learn.

11.1.1 What is a Machine Learning Pipeline?

In simple terms, a machine learning pipeline is a sequence of data processing steps that are chained together. Each step in the pipeline is an individual transformation or model that processes the data in a particular way. Once the data has passed through all steps, the pipeline produces the final output, whether it is a model for predictions or some transformed data.

The key idea behind a pipeline is that it allows you to:

- Automate the entire workflow from data preprocessing to model training and evaluation.
- Ensure that all steps are executed in the correct order.

- Reuse the pipeline across different datasets or experiments without worrying about duplicating code or inconsistent transformations.
- Avoid common errors such as data leakage, where information from the test set unintentionally influences model training.

11.1.2 Components of a Machine Learning Pipeline

A machine learning pipeline typically consists of several components, each of which handles a specific task in the workflow. These components are connected to each other in a sequence, with each step passing data to the next.

The primary components of a pipeline include:

Data Preprocessing: This is often the first step of the pipeline. It involves cleaning the data, handling missing values, encoding categorical variables, and scaling numerical features. Preprocessing can also involve feature extraction or dimensionality reduction techniques like Principal Component Analysis (PCA).

Feature Engineering: This step involves creating new features from the existing data that can better represent the underlying patterns and improve the performance of the model. Techniques such as feature selection, one-hot encoding, and polynomial feature generation are often applied.

Model Training: This is the core of the pipeline, where machine learning models are trained on the processed data. It involves selecting an appropriate algorithm (e.g., logistic regression, decision trees, or neural networks) and training the model using the data.

Model Evaluation: After training, the model is evaluated using various performance metrics like accuracy, precision, recall, F1-score, or mean squared error (MSE). This step ensures that the model is performing as expected and helps in comparing different models.

Hyperparameter Tuning: This involves optimizing the model by adjusting hyperparameters (e.g., learning rate, number of trees, etc.) to improve its performance. This step is crucial for achieving the best possible results.

Model Prediction: The final step of the pipeline involves using the trained model to make predictions on new data.

In practice, not all pipelines contain all of these components. Some may include only data preprocessing and model training, while others may include additional steps such as hyperparameter tuning, feature selection, or model deployment.

11.1.3 Benefits of Using Pipelines

Using pipelines in machine learning workflows offers several key benefits:

Reproducibility: Pipelines allow you to encapsulate the entire workflow in a single object, making it easier to reproduce experiments. This is especially important in research and production environments, where consistency and reproducibility are crucial.

Automation: Pipelines automate repetitive tasks, such as data preprocessing, model training, and evaluation, saving time and reducing the potential for human error. Once a pipeline is defined, you can run it multiple times with minimal intervention.

Consistency: By defining all the steps in a single pipeline, you ensure that the same sequence of operations is applied to the data every time. This reduces the risk of inconsistencies, such as accidentally applying different preprocessing steps to training and test data.

Scalability: Pipelines make it easier to scale machine learning workflows. For example, you can apply pipelines to large datasets, parallelize certain steps, or deploy the pipeline to production systems for real-time predictions.

Cross-validation: Pipelines simplify the process of cross-validation. Instead of manually splitting the dataset into training and test sets for each experiment, you can easily use cross-validation within the pipeline to evaluate your model's performance.

Model Experimentation: Pipelines make it easier to experiment with different models, preprocessing steps, or hyperparameters by swapping out components of the pipeline. This allows for rapid experimentation and comparison of models.

11.1.4 Implementing Pipelines in Scikit-learn

Scikit-learn provides a powerful tool for building and managing machine learning pipelines through the Pipeline class. The Pipeline class allows you to create a sequence of transformations followed by a final estimator (model), ensuring that all steps are applied in the correct order. The general structure of a pipeline is:

```python
from sklearn.pipeline import Pipeline

pipeline = Pipeline([
    ('preprocessor', preprocessing_step),
    ('model', model)
])
```

In this example, 'preprocessor' is a placeholder for the preprocessing steps (such as feature scaling or encoding), and 'model' is the final machine learning model (such as a classifier or regressor). Each step in the pipeline is a tuple, where the first element is a name (which can be used for reference), and the second element is an object that performs the transformation or model fitting.

11.1.5 Example of a Simple Pipeline

Let's create a simple pipeline that performs data preprocessing (scaling) and model training (logistic regression):

```python
from sklearn.datasets import load_iris
from sklearn.model_selection import train_test_split
from sklearn.preprocessing import StandardScaler
from sklearn.linear_model import LogisticRegression
from sklearn.pipeline import Pipeline
from sklearn.metrics import accuracy_score

# Load the iris dataset
data = load_iris()
X = data.data
y = data.target

# Split the data into training and testing sets
X_train, X_test, y_train, y_test = train_test_split(X, y, test_size=0.3, random_state=42)

# Create a pipeline with preprocessing (scaling) and model (logistic regression)
pipeline = Pipeline([
    ('scaler', StandardScaler()),        # Step 1: Scaling the features
    ('classifier', LogisticRegression())  # Step 2: Training a logistic regression model
])

# Fit the pipeline on the training data
```

```
pipeline.fit(X_train, y_train)

# Make predictions on the test set
y_pred = pipeline.predict(X_test)

# Evaluate the model performance
accuracy = accuracy_score(y_test, y_pred)
print(f'Accuracy: {accuracy * 100:.2f}%')
```

In this example:

- We load the iris dataset, which is a simple dataset for classification tasks.
- We split the data into training and test sets using train_test_split.
- We create a pipeline with two steps:
- StandardScaler() for feature scaling.
- LogisticRegression() for training the model.
- We fit the pipeline on the training data and make predictions on the test set.
- Finally, we evaluate the accuracy of the model using the accuracy_score function.

11.1.6 Using Pipelines for Hyperparameter Tuning

One of the major advantages of using pipelines is the ease with which you can perform hyperparameter tuning with methods like GridSearchCV or RandomizedSearchCV. By combining pipelines with hyperparameter tuning, you can automatically search for the best combination of preprocessing steps and model hyperparameters. Below is an example of how to combine Pipeline with GridSearchCV to tune hyperparameters:

```
from sklearn.model_selection import GridSearchCV

# Define the pipeline as before
pipeline = Pipeline([
    ('scaler', StandardScaler()),
    ('classifier', LogisticRegression())
])

# Define the hyperparameters to tune
param_grid = {
    'classifier__C': [0.1, 1, 10],  # Regularization parameter for Logistic Regression
    'classifier__solver': ['liblinear', 'saga'],  # Solvers for Logistic Regression
}
```

```
# Use GridSearchCV to find the best hyperparameters
grid_search = GridSearchCV(pipeline, param_grid, cv=5, verbose=1)

# Fit the grid search
grid_search.fit(X_train, y_train)

# Print the best parameters found by GridSearchCV
print("Best parameters found: ", grid_search.best_params_)
```

In this example:

- We define the param_grid dictionary with hyperparameters for the logistic regression model (C and solver).
- We pass this grid to GridSearchCV, which will automatically search for the best combination of hyperparameters by performing cross-validation.

Machine learning pipelines offer a powerful way to automate and streamline machine learning workflows. By encapsulating the entire process—from data preprocessing to model training and evaluation—into a single object, pipelines ensure consistency, reproducibility, and scalability. Scikit-learn's Pipeline class provides a simple yet effective way to build, maintain, and experiment with machine learning workflows, making it easier to manage complex workflows, optimize hyperparameters, and prevent common pitfalls such as data leakage.

With the use of pipelines, machine learning practitioners can focus on experimentation and innovation, while ensuring that the workflow is efficient, error-free, and easy to reproduce.

11.2 Preprocessing with Pipelines

Preprocessing is a crucial step in any machine learning project. It involves transforming raw data into a format that can be effectively used by machine learning algorithms. The preprocessing pipeline typically includes steps such as data cleaning, scaling, encoding categorical variables, handling missing values, and feature extraction. By automating and organizing preprocessing with pipelines, you ensure consistency, prevent errors, and make the overall machine learning workflow more efficient.

In this section, we will explore how to use Scikit-learn's Pipeline for automating preprocessing steps and integrating them into the larger machine learning workflow. We will cover common preprocessing techniques and demonstrate how to incorporate them into a pipeline to simplify model development.

11.2.1 The Importance of Preprocessing in Machine Learning

The quality and structure of the data play a significant role in the performance of machine learning models. Raw datasets are often incomplete, noisy, or in a format that algorithms cannot interpret directly. Preprocessing prepares the data for the model by addressing several key challenges:

- **Handling Missing Values**: Machine learning algorithms require complete data, and missing values must be appropriately addressed to avoid errors and biased models.
- **Feature Scaling**: Many machine learning models perform better when features are on similar scales. Models like Support Vector Machines (SVMs) and k-nearest neighbors (KNN) are sensitive to the scale of data.
- **Encoding Categorical Variables**: Machine learning models can only process numeric data, so categorical variables must be converted into numerical format using encoding techniques.
- **Feature Extraction and Transformation**: Transformations such as dimensionality reduction or polynomial feature generation can improve model performance by extracting more informative features.

By chaining all these preprocessing steps together into a pipeline, it becomes easier to handle these challenges consistently and efficiently.

11.2.2 Scikit-learn Pipelines for Preprocessing

In Scikit-learn, the Pipeline class allows you to sequentially apply transformations to your data followed by a final estimator (model). This ensures that all preprocessing steps are applied to both the training and testing data in the same manner, reducing the risk of errors like data leakage.

The basic syntax for creating a pipeline in Scikit-learn is:

from sklearn.pipeline import Pipeline

pipeline = Pipeline([

```
    ('step1', transformer_or_estimator1),
    ('step2', transformer_or_estimator2),
    ...
])
```

Here, 'step1', 'step2', etc., are the names of the preprocessing steps, and transformer_or_estimator1, transformer_or_estimator2 are the objects that perform the corresponding transformation or modeling task. These objects could be any transformer (such as scalers or imputers) or estimators (such as classifiers or regressors).

Let's explore some of the most common preprocessing steps you might use in a pipeline.

11.2.3 Common Preprocessing Techniques in Pipelines

Handling Missing Values

One of the first tasks in preprocessing is dealing with missing data. Scikit-learn provides two primary strategies for handling missing values:

Imputation: This involves filling in missing values using a specific strategy such as the mean, median, or most frequent value for numerical features, or the most frequent category for categorical features.

Scikit-learn's SimpleImputer can be used to implement imputation in the pipeline.

```
from sklearn.impute import SimpleImputer
from sklearn.pipeline import Pipeline
from sklearn.preprocessing import StandardScaler
from sklearn.ensemble import RandomForestClassifier

pipeline = Pipeline([
    ('imputer', SimpleImputer(strategy='mean')),  # Impute missing values with the mean
    ('scaler', StandardScaler()),                 # Scale the features
    ('classifier', RandomForestClassifier())     # Train a RandomForest model
])
```

In this example:

- Missing values in the dataset are imputed with the mean value for each column using SimpleImputer.

- Then, the features are scaled using StandardScaler, which standardizes the features by subtracting the mean and dividing by the standard deviation.
- Finally, a Random Forest classifier is trained on the preprocessed data.

Feature Scaling

Scaling is important when using models sensitive to the range of the data, like SVMs, KNN, and logistic regression. Scikit-learn provides several scalers, such as:

- **StandardScaler**: This scales the features to have a mean of 0 and a standard deviation of 1.
- **MinMaxScaler**: This scales the features to a specific range, typically [0, 1].
- **RobustScaler**: This scaler is robust to outliers, as it scales based on the interquartile range rather than the mean and standard deviation.

Example of scaling in a pipeline:

```
from sklearn.preprocessing import MinMaxScaler

pipeline = Pipeline([
    ('scaler', MinMaxScaler()),          # Min-max scale the features
    ('classifier', RandomForestClassifier()) # Random Forest model
])
```

Encoding Categorical Variables

Many machine learning models can only process numerical data. Therefore, categorical features need to be encoded into numerical representations. Scikit-learn provides two common methods for encoding categorical data:

- **OneHotEncoder**: This technique creates binary columns for each category of a categorical feature.
- **LabelEncoder**: This encodes each category with a unique integer.

Here's how you can use OneHotEncoder in a pipeline:

```
from sklearn.preprocessing import OneHotEncoder
from sklearn.compose import ColumnTransformer
from sklearn.ensemble import RandomForestClassifier
```

```
# Specify which columns are categorical
categorical_features = ['column1', 'column2']

# Create a column transformer to apply OneHotEncoder to categorical features
preprocessor = ColumnTransformer(
    transformers=[
        ('cat', OneHotEncoder(), categorical_features)
    ])

# Create a pipeline that applies preprocessing and then a classifier
pipeline = Pipeline([
    ('preprocessor', preprocessor),
    ('classifier', RandomForestClassifier())
])
```

In this example:

- ColumnTransformer is used to apply OneHotEncoder to specific categorical columns in the dataset.
- The transformed features are then passed into a Random Forest classifier for training.

Dimensionality Reduction

Dimensionality reduction techniques like PCA (Principal Component Analysis) can be included in the preprocessing pipeline to reduce the number of features before training a model. PCA is often used to eliminate redundant or irrelevant features, making the model faster and potentially more accurate.

Here's an example that applies PCA before training a classifier:

```
from sklearn.decomposition import PCA
from sklearn.ensemble import RandomForestClassifier
from sklearn.pipeline import Pipeline

pipeline = Pipeline([
    ('pca', PCA(n_components=2)),          # Apply PCA to reduce features to 2
components
    ('classifier', RandomForestClassifier())   # Train a Random Forest model
])
```

In this case:

- PCA is applied to reduce the data to two principal components.
- The model is then trained on the reduced feature set.

11.2.4 Using Pipelines for Cross-Validation

One of the key advantages of using pipelines is that they can simplify the process of applying cross-validation. When using traditional approaches, preprocessing steps such as scaling and imputation might be performed separately for the training and test data, potentially leading to data leakage. However, when you use a pipeline, these preprocessing steps are integrated into the cross-validation process, ensuring that they are applied consistently and correctly.

For example, using a pipeline with GridSearchCV to tune hyperparameters:

```
from sklearn.model_selection import GridSearchCV
from sklearn.ensemble import RandomForestClassifier
from sklearn.preprocessing import StandardScaler
from sklearn.pipeline import Pipeline

pipeline = Pipeline([
    ('scaler', StandardScaler()),            # Feature scaling
    ('classifier', RandomForestClassifier())    # Random Forest classifier
])

# Define the hyperparameters to tune
param_grid = {
    'classifier__n_estimators': [100, 200],
    'classifier__max_depth': [None, 10, 20]
}

# Use GridSearchCV for cross-validation and hyperparameter tuning
grid_search = GridSearchCV(pipeline, param_grid, cv=5)

# Fit the model
grid_search.fit(X_train, y_train)

# Get the best parameters from the grid search
```

```
print("Best parameters:", grid_search.best_params_)
```

In this example, the pipeline ensures that all preprocessing steps are applied correctly during the cross-validation process.

Preprocessing is a vital part of the machine learning workflow, and integrating preprocessing steps into pipelines can significantly streamline the process. Scikit-learn's Pipeline class makes it easy to chain multiple preprocessing steps together and apply them consistently to training and test data.

By automating the preprocessing tasks within a pipeline, you reduce the risk of errors, ensure reproducibility, and increase the efficiency of your machine learning pipeline. This enables better model development and experimentation, making pipelines an essential tool for anyone working with machine learning models.

11.3 Saving and Loading Models with Joblib

Once a machine learning model has been trained, the next step in the workflow often involves saving the trained model so that it can be reused later. Instead of retraining a model every time you need to use it, you can save it to a file and reload it when necessary. This is particularly useful when you have a model that takes a long time to train, or if you need to deploy the model into production environments.

In Scikit-learn, the joblib library is commonly used for saving and loading models, along with other Python objects like NumPy arrays. It provides efficient serialization of large Python objects and is faster and more memory-efficient than the built-in Python pickle module, especially for models involving large NumPy arrays (which are common in machine learning).

In this section, we will cover how to use Joblib to save and load machine learning models in Scikit-learn.

11.3.1 Why Use Joblib?

While Python provides several ways to save objects, Joblib is highly optimized for serializing large objects that are common in machine learning workflows. Some of the key advantages of using joblib over other methods like pickle include:

- **Faster Performance**: joblib is designed for efficiently saving and loading large data structures, making it particularly suitable for machine learning models with large datasets or high-dimensional arrays.
- **Efficient Memory Usage**: It handles large arrays more efficiently by compressing them, reducing the memory usage and improving I/O speed.
- **Cross-platform Compatibility**: Models saved with joblib can be loaded on any system that has the required Python version and dependencies, making it ideal for deployment.

11.3.2 Saving a Model Using Joblib

Once you have trained a model and want to save it, you can use the joblib.dump() function to store the model in a file. Here's a simple example:

```
import joblib
from sklearn.ensemble import RandomForestClassifier
from sklearn.datasets import load_iris
from sklearn.model_selection import train_test_split

# Load dataset
data = load_iris()
X = data.data
y = data.target

# Split the data into training and testing sets
X_train, X_test, y_train, y_test = train_test_split(X, y, test_size=0.3, random_state=42)

# Train a Random Forest model
model = RandomForestClassifier()
model.fit(X_train, y_train)

# Save the trained model to a file
joblib.dump(model, 'random_forest_model.pkl')

print("Model saved successfully!")
```

In this example:

- We train a RandomForestClassifier on the Iris dataset.

- After training, the model is saved using the joblib.dump() function, which serializes the model and writes it to the file 'random_forest_model.pkl'.
- You can replace 'random_forest_model.pkl' with any filename and path you prefer. It is common to use the .pkl extension to indicate a serialized object file, but any file extension is valid.

11.3.3 Loading a Saved Model Using Joblib

Once the model is saved, you can load it back into memory at any time for making predictions or further evaluations. This is done using the joblib.load() function.

```
# Load the saved model
loaded_model = joblib.load('random_forest_model.pkl')

# Make predictions using the loaded model
predictions = loaded_model.predict(X_test)

# Print the first few predictions
print(predictions[:5])
```

In this example:

- The model is loaded from the 'random_forest_model.pkl' file using joblib.load().
- After loading the model, we can use it to make predictions on the test data (X_test).
- Finally, the first five predictions are printed.
- The key takeaway is that after loading the model, you can use it just as if it had been trained in the current session.

11.3.4 Saving and Loading Pipelines with Joblib

In real-world machine learning projects, you may want to save not only the model but also the entire preprocessing pipeline (including scaling, encoding, etc.). The Pipeline class in Scikit-learn allows you to chain preprocessing steps together with a final estimator. Saving a pipeline using joblib works in the same way as saving a single model.

Here's an example of saving and loading a machine learning pipeline:

```
from sklearn.pipeline import Pipeline
from sklearn.preprocessing import StandardScaler
from sklearn.ensemble import RandomForestClassifier
```

```python
from sklearn.model_selection import train_test_split
from sklearn.datasets import load_iris

# Load dataset
data = load_iris()
X = data.data
y = data.target

# Split the dataset
X_train, X_test, y_train, y_test = train_test_split(X, y, test_size=0.3, random_state=42)

# Create a pipeline with scaling and model training
pipeline = Pipeline([
    ('scaler', StandardScaler()),      # Step 1: Feature scaling
    ('classifier', RandomForestClassifier())  # Step 2: Train a Random Forest model
])

# Fit the pipeline
pipeline.fit(X_train, y_train)

# Save the entire pipeline
joblib.dump(pipeline, 'iris_pipeline.pkl')

print("Pipeline saved successfully!")
```

In this example:

- We create a pipeline that first scales the features using StandardScaler and then trains a RandomForestClassifier.
- The entire pipeline is saved to a file named 'iris_pipeline.pkl' using joblib.dump().

To load the saved pipeline and use it for predictions:

```python
# Load the saved pipeline
loaded_pipeline = joblib.load('iris_pipeline.pkl')

# Make predictions with the loaded pipeline
predictions = loaded_pipeline.predict(X_test)

# Print the first few predictions
```

print(predictions[:5])

In this case, the entire pipeline (both preprocessing and model) is loaded and used for making predictions.

11.3.5 Versioning and Dependencies

When saving models, especially in production environments, it is important to consider versioning and dependencies. Over time, libraries, models, and frameworks may be updated, leading to potential compatibility issues.

To avoid these issues:

- Save the version of the model and dependencies: You can save the versions of Scikit-learn and other dependencies (e.g., using pip freeze or a requirements.txt file).
- Ensure that the environment used for saving the model matches the one used for loading it: This ensures that the dependencies and behavior remain consistent across environments.

Example of saving the environment information:

pip freeze > requirements.txt

This will create a requirements.txt file that records the versions of all installed Python packages, including Scikit-learn, NumPy, and other dependencies.

11.3.6 Compressing Models with Joblib

If you're dealing with large models or datasets, you can use compression to reduce the file size when saving models with joblib. This is particularly useful for deployment or when storage is a concern.

You can specify the compression level when saving a model:

```
# Save the model with compression
joblib.dump(model, 'random_forest_model_compressed.pkl', compress=3)
```

The compress argument can be an integer (from 0 to 9, where 0 is no compression and 9 is maximum compression) or a tuple specifying compression and a compression method (e.g., 'xz', 'gzip').

To load a compressed model:

 # Load the compressed model
loaded_model = joblib.load('random_forest_model_compressed.pkl')

Saving and loading machine learning models with Joblib provides a convenient and efficient way to persist your models for future use, making your machine learning workflows more efficient. By using joblib.dump() and joblib.load(), you can serialize both simple models and complex pipelines that include preprocessing steps, ensuring that your models can be easily reused or deployed to production without retraining.

By saving your trained models and pipelines, you can:

- Avoid redundant training, saving time and computational resources.
- Deploy models to production environments quickly.
- Share models across different environments, ensuring consistency and reproducibility.

Using Joblib for saving and loading models is an essential part of a scalable and reproducible machine learning workflow.

11.4 Deploying Scikit-Learn Models with Flask and FastAPI

Once a machine learning model is trained and saved, the next crucial step is deployment. Deployment involves making the model available for real-world use, such as accepting incoming requests, making predictions, and returning results. There are many ways to deploy a machine learning model, and two of the most popular frameworks for building RESTful APIs to serve models are Flask and FastAPI.

In this section, we will discuss how to deploy a trained Scikit-learn model using both Flask and FastAPI. These frameworks allow you to create web services that can expose machine learning models for predictions via HTTP requests.

11.4.1 Deploying with Flask

Flask is a micro web framework in Python that is easy to learn and very flexible. It allows you to create web applications quickly and deploy machine learning models as HTTP-based REST APIs. Flask is widely used due to its simplicity, rich ecosystem, and good documentation.

Steps to Deploy a Scikit-learn Model Using Flask:

Install Flask and joblib

To deploy a Scikit-learn model with Flask, you need to install Flask and Joblib (if not already installed):

pip install Flask joblib

Create the Flask Application

Let's walk through an example of deploying a RandomForest model that predicts flower species using the Iris dataset.

First, make sure you have a trained and saved Scikit-learn model, as demonstrated in the previous section, using joblib.

Now, let's create a Flask application to expose this model via an API.

```
import joblib
from flask import Flask, request, jsonify
import numpy as np

# Load the trained model
model = joblib.load('random_forest_model.pkl')

# Initialize Flask application
app = Flask(__name__)

# Define the API route for making predictions
@app.route('/predict', methods=['POST'])
def predict():
    try:
        # Get input JSON from the request
        data = request.get_json()
```

```python
    # Extract features from the incoming data
    features = np.array(data['features']).reshape(1, -1)

    # Make a prediction using the model
    prediction = model.predict(features)

    # Return the prediction as JSON
    return jsonify({'prediction': int(prediction[0])})

    except Exception as e:
        return jsonify({'error': str(e)})

if __name__ == '__main__':
    # Run the Flask app
    app.run(debug=True)
```

Here's what's happening in the code:

- **Joblib**: We load the previously saved Scikit-learn model using joblib.load().
- **Flask app**: We create a simple Flask application using the Flask class.
- **Predict route**: We define an endpoint /predict that accepts POST requests. The data is passed as a JSON object with a key features (the input data for prediction).
- **Prediction**: We reshape the features into the appropriate shape, make a prediction using the trained model, and return the prediction in JSON format.

Test the Flask API

To test the Flask API locally, you can run the application:

```
python app.py
```

This will start the Flask development server, and your model will be available at http://127.0.0.1:5000/predict.

Now, you can make a POST request to the /predict endpoint with a JSON body containing the feature values. You can use tools like Postman or cURL to make the request.

Here's an example of a POST request using cURL:

```
curl -X POST -H "Content-Type: application/json" -d '{"features": [5.1, 3.5, 1.4, 0.2]}'
http://127.0.0.1:5000/predict
```

If successful, the response will look like:

```
{
  "prediction": 0
}
```

This is the predicted class (in the case of the Iris dataset, 0 represents the species "setosa").

11.4.2 Deploying with FastAPI

FastAPI is a modern, fast, web framework for building APIs with Python. It's designed to be easy to use and highly performant, especially for machine learning deployments, due to its asynchronous capabilities. FastAPI also provides automatic validation and documentation via Swagger UI.

Steps to Deploy a Scikit-learn Model Using FastAPI:

Install FastAPI and Uvicorn

To use FastAPI, you need to install both FastAPI and Uvicorn (for running the server).

```
pip install fastapi uvicorn joblib
```

Create the FastAPI Application

Below is an example of deploying a Scikit-learn model using FastAPI.

```
import joblib
from fastapi import FastAPI
from pydantic import BaseModel
import numpy as np
from typing import List

# Load the trained model
model = joblib.load('random_forest_model.pkl')
```

```python
# Initialize FastAPI app
app = FastAPI()

# Define the input data format (features) using Pydantic
class PredictionRequest(BaseModel):
    features: List[float]

# Define the API route for making predictions
@app.post('/predict')
async def predict(request: PredictionRequest):
    try:
        # Extract features from the request
        features = np.array(request.features).reshape(1, -1)

        # Make the prediction
        prediction = model.predict(features)

        # Return the prediction as a response
        return {'prediction': int(prediction[0])}

    except Exception as e:
        return {'error': str(e)}

# Run the FastAPI app with Uvicorn
if __name__ == '__main__':
    import uvicorn
    uvicorn.run(app, host="0.0.0.0", port=8000)
```

Here's what's happening in the code:

- **FastAPI app**: We create a FastAPI application with the FastAPI() class.
- **Pydantic model**: We define a PredictionRequest class using Pydantic to enforce input validation for the request body.
- **Prediction endpoint**: The /predict endpoint receives a POST request containing the features in JSON format, makes a prediction, and returns the result.
- **Asynchronous support**: FastAPI supports asynchronous endpoints, improving scalability.

Test the FastAPI API

To run the FastAPI application, execute:

python app.py

This will start the FastAPI server, and the API will be available at http://127.0.0.1:8000/predict.

FastAPI automatically generates Swagger UI documentation, which you can access by navigating to http://127.0.0.1:8000/docs in your browser.

Making Predictions with FastAPI

You can make a POST request to FastAPI using Postman, cURL, or Swagger UI.

Here's an example of making a prediction using cURL:

curl -X POST "http://127.0.0.1:8000/predict" -H "Content-Type: application/json" -d '{"features": [5.1, 3.5, 1.4, 0.2]}'

The response will look like:

```
{
  "prediction": 0
}
```

11.4.3 Comparison of Flask vs. FastAPI

While both Flask and FastAPI are popular frameworks for deploying machine learning models, they have some key differences:

Flask:

- Simpler to set up, widely used, and has a large ecosystem.
- Synchronous (blocking) by default.
- Less performant than FastAPI for high-throughput applications due to its synchronous nature.

FastAPI:

- Asynchronous by default, making it more scalable for high-traffic or real-time prediction applications.
- Automatically generates interactive API documentation (Swagger UI) and handles input validation using Pydantic.
- Faster performance due to asynchronous nature and modern features.

For real-time applications with high concurrency or when you need automatic API documentation, FastAPI may be the better choice. For simpler projects or when you're looking for simplicity, Flask works just fine.

Deploying a machine learning model using Flask or FastAPI provides an easy way to make your model accessible via RESTful APIs. Both frameworks are lightweight, flexible, and capable of handling HTTP requests for predictions.

- Flask is ideal for small to medium-scale applications and for developers who prefer simplicity and flexibility.
- FastAPI is highly recommended for more complex, high-performance applications, especially when scalability, asynchronous processing, and automatic API documentation are important.

By deploying your Scikit-learn models with these frameworks, you can make predictions in real-time, integrate the models into larger systems, and provide a user-friendly interface for external applications to interact with your model.

12. Building a Machine Learning Project from Scratch

Applying machine learning in practice requires a structured approach. In this chapter, we walk through an end-to-end ML project, from defining the problem and collecting data to training, evaluating, and refining the model. You'll gain insights into best practices for handling real-world projects.

12.1 Defining the Problem and Collecting Data

Before embarking on any machine learning project, the very first step is to clearly define the problem you aim to solve and gather the relevant data that will help in solving that problem. This phase is crucial because it sets the foundation for the entire project, impacting all subsequent stages, from model selection to evaluation.

In machine learning, a well-defined problem statement and high-quality data are key to building successful models. If the problem is poorly defined or if the data is inadequate, even the most sophisticated algorithms may fail to deliver meaningful results. In this section, we will explore the process of defining the problem and collecting the data, focusing on how these steps shape the direction of the project and contribute to its success.

12.1.1 Defining the Problem

A clearly defined problem is the backbone of any machine learning project. Without a clear objective, the project can quickly lose focus, and efforts might be wasted on irrelevant tasks. To define the problem, it's essential to answer the following questions:

What is the objective?

- The primary objective of the project needs to be clearly articulated. Are you trying to classify data into categories (e.g., spam detection), predict a numerical value (e.g., house prices), or discover hidden patterns (e.g., clustering customers)?
- **Example**: The objective could be to build a model that predicts whether an email is spam or not (classification problem) or a model that forecasts the sales for the next quarter (regression problem).

What type of problem is it?

Machine learning problems can broadly be categorized into three types:

- **Supervised Learning**: Involves training a model on labeled data to predict outcomes (e.g., classification or regression).
- **Unsupervised Learning**: Involves identifying patterns or groupings in data without predefined labels (e.g., clustering or dimensionality reduction).
- **Reinforcement Learning**: Involves training models to make decisions by interacting with an environment to maximize a reward.
- **Example**: In the spam detection example, you are working on a supervised classification problem since you have labeled data with emails marked as "spam" or "not spam".

What are the success criteria?

- Clearly defining how success will be measured is important. Success metrics could include accuracy, precision, recall, F1-score, or mean squared error, depending on the problem.
- **Example**: In a classification task, you might use accuracy as a metric, while in a regression task, you might use the mean squared error (MSE).

What are the constraints and limitations?

- Every project has constraints such as time, computational resources, budget, or data availability. Defining these early on helps to focus efforts and manage expectations.
- **Example**: If the data is limited, you might not have the resources to gather a large dataset, which could affect model performance.

What stakeholders are involved?

- Machine learning projects are often carried out in teams or organizations, so identifying the stakeholders (e.g., business owners, data scientists, developers) and understanding their needs will shape the problem definition.
- **Example**: If you're building a model to predict customer churn, your stakeholders could include marketing managers, customer service teams, and business executives.
- The goal of this stage is to create a problem statement that is specific, actionable, and aligned with the project's business or scientific objectives.

12.1.2 Collecting the Data

Once the problem has been defined, the next step is to gather the data that will be used to train, test, and evaluate the model. The quality of the data is paramount since machine learning algorithms are only as good as the data they are trained on. Data collection involves several key considerations:

Identify Data Sources:

Depending on the problem you're trying to solve, you will need to identify where the relevant data resides. There are several potential data sources:

- **Internal Data**: Data that already exists within the organization, such as customer records, transaction logs, or website analytics.
- **Public Datasets**: Many open-source datasets are available for various domains, such as Kaggle, UCI Machine Learning Repository, or government databases.
- **External APIs**: You may need to collect data from external services like social media (Twitter API, Facebook Graph API), financial data providers, or IoT sensors.
- **Web Scraping**: In cases where relevant data is publicly available on websites, web scraping can be used to extract data programmatically.

Data Collection Methods:

Depending on the project, you may use different methods to collect the data:

- **Surveys**: If primary data collection is needed, surveys or questionnaires can be used to gather responses.
- **Sensors and IoT Devices**: In projects like smart homes or autonomous vehicles, data is often collected through physical devices or sensors.
- **Logs and Records**: For systems like e-commerce platforms or customer support, data may already exist in the form of logs, records, or transaction histories.
- **Example**: For an email spam detection model, the data could be collected by scraping a labeled email dataset or using an internal company database of emails.

Data Quality:

The quality of the data you collect will significantly impact the performance of your model. Data quality encompasses several factors:

- **Completeness**: Missing data can result in biased or incorrect predictions. It's important to understand where data is missing and how to handle it (e.g., imputation or removal).
- **Consistency**: The data should be free from contradictions and errors. For example, numerical values should be formatted consistently (e.g., currency values should be in the same currency).
- **Relevance**: The data must be relevant to the problem at hand. Collecting unnecessary or unrelated data can reduce the effectiveness of the model.
- **Accuracy**: Data should be accurate and reflect reality as much as possible. Inaccurate data can lead to faulty predictions and biased results.
- **Example**: If you're building a fraud detection system for credit card transactions, you need accurate records of all transactions, including both legitimate and fraudulent transactions.

Data Labeling:

- For supervised learning tasks, the data needs to be labeled (i.e., for classification tasks, each data point should have a corresponding class). Labeling can be done manually, semi-automatically, or by leveraging existing systems that have already categorized data.
- **Example**: In a binary classification problem, emails need to be labeled as "spam" or "not spam". If this is not available, you may need to manually label a sample of emails or use heuristics for labeling.

Ethical Considerations:

- It's essential to ensure that the data collected respects privacy, consent, and fairness. Ethical issues could arise if the data includes personally identifiable information (PII) or if the data is collected without informed consent.
- **Example**: If you are building a model that analyzes medical data, you must ensure compliance with regulations like HIPAA (Health Insurance Portability and Accountability Act) or GDPR (General Data Protection Regulation).

Data Size:

- Machine learning models perform better when they are trained on large amounts of data. However, depending on the problem and available resources, collecting large datasets may not always be feasible. In such cases, strategies like data augmentation, synthetic data generation, or sampling can be used to address data limitations.

- **Example**: If your dataset is small, you might want to augment it by generating synthetic data or using techniques like bootstrapping to create a larger dataset.

Handling Data Imbalances:

In many real-world problems, the data may be imbalanced (i.e., certain classes or outcomes are underrepresented). For example, in a fraud detection system, fraudulent transactions might make up only a small fraction of the data. Handling this class imbalance is crucial, and techniques such as resampling, SMOTE (Synthetic Minority Over-sampling Technique), or class weighting can be applied.

Exploratory Data Analysis (EDA):

- Before diving into model building, it's important to explore and understand the dataset. EDA involves examining the data's distribution, correlations, trends, and potential outliers. Visualizations like histograms, box plots, and scatter plots can help reveal important insights and guide data preprocessing steps.
- **Example**: In an EDA for a customer churn prediction dataset, you might explore relationships between features like age, tenure, and account type with the target variable (churned or not).

12.1.3 Key Takeaways

- Defining the problem clearly is essential for setting a clear direction for the project and identifying the correct machine learning techniques and performance metrics.
- Data collection is an iterative and critical phase that requires you to gather relevant, high-quality, and sufficient data. The methods used to collect data will depend on the nature of the problem.
- Quality, completeness, and relevance are paramount when gathering data to ensure the model learns from meaningful and accurate information.
- Ethical considerations and regulatory compliance should always be taken into account when collecting and handling data, especially when dealing with sensitive or personal information.

By clearly defining the problem and collecting high-quality, relevant data, you lay a solid foundation for building a successful machine learning model that can provide valuable insights or accurate predictions.

12.2 Data Preprocessing and Exploratory Data Analysis

Once the problem is defined and the data has been collected, the next crucial step in a machine learning project is data preprocessing and exploratory data analysis (EDA). These steps are pivotal because they help ensure that the data is clean, structured, and ready for model training. Poorly prepared data can lead to inaccurate or misleading model results, which can impact the success of the machine learning project. In this section, we will explore the key aspects of data preprocessing and EDA, focusing on how these processes help improve model performance.

12.2.1 Data Preprocessing

Data preprocessing is a series of techniques and transformations applied to raw data to convert it into a format suitable for machine learning algorithms. The objective of preprocessing is to ensure that the data is clean, consistent, and free from biases, missing values, or errors.

Key Steps in Data Preprocessing:

Handling Missing Values:

Missing values are common in real-world datasets and can arise for various reasons (e.g., errors during data collection, incomplete records). Most machine learning models require that there are no missing values in the data, as these can introduce bias or errors.

Common strategies to handle missing values include:

- **Imputation**: Replacing missing values with statistical measures like mean, median, or mode for numerical columns. For categorical variables, the mode (most frequent value) is commonly used.
- **Forward or Backward Filling**: For time-series data, missing values can be filled with previous or next available values.
- **Removal**: In cases where missing values are sparse, rows or columns with missing data can be removed from the dataset. However, this may lead to data loss.
- **Prediction**: In some cases, a machine learning model can be used to predict missing values based on other data features.
- **Example**: In a customer dataset, if the "Age" column has missing values, we might fill those gaps with the median age of all customers to preserve the data distribution.

Dealing with Outliers:

Outliers are data points that are significantly different from the rest of the data. They may result from errors in data collection or genuine variations, but they can skew statistical analysis and negatively affect model performance.

Common techniques for handling outliers include:

- **Z-Score**: Data points that lie more than a certain number of standard deviations (e.g., 3) from the mean can be considered outliers.
- **IQR (Interquartile Range)**: Outliers can also be detected by looking at values that fall outside of the range defined by the first quartile (Q1) and the third quartile (Q3). Values beyond Q1 - 1.5*IQR or Q3 + 1.5*IQR can be flagged as outliers.
- **Winsorizing**: This involves limiting extreme values to a certain percentile to reduce the impact of outliers.
- **Transformation**: In some cases, applying transformations like the logarithmic or square root transformations can help reduce the impact of outliers.
- **Example**: If the "Income" column in a customer dataset contains values like $1,000,000, which are unusually high, those might be considered outliers and could either be removed or capped at a specific threshold.

Encoding Categorical Variables:

Many machine learning algorithms require numerical data to work effectively. Therefore, categorical variables (i.e., variables that represent categories or classes, such as "Gender", "City", etc.) need to be converted into a numerical format.

Common methods of encoding categorical variables include:

- **Label Encoding**: Assigns a unique integer to each category. For example, "Red", "Blue", and "Green" may be encoded as 0, 1, and 2, respectively.
- **One-Hot Encoding**: Converts each category into a separate binary column. For example, "Color" with values "Red", "Blue", and "Green" would create three columns: "Color_Red", "Color_Blue", and "Color_Green". Each row would have a 1 in the column corresponding to its category and 0s in the others.
- **Binary Encoding**: Combines features of both Label Encoding and One-Hot Encoding, but it uses fewer columns than One-Hot Encoding, which can be useful when the number of categories is large.

- **Example**: If a "City" column has values "New York", "Los Angeles", and "Chicago", One-Hot Encoding would create three new columns, each representing one of the cities.

Feature Scaling and Normalization:

Feature scaling is essential for machine learning algorithms that are sensitive to the scale of input features, such as distance-based algorithms (e.g., k-Nearest Neighbors, Support Vector Machines) or gradient-based optimization algorithms (e.g., Gradient Descent).

Common scaling techniques include:

- **Min-Max Scaling**: Scales the data to a fixed range, usually between 0 and 1. The formula is: $X\_scaled = (X - X\_min) / (X\_max - X\_min)$.
- **Standardization**: Centers the data by subtracting the mean and scaling it by the standard deviation. This transforms the data to have a mean of 0 and a standard deviation of 1. The formula is: $X\_scaled = (X - mean) / standard\ deviation$.
- **Example**: If you have a feature like "Income" with a wide range (e.g., \$1,000 to \$1,000,000), Min-Max Scaling or Standardization can be applied to normalize the feature so that all values are on a similar scale.

Feature Engineering:

Feature engineering is the process of creating new features from existing ones to improve model performance. This can involve transforming variables, combining multiple features, or extracting new insights from raw data.

Common feature engineering techniques include:

- **Polynomial Features**: Creating new features by raising existing features to higher powers (e.g., squared or cubic terms).
- **Interaction Features**: Combining features through multiplication or addition to capture interactions between them.
- **Binning**: Converting continuous variables into categorical ones by grouping them into bins.
- **Datetime Features**: Extracting features like day of the week, month, or year from datetime variables to capture cyclical patterns.
- **Example**: In a dataset about house prices, a feature like "Square Feet" might be combined with "Number of Bedrooms" to create a new feature, "Price per Bedroom."

12.2.2 Exploratory Data Analysis (EDA)

Exploratory Data Analysis (EDA) is the process of analyzing datasets to summarize their main characteristics, often with the help of visual methods. The goal of EDA is to understand the underlying patterns, spot anomalies, check assumptions, and discover relationships between variables. It helps you gain insights into the data, guiding decisions about preprocessing and feature engineering.

Key Steps in EDA:

Understanding the Distribution of Features:

Visualizing the distribution of each feature can provide valuable insights into the nature of the data and help identify any skewed distributions, outliers, or data imbalances.

Common visualization techniques:

- **Histograms**: To understand the distribution of continuous features.
- **Box Plots**: To visualize the spread and detect outliers.
- **Bar Charts**: To show the distribution of categorical variables.
- **Example**: A histogram of the "Age" feature might reveal a skewed distribution, with most customers falling within a certain age range.

Exploring Relationships Between Features:

Understanding the relationships between features can help uncover important interactions or correlations that might influence model performance.

Common techniques:

- **Scatter Plots**: To show relationships between two continuous variables.
- **Correlation Matrix**: To check correlations between numerical features and identify highly correlated features that might be redundant.
- **Pair Plots**: To visualize the pairwise relationships between multiple features.
- **Example**: A scatter plot between "Age" and "Income" might show that older customers tend to have higher incomes.

Identifying Missing Values and Outliers:

- As part of the EDA process, it's crucial to inspect whether any features contain missing or inconsistent values. Data visualization tools like heatmaps or bar charts can be helpful in identifying the presence of missing data.
- **Example**: A heatmap can reveal patterns of missingness across different features, indicating whether certain columns have more missing values than others.

Class Imbalance:

- In classification problems, it is important to check if the dataset has imbalanced classes (i.e., one class is significantly more frequent than the other). Class imbalance can affect the model's performance and lead to biased predictions.
- **Example**: A class distribution plot can show if, for instance, 90% of emails are "not spam" and only 10% are "spam." In this case, techniques like oversampling or under-sampling may be needed.

Statistical Summary:

- A basic statistical summary of the data (such as mean, median, mode, standard deviation, and percentiles) can give a quick overview of the central tendency, spread, and skewness of features.
- **Example**: A statistical summary might show that the median "Age" is 35, with a standard deviation of 10, indicating that the majority of customers are between 25 and 45 years old.

12.2.3 Key Takeaways

- Data Preprocessing involves cleaning, transforming, and scaling the data to ensure it is ready for machine learning algorithms. Handling missing values, outliers, encoding categorical variables, and scaling features are essential preprocessing steps.
- Exploratory Data Analysis (EDA) helps in understanding the data's structure, identifying patterns, detecting anomalies, and ensuring the quality of the data. EDA also helps in feature selection and the discovery of relationships between features.
- Both preprocessing and EDA are iterative processes that require attention to detail and can have a significant impact on the performance of your machine learning models.

Together, data preprocessing and exploratory data analysis are vital stages that ensure the data is of high quality, relevant, and ready to be used for training machine learning models.

12.3 Choosing the Right Model and Training It

After collecting and preprocessing the data, and performing exploratory data analysis (EDA), the next critical step in a machine learning project is to choose the right model and train it effectively. This decision depends on various factors, including the type of problem you're solving (e.g., classification, regression), the nature of your data, the performance metrics you care about, and the computational resources at your disposal. The goal is to select a model that balances complexity, interpretability, and performance, and then properly train it using the prepared data.

In this section, we will guide you through the process of selecting the right machine learning model and training it. We will also discuss common considerations, evaluation techniques, and practical tips for achieving the best model performance.

12.3.1 Types of Machine Learning Problems

The first step in choosing a model is understanding the type of machine learning problem you're dealing with. There are three main categories of problems in machine learning: classification, regression, and clustering. The choice of model depends on the specific problem you aim to solve.

Classification:

- In classification problems, the goal is to predict categorical labels (e.g., yes/no, spam/ham, disease/no disease). Each input is assigned to a particular class.
- **Examples**: Email spam detection, image recognition (cat vs. dog), medical diagnoses (disease vs. no disease).

Common Models:

- **Logistic Regression**: A simple and effective model for binary classification problems.
- **k-Nearest Neighbors (KNN):** A distance-based model that classifies points based on their proximity to labeled data.
- **Decision Trees and Random Forests**: Suitable for handling both categorical and numerical data, offering interpretability.
- **Support Vector Machines (SVM):** Effective in high-dimensional spaces, used for both linear and non-linear classification.

- **Neural Networks**: Powerful models for complex classification problems, particularly when dealing with large datasets and non-linear decision boundaries.

Regression:

- Regression problems aim to predict continuous values (e.g., sales numbers, temperature, housing prices).
- **Examples**: Predicting house prices, forecasting sales, predicting stock prices.

Common Models:

- **Linear Regression**: A simple, interpretable model for predicting a continuous target variable.
- **Ridge/Lasso Regression**: Variations of linear regression that help prevent overfitting by adding regularization.
- **Decision Trees and Random Forests**: These models can be used for regression tasks, allowing for non-linear relationships between features and the target variable.
- **Gradient Boosting**: Powerful algorithms like XGBoost, LightGBM, and CatBoost are effective for regression tasks, providing high predictive accuracy.
- **Neural Networks**: Can be used for complex regression tasks where relationships between variables are non-linear and require deep learning techniques.

Clustering:

- Clustering is an unsupervised learning technique used to group similar data points together into clusters without labeled data.
- **Examples**: Customer segmentation, grouping similar documents, image compression.

Common Models:

- **K-Means**: One of the most popular clustering algorithms, effective for partitioning data into k clusters.
- **DBSCAN**: A density-based clustering algorithm that can detect clusters of varying shapes.
- **Hierarchical Clustering**: Builds a tree-like structure of clusters and is useful when you want to visualize the relationships between clusters.

12.3.2 Choosing the Right Model

Once the problem type is identified, the next step is to choose the model that is best suited for your data and objectives. Here are some important considerations for choosing the right machine learning model:

Problem Characteristics:

- **Type of Data**: The nature of the features (e.g., numerical, categorical, or mixed data types) plays a significant role in model selection. For example, tree-based models like Decision Trees and Random Forests can handle both numerical and categorical data, while linear models typically require numerical input.
- **Size of Dataset**: For large datasets, complex models like neural networks or gradient boosting models may perform well, but they may be computationally expensive. For smaller datasets, simpler models like logistic regression or k-NN might work better.
- **Output Type**: Determine whether the model should output a categorical value (classification), a continuous value (regression), or groupings (clustering).

Model Complexity vs. Interpretability:

- **Simple Models**: If interpretability is important, consider simple models like linear regression or decision trees. These models are easy to explain and provide clear insights into how predictions are made.
- **Complex Models**: If high accuracy is critical and interpretability is less important, more complex models like gradient boosting (XGBoost, LightGBM) or deep learning models (neural networks) may be more appropriate. However, these models often act as "black boxes" and can be harder to interpret.

Training Time and Resources:

More complex models, particularly neural networks, require significant computational resources and time for training. If the problem is simple or the dataset is small, less computationally intensive models like logistic regression or decision trees may be a better fit.

Performance Metrics:

- Think about the evaluation metrics you will use to measure the performance of the model. For classification tasks, accuracy, precision, recall, F1-score, or ROC-AUC are common metrics. For regression, metrics like Mean Squared Error (MSE), Root Mean Squared Error (RMSE), and R-squared are frequently used.

- Certain models may be better suited for optimizing specific metrics. For example, Random Forests and Gradient Boosting models generally provide high accuracy, while simpler models may not be as robust.

12.3.3 Training the Model

Once the model is selected, the next step is to train it using your data. The training process involves adjusting the model's parameters based on the data to minimize the error in predictions.

Splitting the Data:

- Before training, it's crucial to split your data into training and testing datasets. Typically, you use about 70–80% of the data for training and 20–30% for testing.
- Cross-validation: In addition to a simple train-test split, cross-validation techniques like k-fold cross-validation can be used to ensure that the model generalizes well to unseen data. Cross-validation helps prevent overfitting by training and evaluating the model on different subsets of the data.
- **Example**: In a 5-fold cross-validation, the dataset is split into five equal parts, and the model is trained on four parts while tested on the remaining part. This process is repeated five times, ensuring that every data point is used for both training and testing.

Model Fitting:

- Fitting the model involves training it on the training data. This step adjusts the internal parameters (e.g., coefficients for linear regression, decision thresholds for decision trees) so that the model can make accurate predictions.
- During this process, the model will learn patterns from the data and improve its ability to predict the target variable.

Hyperparameter Tuning:

Most machine learning models come with hyperparameters that control the learning process (e.g., learning rate, regularization strength, number of trees in a Random Forest). Tuning these hyperparameters can have a significant impact on the model's performance.

Techniques for hyperparameter tuning include:

- **Grid Search**: Exhaustively searching through a predefined set of hyperparameters.
- **Random Search**: Randomly sampling hyperparameters from a specified range, which is less computationally expensive than Grid Search.
- **Bayesian Optimization**: Using probabilistic models to find the most promising hyperparameters in a more efficient manner.
- **Example**: For a Random Forest model, you may tune hyperparameters such as the number of trees (n_estimators), the maximum depth of trees (max_depth), and the minimum samples required to split a node (min_samples_split).

Training the Model (Example in Scikit-Learn):

In Scikit-Learn, training a model typically involves calling the fit() method on the model object, passing in the training data and corresponding labels.

```
from sklearn.ensemble import RandomForestClassifier
from sklearn.model_selection import train_test_split

# Load the dataset and split it into features and target
X = data.drop(columns=["target"])
y = data["target"]

# Split data into train and test sets
X_train, X_test, y_train, y_test = train_test_split(X, y, test_size=0.2, random_state=42)

# Initialize the model
model = RandomForestClassifier(n_estimators=100)

# Train the model
model.fit(X_train, y_train)
```

Evaluating the Model:

- After training, the model's performance should be evaluated on the test set (or using cross-validation) to ensure it generalizes well to unseen data.
- **Example Evaluation**: For classification, you could use metrics like accuracy, precision, recall, or F1-score. For regression, metrics like Mean Squared Error (MSE) or R-squared might be used.

```
from sklearn.metrics import accuracy_score

# Predict on the test set
y_pred = model.predict(X_test)

# Evaluate accuracy
accuracy = accuracy_score(y_test, y_pred)
print(f"Accuracy: {accuracy:.4f}")
```

12.3.4 Key Takeaways

- Choosing the right model is a critical step and depends on the problem type (classification, regression, or clustering), the data characteristics, the model complexity, and performance metrics.
- Training a model involves splitting the data, fitting the model to the training data, and tuning hyperparameters to optimize performance.
- Model evaluation ensures that the trained model performs well on unseen data and generalizes to real-world scenarios. Proper evaluation metrics are essential for understanding model performance.

By carefully selecting the appropriate model, training it with the right techniques, and evaluating its performance, you can build powerful machine learning models that provide meaningful insights and predictions.

12.4 Model Evaluation and Iteration

Once a machine learning model has been trained, the next crucial step is model evaluation. This process helps you understand how well your model is performing, identify potential weaknesses, and determine if it is suitable for deployment. In real-world machine learning projects, model evaluation is not a one-time task but an iterative process. Based on the evaluation results, you may need to return to previous stages of the workflow, such as data preprocessing, feature engineering, or model selection, to improve the performance of the model.

In this section, we will cover various aspects of model evaluation and the iterative process that helps refine and improve your machine learning model. This includes evaluating the model's performance using different metrics, performing error analysis, and making adjustments based on the results to ensure optimal outcomes.

12.4.1 Model Evaluation Metrics

The first step in model evaluation is to measure its performance using suitable evaluation metrics. Different types of problems (classification, regression, clustering) require different metrics, and choosing the right ones is essential for gaining useful insights.

Classification Metrics:

Accuracy: This is the simplest and most commonly used metric. It calculates the ratio of correct predictions to the total number of predictions:

$$\text{Accuracy} = \frac{\text{Number of Correct Predictions}}{\text{Total Number of Predictions}}$$

While accuracy is useful, it can be misleading in the case of imbalanced datasets, where one class is significantly more frequent than the other.

Precision and Recall:

Precision measures the proportion of true positive predictions relative to the total positive predictions made:

$$\text{Precision} = \frac{\text{True Positives}}{\text{True Positives} + \text{False Positives}}$$

Recall (or Sensitivity) measures the proportion of true positives relative to the actual positives in the dataset:

$$\text{Recall} = \frac{\text{True Positives}}{\text{True Positives} + \text{False Negatives}}$$

These metrics are especially useful in imbalanced datasets. For example, in medical diagnosis, detecting all positive cases (high recall) is critical, even if some false positives are allowed.

F1-score: The F1-score is the harmonic mean of precision and recall, providing a balance between the two. It is especially useful when you need to balance precision and recall in cases of imbalanced datasets:

$$\text{F1-score} = 2 \times \frac{\text{Precision} \times \text{Recall}}{\text{Precision} + \text{Recall}}$$

The F1-score is useful when the cost of false positives and false negatives are roughly equal.

ROC Curve and AUC:

- **ROC Curve** (Receiver Operating Characteristic) plots the true positive rate (recall) against the false positive rate (1-specificity) at various threshold settings. It helps visualize the performance of a classifier.
- **AUC** (Area Under the Curve) measures the area under the ROC curve. A model with AUC = 1 has perfect classification, while AUC = 0.5 indicates a random classifier.

Regression Metrics:

Mean Absolute Error (MAE): MAE calculates the average of the absolute differences between the predicted and actual values. It is simple and interpretable, but it treats all errors equally without considering the magnitude of the errors.

$$\text{MAE} = \frac{1}{n} \sum_{i=1}^{n} \left| y_{\text{true}}^{i} - y_{\text{pred}}^{i} \right|$$

Mean Squared Error (MSE): MSE is the average of the squared differences between predicted and actual values. It penalizes larger errors more heavily due to the squaring of residuals:

$$\text{MSE} = \frac{1}{n} \sum_{i=1}^{n} \left(y_{\text{true}}^{i} - y_{\text{pred}}^{i} \right)^{2}$$

While it is more sensitive to outliers than MAE, it gives more importance to larger errors.

Root Mean Squared Error (RMSE): RMSE is the square root of MSE, bringing the metric back to the original units of the target variable, making it more interpretable:

$$\text{RMSE} = \sqrt{\frac{1}{n} \sum_{i=1}^{n} \left(y_{\text{true}}^{i} - y_{\text{pred}}^{i} \right)^2}$$

R-squared (R²): R^2 is a measure of how well the model's predictions match the actual values. It represents the proportion of the variance in the dependent variable that is predictable from the independent variables. A higher R^2 indicates a better fit of the model.

Clustering Metrics:

- **Silhouette Score:** This metric measures how similar an object is to its own cluster compared to other clusters. A higher silhouette score indicates better-defined clusters.
- **Adjusted Rand Index (ARI):** ARI measures the similarity between two data clusterings, accounting for chance grouping.

12.4.2 Error Analysis

Model evaluation doesn't stop at calculating performance metrics. Error analysis is crucial for understanding the model's shortcomings and identifying areas for improvement.

Analyzing Misclassifications (Classification):

- After evaluating the classification model, examine the types of errors the model makes by reviewing the confusion matrix. The confusion matrix shows the counts of true positives, true negatives, false positives, and false negatives.
- Misclassifications could reveal patterns that suggest feature engineering opportunities, data quality issues, or model limitations. For example, if your model frequently misclassifies a specific class, you might want to collect more data for that class or adjust the model's thresholds.

Residual Analysis (Regression):

In regression tasks, the residuals (the difference between the actual and predicted values) should ideally be randomly distributed. By plotting residuals against the predicted values, you can assess whether the model is underfitting or overfitting. Non-random patterns in the residuals could indicate that the model isn't capturing certain aspects of the data.

Outlier Detection:

Identifying outliers in the dataset can provide insights into whether the model is underperforming due to extreme values. Outliers may need to be treated differently or removed, especially if they have a large impact on the model's accuracy.

Bias-Variance Tradeoff:

When analyzing errors, it's essential to consider the bias-variance tradeoff. A model with high bias tends to underfit the data (e.g., a linear regression model for a non-linear problem), while a model with high variance overfits the data (e.g., a deep decision tree). Balancing bias and variance is crucial for achieving a model that generalizes well.

12.4.3 Iterating on the Model

Machine learning is an iterative process, and the model evaluation phase often leads to the need for adjustments. Based on the evaluation and error analysis, here are some possible iterations you can perform to improve your model:

Feature Engineering: Based on performance evaluation, you may decide to create new features or refine existing ones. Feature importance scores from tree-based models or correlation matrices can guide you in selecting which features to keep or drop.

Hyperparameter Tuning: If your model's performance is not optimal, hyperparameter tuning can help improve it. Methods like Grid Search or Random Search can help explore different combinations of hyperparameters. Additionally, more sophisticated methods such as Bayesian Optimization can be used to efficiently find the best hyperparameters.

Model Selection: If the current model is not performing well despite optimizations, you may need to experiment with different algorithms. For example, if a simple linear model is underperforming, you could try more complex models like decision trees, random forests, or gradient boosting machines.

Ensemble Methods: Combining multiple models using techniques like bagging (e.g., Random Forest) or boosting (e.g., XGBoost) can help increase accuracy and reduce overfitting.

Data Augmentation or Additional Data: If the model is underfitting or biased due to a lack of sufficient data, consider obtaining more data or using data augmentation techniques.

Cross-validation: Use cross-validation to ensure that your model performs consistently across different subsets of the data. This helps in identifying overfitting and improving model stability.

12.4.4 Key Takeaways

- Model evaluation is essential to understanding how well your model performs and whether it is suitable for deployment.
- Different types of problems require different evaluation metrics, such as accuracy, precision, recall, F1-score for classification, and MAE, MSE, RMSE, and R^2 for regression.
- Error analysis helps uncover misclassifications or residual patterns, providing insights into how the model can be improved.
- Iteration is key in machine learning. Based on the evaluation results, iterating on the model through feature engineering, hyperparameter tuning, model selection, or even data augmentation helps refine the model and improve its performance.

By continuously evaluating, analyzing, and iterating on your model, you can ensure it reaches its full potential and performs well in real-world applications.

13. Using Scikit-Learn with Deep Learning Frameworks

Machine learning and deep learning often complement each other. This chapter explores how to integrate Scikit-Learn with TensorFlow and PyTorch, allowing you to use traditional ML techniques alongside deep neural networks for hybrid models and feature extraction.

13.1 Integrating Scikit-Learn with TensorFlow and Keras

In the world of machine learning and deep learning, Scikit-Learn, TensorFlow, and Keras are three of the most widely used libraries. While Scikit-Learn is primarily designed for traditional machine learning algorithms, TensorFlow and Keras are used for building deep learning models. Integrating Scikit-Learn with TensorFlow and Keras can enable users to leverage the strengths of both libraries, such as utilizing Scikit-Learn's preprocessing tools and model evaluation techniques alongside the power of TensorFlow/Keras for complex neural networks.

In this section, we'll explore how to integrate Scikit-Learn with TensorFlow and Keras, which allows seamless data preprocessing, model evaluation, and efficient deep learning model development in a unified workflow.

13.1.1 Why Integrate Scikit-Learn with TensorFlow and Keras?

There are several reasons why integrating Scikit-Learn with TensorFlow and Keras is beneficial:

Data Preprocessing: Scikit-Learn provides a rich suite of preprocessing tools, such as scaling, normalization, encoding categorical variables, imputation of missing values, and more. These tools are essential for preparing data before feeding it into a neural network.

Pipeline Integration: Scikit-Learn offers a pipeline framework that helps in chaining multiple data preprocessing steps, as well as combining preprocessing and modeling into a single coherent workflow. This can be particularly useful when integrating with deep learning models created using TensorFlow/Keras.

Model Evaluation: Scikit-Learn has a set of useful metrics and evaluation tools, such as confusion matrices, cross-validation, and performance metrics like accuracy, precision, recall, and F1-score. These can be easily applied to evaluate the performance of TensorFlow and Keras models.

Hyperparameter Tuning: Scikit-Learn provides GridSearchCV and RandomizedSearchCV, which are powerful tools for performing hyperparameter tuning. These can be applied to both Scikit-Learn models as well as deep learning models built using TensorFlow and Keras.

Cross-Platform Compatibility: Scikit-Learn works seamlessly with both TensorFlow and Keras. This allows data scientists to experiment with both traditional machine learning models and deep learning models, all within the same environment.

13.1.2 Using Scikit-Learn for Preprocessing with Keras Models

One of the most common ways Scikit-Learn integrates with TensorFlow and Keras is through data preprocessing. Data preprocessing is an important step before training any machine learning model, including deep learning models.

Here's how you can use Scikit-Learn preprocessing tools and integrate them with a Keras model.

Example: Scaling data with StandardScaler and using it in a Keras model

```
import numpy as np
from sklearn.preprocessing import StandardScaler
from tensorflow.keras.models import Sequential
from tensorflow.keras.layers import Dense
from sklearn.model_selection import train_test_split

# Sample dataset (e.g., using NumPy)
X = np.random.rand(100, 10)  # 100 samples with 10 features
y = np.random.randint(0, 2, 100)  # Binary classification target

# Step 1: Preprocess the data using Scikit-Learn's StandardScaler
scaler = StandardScaler()
X_scaled = scaler.fit_transform(X)

# Step 2: Split the data into training and testing sets
```

```
X_train, X_test, y_train, y_test = train_test_split(X_scaled, y, test_size=0.2,
random_state=42)

# Step 3: Build a simple Keras model
model = Sequential([
    Dense(64, input_dim=X_train.shape[1], activation='relu'),
    Dense(32, activation='relu'),
    Dense(1, activation='sigmoid')
])

# Step 4: Compile and train the model
model.compile(optimizer='adam', loss='binary_crossentropy', metrics=['accuracy'])
model.fit(X_train, y_train, epochs=10, batch_size=32)

# Step 5: Evaluate the model on the test data
test_loss, test_acc = model.evaluate(X_test, y_test)
print(f'Test accuracy: {test_acc}')
```

In this example:

- We first use Scikit-Learn's StandardScaler to scale the input features, which is a common preprocessing step when working with neural networks. This step ensures that the data is centered around zero with a standard deviation of one.
- Then, the data is split into training and testing sets using Scikit-Learn's train_test_split function.
- Finally, a simple Keras model is built, trained, and evaluated on the scaled data.

By using Scikit-Learn's preprocessing tools and Keras for deep learning, we have a powerful combination for building, tuning, and evaluating models.

13.1.3 Hyperparameter Tuning with Scikit-Learn for Keras Models

Hyperparameter tuning plays a vital role in improving the performance of machine learning and deep learning models. While Keras provides functions like GridSearchCV and RandomizedSearchCV for deep learning, you can also use Scikit-Learn's GridSearchCV or RandomizedSearchCV to tune hyperparameters for Keras models.

Example: Using Scikit-Learn's GridSearchCV with a Keras Model

```
from sklearn.model_selection import GridSearchCV
```

```python
from tensorflow.keras.wrappers.scikit_learn import KerasClassifier

# Function to create the Keras model
def create_model(optimizer='adam'):
    model = Sequential([
        Dense(64, input_dim=X_train.shape[1], activation='relu'),
        Dense(32, activation='relu'),
        Dense(1, activation='sigmoid')
    ])
    model.compile(optimizer=optimizer, loss='binary_crossentropy', metrics=['accuracy'])
    return model

# Step 1: Convert the Keras model into a Scikit-Learn classifier
model = KerasClassifier(build_fn=create_model, epochs=10, batch_size=32,
verbose=0)

# Step 2: Define the parameter grid for hyperparameter tuning
param_grid = {'optimizer': ['adam', 'sgd']}

# Step 3: Apply GridSearchCV to find the best optimizer
grid = GridSearchCV(estimator=model, param_grid=param_grid, n_jobs=-1, cv=3)
grid_result = grid.fit(X_train, y_train)

# Step 4: Print the best parameters and the best score
print(f'Best Params: {grid_result.best_params_}')
print(f'Best Score: {grid_result.best_score_}')
```

In this example:

- We define a Keras model-building function, create_model(), which accepts hyperparameters like the optimizer type.
- We use KerasClassifier from the tensorflow.keras.wrappers.scikit_learn module to wrap the Keras model and make it compatible with Scikit-Learn.
- The GridSearchCV is used to find the best optimizer by evaluating the model with different hyperparameter values and using cross-validation.

13.1.4 Cross-Validation with Scikit-Learn and Keras

Cross-validation is an essential technique for assessing the generalization performance of machine learning models. You can integrate Scikit-Learn's cross-validation tools with

Keras models by using KerasClassifier or KerasRegressor in conjunction with Scikit-Learn's cross_val_score function.

Example: Using Cross-Validation with a Keras Model

```
from sklearn.model_selection import cross_val_score
from tensorflow.keras.wrappers.scikit_learn import KerasClassifier

# Use the same create_model function from the previous example
model = KerasClassifier(build_fn=create_model, epochs=10, batch_size=32,
verbose=0)

# Step 1: Perform 3-fold cross-validation
cv_scores = cross_val_score(model, X_train, y_train, cv=3)

# Step 2: Print the cross-validation results
print(f'Cross-validation scores: {cv_scores}')
print(f'Mean CV score: {cv_scores.mean()}')
```

This allows you to assess the model's performance across different subsets of the training data, helping prevent overfitting and giving a better estimate of how well the model will perform on unseen data.

13.1.5 Using TensorFlow/Keras in Scikit-Learn Pipelines

Another powerful integration technique is to include Keras models within Scikit-Learn's Pipeline structure. This allows you to combine preprocessing steps with deep learning models into a single, cohesive workflow. Pipelines ensure that all data transformations and model training steps are applied correctly in a reproducible manner.

Example: Using a Keras Model in a Scikit-Learn Pipeline

```
from sklearn.pipeline import Pipeline
from sklearn.preprocessing import StandardScaler
from tensorflow.keras.wrappers.scikit_learn import KerasClassifier

# Step 1: Define the Keras model function
def create_model():
    model = Sequential([
        Dense(64, input_dim=X_train.shape[1], activation='relu'),
```

```
    Dense(32, activation='relu'),
    Dense(1, activation='sigmoid')
])
model.compile(optimizer='adam', loss='binary_crossentropy', metrics=['accuracy'])
return model

# Step 2: Create a pipeline with a scaler and Keras model
pipeline = Pipeline([
    ('scaler', StandardScaler()),
    ('model', KerasClassifier(build_fn=create_model, epochs=10, batch_size=32,
verbose=0))
])

# Step 3: Fit the pipeline to the training data
pipeline.fit(X_train, y_train)

# Step 4: Evaluate the pipeline on the test data
test_acc = pipeline.score(X_test, y_test)
print(f'Test accuracy: {test_acc}')
```

In this example:

- We create a pipeline that first applies a StandardScaler to the data, followed by fitting a Keras model.
- The pipeline structure ensures that all necessary preprocessing steps are applied automatically each time you call fit or predict on the pipeline.

Integrating Scikit-Learn with TensorFlow and Keras provides several advantages, including the ability to utilize Scikit-Learn's powerful preprocessing tools, model evaluation metrics, and hyperparameter tuning alongside the deep learning power of TensorFlow/Keras. The integration simplifies workflows and helps build end-to-end machine learning pipelines that include both traditional machine learning and deep learning models. Whether you're preprocessing data, tuning hyperparameters, or evaluating models, combining the strengths of these libraries will lead to more robust, efficient, and effective machine learning solutions.

13.2 Combining Scikit-Learn with PyTorch for Hybrid Models

In machine learning and deep learning, Scikit-Learn and PyTorch are two of the most popular libraries used for building models. Scikit-Learn is widely recognized for its versatility in handling traditional machine learning tasks, such as classification, regression, clustering, and feature engineering, while PyTorch has become one of the most widely used frameworks for building deep learning models. Integrating these two libraries can help take advantage of the strengths of both worlds—combining the flexibility and simplicity of Scikit-Learn with the power and extensibility of PyTorch.

In this section, we will explore how to combine Scikit-Learn and PyTorch to create hybrid models. These hybrid models may use Scikit-Learn for preprocessing, feature engineering, and evaluation, while leveraging PyTorch for building more complex neural networks. By using Scikit-Learn in tandem with PyTorch, you can enhance the machine learning workflow, allowing for more efficient experimentation and model building.

13.2.1 Why Combine Scikit-Learn with PyTorch?

There are several reasons to integrate Scikit-Learn with PyTorch for hybrid models:

Preprocessing and Feature Engineering: Scikit-Learn excels at preprocessing tasks such as scaling, encoding categorical variables, and imputing missing values. These tools can be applied before passing the data to PyTorch models for training, ensuring that the data is ready for deep learning algorithms.

Pipelines: Scikit-Learn's pipeline feature allows for easy chaining of preprocessing and modeling steps, making it simple to apply multiple transformations sequentially. This can be particularly helpful when using Scikit-Learn for feature engineering and PyTorch for model building.

Model Evaluation: Scikit-Learn provides a variety of model evaluation metrics and techniques (e.g., cross-validation, confusion matrix, classification report) that can be easily used to assess the performance of PyTorch models. These metrics help evaluate deep learning models on the same metrics that are commonly used for traditional machine learning models.

Hyperparameter Tuning: Scikit-Learn's GridSearchCV and RandomizedSearchCV provide excellent tools for hyperparameter optimization, and these can be applied to PyTorch models to fine-tune the architecture and hyperparameters of neural networks.

Seamless Integration: Combining Scikit-Learn and PyTorch allows for more seamless model-building workflows where Scikit-Learn handles the easier tasks (data manipulation, preprocessing, evaluation) while PyTorch focuses on building and training deep learning models. This division of labor can streamline development and experimentation.

13.2.2 Using Scikit-Learn for Data Preprocessing with PyTorch Models

Scikit-Learn's powerful preprocessing tools can be used to prepare your data before passing it into a PyTorch model. For example, you can use StandardScaler, OneHotEncoder, or SimpleImputer from Scikit-Learn to prepare your features before training a PyTorch model.

Example: Preprocessing Data with Scikit-Learn and Using It in a PyTorch Model

```
import numpy as np
from sklearn.preprocessing import StandardScaler
from sklearn.model_selection import train_test_split
import torch
import torch.nn as nn
import torch.optim as optim


# Sample dataset (e.g., using NumPy)
X = np.random.rand(100, 10)  # 100 samples with 10 features
y = np.random.randint(0, 2, 100)  # Binary classification target


# Step 1: Preprocess the data using Scikit-Learn's StandardScaler
scaler = StandardScaler()
X_scaled = scaler.fit_transform(X)


# Step 2: Split the data into training and testing sets
X_train, X_test, y_train, y_test = train_test_split(X_scaled, y, test_size=0.2,
random_state=42)


# Convert data to PyTorch tensors
X_train_tensor = torch.tensor(X_train, dtype=torch.float32)
X_test_tensor = torch.tensor(X_test, dtype=torch.float32)
y_train_tensor = torch.tensor(y_train, dtype=torch.long)
y_test_tensor = torch.tensor(y_test, dtype=torch.long)


# Step 3: Define a simple PyTorch model
class SimpleNN(nn.Module):
    def __init__(self):
```

```python
        super(SimpleNN, self).__init__()
        self.layer1 = nn.Linear(X_train.shape[1], 64)  # 64 units in the hidden layer
        self.layer2 = nn.Linear(64, 32)  # 32 units in the second hidden layer
        self.output = nn.Linear(32, 2)  # 2 output units for binary classification

    def forward(self, x):
        x = torch.relu(self.layer1(x))
        x = torch.relu(self.layer2(x))
        x = self.output(x)
        return x

# Step 4: Instantiate the model, loss function, and optimizer
model = SimpleNN()
criterion = nn.CrossEntropyLoss()  # Loss for binary classification
optimizer = optim.Adam(model.parameters(), lr=0.001)

# Step 5: Train the model
for epoch in range(10):
    model.train()
    optimizer.zero_grad()

    # Forward pass
    output = model(X_train_tensor)
    loss = criterion(output, y_train_tensor)

    # Backward pass
    loss.backward()
    optimizer.step()

    print(f"Epoch {epoch+1}, Loss: {loss.item()}")

# Step 6: Evaluate the model
model.eval()
with torch.no_grad():
    predictions = model(X_test_tensor)
    predicted_classes = torch.argmax(predictions, dim=1)
    accuracy = (predicted_classes == y_test_tensor).sum().item() / len(y_test_tensor)
    print(f"Test Accuracy: {accuracy:.4f}")
```

In this example:

- We use Scikit-Learn's StandardScaler to scale the features of the dataset, which is an essential preprocessing step before feeding data into a neural network. This is particularly useful for models like neural networks that are sensitive to the scale of input features.
- The data is split into training and testing sets using Scikit-Learn's train_test_split function.
- We define a simple feedforward neural network using PyTorch's nn.Module, compile it with a loss function (CrossEntropyLoss) and optimizer (Adam), and then train the model on the preprocessed data.
- Finally, we evaluate the model's accuracy on the test set.

13.2.3 Hyperparameter Tuning with Scikit-Learn and PyTorch

Scikit-Learn provides excellent tools for hyperparameter tuning, such as GridSearchCV and RandomizedSearchCV, but these tools are designed for Scikit-Learn models. To use them with PyTorch models, we need to use the sklearn.model_selection module in combination with the PyTorch model wrapper, KerasClassifier or KerasRegressor equivalents, to perform hyperparameter search for the neural network's hyperparameters.

Example: Hyperparameter Tuning Using GridSearchCV for a PyTorch Model

To use Scikit-Learn's GridSearchCV for tuning PyTorch hyperparameters, you can wrap the model into a Scikit-Learn compatible model using torch.utils.data.Dataset and torch.utils.data.DataLoader. Here's how it can be done:

```
from sklearn.model_selection import GridSearchCV
from sklearn.base import BaseEstimator, ClassifierMixin
import torch
import torch.nn as nn
import torch.optim as optim

# Step 1: Define a wrapper for PyTorch model to use in GridSearchCV
class PyTorchWrapper(BaseEstimator, ClassifierMixin):
    def __init__(self, model, optimizer, criterion, epochs=10):
        self.model = model
        self.optimizer = optimizer
        self.criterion = criterion
        self.epochs = epochs
```

```python
    def fit(self, X, y):
        self.model.train()
        for epoch in range(self.epochs):
            self.optimizer.zero_grad()
            output = self.model(X)
            loss = self.criterion(output, y)
            loss.backward()
            self.optimizer.step()
        return self

    def predict(self, X):
        self.model.eval()
        with torch.no_grad():
            output = self.model(X)
            _, predicted = torch.max(output, 1)
        return predicted.numpy()


# Step 2: Wrap your PyTorch model and use it in GridSearchCV
model = SimpleNN()
optimizer = optim.Adam(model.parameters())
criterion = nn.CrossEntropyLoss()
pytorch_model = PyTorchWrapper(model, optimizer, criterion)


# Define the parameter grid
param_grid = {
    'epochs': [5, 10],
    'optimizer': [optim.Adam, optim.SGD]
}


# Step 3: Perform hyperparameter tuning with GridSearchCV
grid_search = GridSearchCV(estimator=pytorch_model, param_grid=param_grid, cv=3)
grid_search.fit(X_train_tensor, y_train_tensor)

# Print the best parameters
print(f"Best Parameters: {grid_search.best_params_}")
```

In this example:

- We define a wrapper class PyTorchWrapper, which implements the fit and predict methods required by Scikit-Learn. This wrapper allows us to use the PyTorch model inside Scikit-Learn's GridSearchCV for hyperparameter tuning.
- We create a simple model using PyTorch, define the optimizer and loss function, and pass everything into the GridSearchCV.
- We perform hyperparameter tuning over different values of epochs and optimizers.

13.2.4 Using PyTorch Models in Scikit-Learn Pipelines

You can also include PyTorch models in Scikit-Learn pipelines, which allows you to chain together preprocessing, feature engineering, and deep learning into a unified workflow. By doing this, Scikit-Learn handles all the preprocessing and feature engineering, while PyTorch takes care of training the deep learning model.

Example: PyTorch Model in a Scikit-Learn Pipeline

```
from sklearn.pipeline import Pipeline
from sklearn.preprocessing import StandardScaler
from sklearn.model_selection import train_test_split

# Define the model and the pipeline
pipeline = Pipeline([
    ('scaler', StandardScaler()),
    ('model', PyTorchWrapper(model, optimizer, criterion))
])

# Step 1: Train the pipeline
pipeline.fit(X_train_tensor, y_train_tensor)

# Step 2: Evaluate the pipeline
accuracy = pipeline.score(X_test_tensor, y_test_tensor)
print(f"Test accuracy: {accuracy:.4f}")
```

In this case:

- We use Scikit-Learn's pipeline to combine scaling and model training steps.
- The StandardScaler is used to scale the features, and the PyTorch model is trained as part of the pipeline.

Integrating Scikit-Learn and PyTorch allows data scientists and machine learning engineers to combine the strengths of traditional machine learning with deep learning. Scikit-Learn provides easy-to-use tools for preprocessing, feature engineering, evaluation, and hyperparameter tuning, while PyTorch excels at building and training complex neural network architectures. By combining these two powerful libraries, you can create more efficient workflows, tune hyperparameters effectively, and build hybrid models that can take full advantage of the strengths of both traditional machine learning and deep learning techniques.

13.3 Feature Extraction for Deep Learning Models

Feature extraction is a critical step in the machine learning pipeline, especially when working with high-dimensional data such as images, audio, or text. In traditional machine learning, feature extraction refers to the process of selecting, modifying, or transforming raw data into features that better represent the underlying patterns. For deep learning models, feature extraction is often handled implicitly through multiple layers of the network, but the concept still holds significant importance in certain cases, particularly when pre-trained models are used or when dealing with structured data where automatic feature extraction may not be sufficient.

In this section, we will explore how feature extraction works for deep learning models, the various techniques for extracting features, and how Scikit-Learn can complement deep learning workflows in feature extraction.

13.3.1 Feature Extraction in Deep Learning

In deep learning, particularly in neural networks, the term "feature extraction" is typically associated with the automatic learning of relevant features from raw data through the use of layers such as convolutional layers (in CNNs), recurrent layers (in RNNs), or fully connected layers (in dense networks). While these models can learn hierarchical features through training, feature extraction may still be relevant in scenarios where:

- Pre-trained models are used and fine-tuned for specific tasks.
- High-level representations of data are needed.

Data pre-processing or manual extraction is necessary to improve model performance. In a deep learning context, the network learns features in successive layers. For instance, in Convolutional Neural Networks (CNNs) for image classification, the lower layers learn basic features like edges, textures, and colors, while the higher layers learn more abstract and complex patterns, such as shapes or objects. This learning process allows deep learning models to automatically perform feature extraction on raw input data, making them highly effective for many tasks.

13.3.2 Using Pre-Trained Models for Feature Extraction

One of the most popular ways to leverage feature extraction for deep learning models is by using pre-trained models. Pre-trained models are deep learning models that have been trained on a large dataset, often on a task like image classification or natural language processing, and can be used to extract high-level features from new data. This technique is called transfer learning.

In transfer learning, you use the feature extraction capabilities of a pre-trained model and adapt it to your specific problem. You can either use the entire pre-trained model as a feature extractor or fine-tune specific layers for your own task. In many cases, using a pre-trained model significantly reduces the time needed to train the network and improves performance on smaller datasets.

Example: Using a Pre-Trained CNN for Feature Extraction

In this example, we will use a pre-trained convolutional neural network (e.g., VGG16 or ResNet) to extract features from images.

```
import torch
from torchvision import models, transforms
from PIL import Image
import numpy as np

# Load a pre-trained ResNet model
resnet = models.resnet50(pretrained=True)
resnet.eval()  # Set the model to evaluation mode

# Define a transform to preprocess the image
transform = transforms.Compose([
    transforms.Resize((224, 224)),
    transforms.ToTensor(),
    transforms.Normalize(mean=[0.485, 0.456, 0.406], std=[0.229, 0.224, 0.225])
])

# Load an example image
```

```
img_path = "example_image.jpg"
img = Image.open(img_path)

# Apply the transformation
img_tensor = transform(img).unsqueeze(0)  # Add batch dimension

# Pass the image through the model to extract features
with torch.no_grad():  # Disable gradient computation
    features = resnet(img_tensor)

# Extract the features from the final fully connected layer
feature_vector = features.flatten()  # Flatten the feature map into a 1D vector
print("Extracted Feature Vector Shape:", feature_vector.shape)
```

In this example:

- A pre-trained ResNet50 model is used to extract features from an input image.
- The image is resized, normalized, and transformed into a tensor before being passed through the network.
- The output of the ResNet model is a high-level feature vector that represents the image.
- The feature vector can be used for downstream tasks like classification, clustering, or even as input to another machine learning model.

By using pre-trained models, the feature extraction process becomes highly efficient and allows for leveraging models that have already been trained on large, diverse datasets (such as ImageNet for images or BERT for text).

13.3.3 Feature Extraction in NLP with Pre-Trained Models

For natural language processing (NLP) tasks, pre-trained models like BERT, GPT, or Word2Vec are often used to extract meaningful features from text data. These models transform text into high-dimensional embeddings that capture semantic meaning. The embeddings can then be used as features for downstream tasks, such as sentiment analysis, text classification, or named entity recognition.

Example: Using BERT for Feature Extraction in NLP

Here's an example of using the pre-trained BERT model from the Hugging Face transformers library for feature extraction in NLP:

```
from transformers import BertTokenizer, BertModel
import torch

# Initialize the tokenizer and model
tokenizer = BertTokenizer.from_pretrained('bert-base-uncased')
model = BertModel.from_pretrained('bert-base-uncased')

# Example sentence
sentence = "Feature extraction is crucial in deep learning."

# Tokenize the sentence
inputs = tokenizer(sentence, return_tensors="pt", padding=True, truncation=True)

# Extract features from BERT
with torch.no_grad():
    outputs = model(**inputs)

# The 'outputs' object contains hidden states from BERT's layers
# We can extract the last hidden state (word embeddings) as features
last_hidden_states = outputs.last_hidden_state
sentence_embedding = last_hidden_states.mean(dim=1)  # Average across tokens to get
sentence-level features

print("Sentence Embedding Shape:", sentence_embedding.shape)
```

In this example:

- We use the BERT tokenizer to tokenize a sentence and convert it into the required format for input into the pre-trained BERT model.
- The BERT model generates word-level embeddings, which are high-dimensional feature vectors.
- We average the embeddings across all tokens to obtain a fixed-length sentence embedding that can be used for downstream tasks.

By leveraging pre-trained models like BERT, you can extract rich, contextual features from text without having to manually design features. These embeddings capture a wide range of semantic information and are suitable for a variety of NLP tasks.

13.3.4 Combining Feature Extraction with Scikit-Learn Models

After extracting features using deep learning models like CNNs or BERT, you may want to feed those features into traditional machine learning models, such as SVMs, random forests, or logistic regression. Scikit-Learn models are effective for such tasks when the input features are extracted by deep learning models.

For example, in image classification, you could use a CNN (or a pre-trained model) to extract features from images and then use Scikit-Learn models like Random Forest or SVM to perform the final classification.

Example: Using Extracted Features with Scikit-Learn

```
from sklearn.ensemble import RandomForestClassifier
from sklearn.model_selection import train_test_split
from sklearn.metrics import accuracy_score

# Let's assume 'feature_vector' is the extracted feature from a pre-trained model
# Prepare a dataset
X = np.random.rand(100, 2048)  # 100 samples with 2048 feature dimensions (e.g., from ResNet50)
y = np.random.randint(0, 2, 100)  # Binary target variable (0 or 1)

# Split data into training and testing sets
X_train, X_test, y_train, y_test = train_test_split(X, y, test_size=0.2, random_state=42)

# Train a Random Forest Classifier
clf = RandomForestClassifier(n_estimators=100)
clf.fit(X_train, y_train)

# Evaluate the model
y_pred = clf.predict(X_test)
accuracy = accuracy_score(y_test, y_pred)
print(f"Random Forest Accuracy: {accuracy:.4f}")
```

In this case:

- We assume the feature vectors were extracted from a pre-trained CNN (e.g., ResNet).
- These features are used as input to a Scikit-Learn RandomForestClassifier.
- After training, we evaluate the model on a test set.

13.3.5 Feature Extraction in Autoencoders

Autoencoders are unsupervised neural networks that learn efficient representations (or features) of input data. Autoencoders are often used for feature extraction, especially when you want to reduce dimensionality or find patterns in the data without labeled training examples.

Example: Feature Extraction Using an Autoencoder

```python
import torch
import torch.nn as nn

# Define a simple autoencoder architecture
class Autoencoder(nn.Module):
    def __init__(self):
        super(Autoencoder, self).__init__()
        self.encoder = nn.Sequential(
            nn.Linear(784, 128),
            nn.ReLU(),
            nn.Linear(128, 32)
        )
        self.decoder = nn.Sequential(
            nn.Linear(32, 128),
            nn.ReLU(),
            nn.Linear(128, 784),
            nn.Sigmoid()
        )

    def forward(self, x):
        encoded = self.encoder(x)
        decoded = self.decoder(encoded)
        return encoded, decoded

# Example data (e.g., flattened MNIST images)
X = torch.rand(64, 784)  # 64 samples with 784 features (28x28 images)

# Instantiate and train the autoencoder (not shown for brevity)
autoencoder = Autoencoder()
```

```
# Extract features using the encoder
encoded_features, _ = autoencoder(X)

print("Encoded Feature Shape:", encoded_features.shape)
```

In this example:

- We define a simple autoencoder with an encoder and decoder.
- The encoder learns to extract compressed features from high-dimensional data (e.g., flattened MNIST images).
- We use the encoder to extract the features.

Feature extraction for deep learning models is a powerful tool that allows you to extract meaningful, high-level representations of data. Pre-trained models like ResNet, VGG, and BERT are commonly used for feature extraction in fields like computer vision and NLP. These models can be used for transfer learning, where the extracted features can be fed into Scikit-Learn models for further processing. Whether you're working with images, text, or structured data, feature extraction techniques can significantly improve the performance of deep learning models by providing rich, contextual representations.

14. Automating Machine Learning with Scikit-Learn

AutoML is revolutionizing machine learning by automating feature selection, model selection, and hyperparameter tuning. This chapter introduces tools like TPOT and Auto-Sklearn, helping you leverage automation to streamline your ML workflow and improve model performance.

14.1 What is Automated Machine Learning (AutoML)?

Automated Machine Learning (AutoML) refers to the process of automating the end-to-end process of applying machine learning to real-world problems. The goal of AutoML is to make machine learning more accessible to non-experts and more efficient for experienced data scientists by automating tasks that traditionally require manual intervention and expert knowledge. In essence, AutoML aims to simplify and streamline the development of machine learning models, making it easier to build, train, and deploy predictive models with minimal human involvement.

AutoML covers a wide range of tasks involved in the machine learning pipeline, from data preprocessing and feature engineering to model selection and hyperparameter tuning. By automating these aspects of the machine learning process, AutoML tools help users save time and resources while improving the overall efficiency and performance of their models.

Key Aspects of AutoML

Data Preprocessing: Data preprocessing is a crucial step in any machine learning pipeline, involving tasks such as handling missing values, normalizing data, encoding categorical variables, and feature scaling. AutoML platforms often automate these tasks by applying different techniques based on the nature of the dataset.

Feature Engineering: Feature engineering involves creating new features from raw data, which can significantly improve model performance. AutoML systems typically automate the feature extraction and selection process by exploring various transformations and combinations of the original features.

Model Selection: Choosing the right machine learning algorithm for a specific task can be time-consuming and requires expertise. AutoML systems automate the process of selecting the best model from a wide range of algorithms, including decision trees, random forests, support vector machines, deep learning models, and more. The system evaluates each model's performance and chooses the one that performs the best for the given dataset.

Hyperparameter Optimization: Every machine learning model comes with a set of hyperparameters that need to be tuned for optimal performance. Manual tuning of these hyperparameters is often a tedious and computationally expensive process. AutoML platforms automate this task by using techniques like grid search, random search, or more advanced methods like Bayesian optimization to find the best hyperparameters for the chosen model.

Model Training and Evaluation: After selecting the model and tuning the hyperparameters, AutoML systems automate the training process and evaluate the model's performance using various metrics, such as accuracy, precision, recall, F1-score, and AUC-ROC curve. AutoML platforms often provide tools for model validation and cross-validation to ensure the model generalizes well to unseen data.

Model Deployment: Once the model is trained and optimized, AutoML tools help with the deployment process. They generate the necessary code or APIs for integrating the model into production environments, making it easier for users to deploy their models without deep technical knowledge of deployment strategies.

Model Monitoring and Maintenance: In real-world applications, machine learning models may degrade over time due to changes in data distribution (data drift) or other factors. AutoML platforms often provide tools to monitor the performance of deployed models and retrain them automatically when necessary, ensuring that the model remains accurate and effective.

Benefits of AutoML

Accessibility: One of the primary benefits of AutoML is its ability to democratize machine learning by making it accessible to non-experts. People without deep knowledge of machine learning algorithms, statistics, or data science can use AutoML tools to build models and solve problems. This is especially important for business professionals and analysts who want to use machine learning to derive insights from data but do not have the technical skills required to do so manually.

Time and Cost Efficiency: AutoML significantly reduces the amount of time and effort spent on building machine learning models. By automating the tedious and time-consuming aspects of model development, such as data preprocessing, feature engineering, and hyperparameter tuning, AutoML allows data scientists to focus on higher-level tasks and analysis. This not only saves time but also reduces the costs associated with developing machine learning models.

Improved Model Performance: AutoML systems often employ advanced algorithms and techniques to search through the space of possible models and hyperparameters more effectively than human experts. This can lead to the discovery of better-performing models that might not have been found through manual experimentation. Additionally, AutoML platforms may apply techniques like ensemble learning to combine multiple models and improve performance further.

Scalability: AutoML systems can automatically scale the model development process to handle large datasets or complex tasks that might be too challenging for human experts to tackle manually. AutoML can optimize models for both small-scale and large-scale datasets, making it a versatile tool for a wide range of use cases.

Standardization and Best Practices: AutoML tools often incorporate best practices and the latest research in machine learning, ensuring that users benefit from state-of-the-art techniques. This helps standardize the machine learning process, making it more reproducible and consistent across different projects.

Popular AutoML Tools and Frameworks

Several tools and frameworks have emerged to facilitate the adoption of AutoML, each with its unique features and capabilities:

Google Cloud AutoML: Google's Cloud AutoML offers a suite of machine learning services that help users with tasks like image classification, text sentiment analysis, and object detection. Google Cloud AutoML provides a user-friendly interface for building custom models with minimal coding required. It also offers pre-trained models for various use cases, making it easier for users to build powerful machine learning applications.

H2O.ai: H2O.ai is an open-source machine learning platform that provides AutoML capabilities, including automatic model selection, hyperparameter optimization, and model interpretation. H2O's AutoML is designed to work with large-scale datasets and is used by companies across various industries to automate the process of building and deploying machine learning models.

TPOT: TPOT is an open-source Python library for AutoML that uses genetic algorithms to optimize machine learning pipelines. TPOT automates the process of model selection, preprocessing, and hyperparameter tuning by searching through a wide range of possible solutions and selecting the best-performing ones. It integrates seamlessly with Scikit-Learn, allowing users to apply AutoML to Scikit-Learn models.

AutoKeras: AutoKeras is an open-source AutoML library built on top of Keras. It provides an easy-to-use interface for deep learning tasks, such as image classification, text classification, and regression. AutoKeras uses neural architecture search (NAS) to automatically find the best neural network architecture for a given problem, making it easier for users to build deep learning models without manual intervention.

Azure AutoML: Microsoft's Azure AutoML provides a cloud-based platform for building, training, and deploying machine learning models. It automates various stages of the machine learning process, including data preprocessing, model selection, and hyperparameter tuning. Azure AutoML is integrated with the Azure cloud ecosystem, making it a powerful tool for enterprise machine learning applications.

DataRobot: DataRobot is an enterprise-level AutoML platform that automates the entire machine learning pipeline, from data preprocessing and feature engineering to model selection and deployment. DataRobot is designed for business users and data scientists alike, offering an intuitive interface and advanced model interpretability tools to explain how the model makes decisions.

Challenges of AutoML

While AutoML has made machine learning more accessible and efficient, it also comes with some challenges:

Interpretability: Many AutoML systems generate complex models, which can be difficult to interpret. While AutoML platforms improve model performance, they may not always provide clear insights into how or why a model makes certain predictions, which can be a limitation in industries where explainability is crucial (e.g., healthcare and finance).

Black-box Nature: AutoML can sometimes be seen as a "black box" because it automates many of the decision-making processes involved in building a machine learning model. Users may not always have visibility into how certain features, models, or hyperparameters were selected, which can limit their ability to troubleshoot or modify the model.

Computational Cost: AutoML systems often require significant computational resources, especially when performing tasks like hyperparameter tuning or neural architecture search. This can lead to high costs for users, particularly when working with large datasets or complex models.

Overfitting: Despite the use of cross-validation and other techniques to prevent overfitting, AutoML systems can sometimes produce models that overfit to the training data, especially when the dataset is small or noisy. This can result in poor generalization to unseen data.

Automated Machine Learning (AutoML) is transforming the way machine learning models are developed, making it easier for non-experts to build and deploy machine learning models while also improving the efficiency and performance of data scientists. By automating tasks like data preprocessing, model selection, and hyperparameter tuning, AutoML tools help users save time, reduce costs, and improve model performance. However, the technology is not without its challenges, including interpretability, computational cost, and the risk of overfitting. As AutoML continues to evolve, it has the potential to further democratize machine learning and accelerate the adoption of AI across various industries.

14.2 Using TPOT for AutoML in Scikit-Learn

In the world of machine learning, automating the process of model selection, hyperparameter tuning, and feature engineering can greatly enhance productivity and reduce the time spent on model development. One of the most promising tools to achieve this is TPOT, which stands for Tree-based Pipeline Optimization Tool. TPOT is an open-source Python library that automates the process of designing machine learning pipelines, making it easier for data scientists and non-experts alike to apply machine learning without needing to manually tune parameters or select models. TPOT is built on top of Scikit-Learn, which makes it seamlessly compatible with the wide range of machine learning algorithms available in the Scikit-Learn ecosystem.

In this section, we will explore how TPOT works, how to use it for AutoML tasks, and how it integrates with Scikit-Learn to simplify machine learning workflows.

What is TPOT?

TPOT is an AutoML tool that uses genetic algorithms to automate the process of selecting models and optimizing hyperparameters. Genetic algorithms are a class of optimization algorithms inspired by natural selection, where solutions evolve over successive generations, with the fittest solutions being selected to pass their traits to the next generation.

In the case of TPOT, genetic algorithms are used to:

- **Generate and evolve machine learning pipelines**: TPOT automatically searches through a wide variety of machine learning models and feature engineering techniques, building pipelines by combining models and preprocessing steps that are most likely to perform well on the given dataset.
- **Tune hyperparameters**: As part of its pipeline optimization, TPOT also tunes hyperparameters, finding the best combination of parameters for the chosen model.
- **Evaluate pipeline performance**: TPOT uses cross-validation to evaluate the performance of pipelines, ensuring the selected model generalizes well to unseen data.
- **Select the best pipeline**: After running for a predefined number of generations or iterations, TPOT returns the best pipeline (i.e., the model and its hyperparameters) for the given task.

TPOT and Scikit-Learn Integration

Since TPOT is built on top of Scikit-Learn, it can be easily integrated into any machine learning project that uses the Scikit-Learn library. TPOT utilizes Scikit-Learn's powerful machine learning algorithms, transformers, and metrics, allowing users to leverage the best features of both libraries.

Here are some key Scikit-Learn components that TPOT uses:

- **Models (Classifiers/Regressors):** TPOT selects from a wide range of models, including decision trees, support vector machines (SVMs), logistic regression, random forests, and gradient boosting, among others.
- **Preprocessing and Transformers**: TPOT includes preprocessing steps such as standard scaling, normalization, imputation of missing values, and feature selection (via transformers like PCA and feature scaling) from Scikit-Learn.
- **Cross-validation and Model Evaluation**: TPOT uses Scikit-Learn's cross_val_score and other evaluation metrics like accuracy, F1-score, and mean

squared error (MSE) to assess the performance of pipelines and select the best one.

How TPOT Works

To use TPOT, the process can be broken down into several key steps:

Install TPOT: First, make sure TPOT and its dependencies are installed. You can install TPOT using pip:

pip install tpot

TPOT requires certain dependencies, such as scikit-learn, pandas, and deap (the library for genetic algorithms), which will automatically be installed when you install TPOT.

Import Libraries: In the Python script or Jupyter Notebook, import the necessary libraries, including TPOT and Scikit-Learn.

from tpot import TPOTClassifier
from sklearn.datasets import load_digits
from sklearn.model_selection import train_test_split

Load and Preprocess the Dataset: Next, load the dataset and split it into training and test sets. You can use Scikit-Learn's built-in datasets or any custom dataset.

 # Load the Digits dataset
digits = load_digits()
X = digits.data
y = digits.target

 # Split the data into training and testing sets

X_train, X_test, y_train, y_test = train_test_split(X, y, test_size=0.25, random_state=42)

Create a TPOT Instance: Now, you can create an instance of TPOTClassifier (for classification problems) or TPOTRegressor (for regression problems). Set the generations parameter to define the number of iterations (or generations) TPOT will run to optimize the pipeline, and the population_size parameter to specify how many pipelines TPOT will evolve per generation.

```
# Create a TPOTClassifier instance
tpot = TPOTClassifier(generations=5, population_size=20, random_state=42)
generations=5: The number of generations (iterations) of pipeline optimization.
population_size=20: The number of pipelines to evaluate per generation.
random_state=42: To ensure reproducibility.
```

Fit the Model: Call the fit method on the TPOT instance to begin the optimization process. TPOT will automatically perform data preprocessing, model selection, hyperparameter tuning, and evaluation.

```
# Fit the model using TPOT
tpot.fit(X_train, y_train)
```

During the fitting process, TPOT will iteratively evaluate different combinations of models and preprocessing techniques. It uses cross-validation to assess the performance of each pipeline. The process can take some time depending on the complexity of the task, the size of the dataset, and the number of generations and pipelines specified.

Evaluate the Best Model: Once TPOT has finished optimizing the pipeline, you can evaluate the best pipeline found by TPOT on the test set.

```
# Evaluate the best model
print(f'Test Accuracy: {tpot.score(X_test, y_test)}')
```

Export the Best Pipeline: After TPOT has found the best pipeline, you can export the optimized model as Python code, allowing you to save it and use it in the future.

```
# Export the best pipeline
tpot.export('best_model.py')
```

This code will generate a Python script containing the best pipeline with the chosen model, preprocessing steps, and hyperparameters. You can then load this script to use the trained model for predictions or further development.

Example Use Case

Let's consider a simple classification task using the Digits dataset. This dataset contains 8x8 pixel images of handwritten digits (0-9). The goal is to classify the digits into one of the 10 classes (0-9).

Here is how TPOT can be used for this task:

```
from tpot import TPOTClassifier
from sklearn.datasets import load_digits
from sklearn.model_selection import train_test_split

# Load and split the Digits dataset
digits = load_digits()
X = digits.data
y = digits.target
X_train, X_test, y_train, y_test = train_test_split(X, y, test_size=0.25, random_state=42)

# Initialize the TPOT classifier
tpot = TPOTClassifier(generations=5, population_size=20, random_state=42)

# Fit the model
tpot.fit(X_train, y_train)

# Evaluate the best model
print(f'Test Accuracy: {tpot.score(X_test, y_test)}')

# Export the best pipeline to a Python file
tpot.export('best_model.py')
```

This process will search for the optimal pipeline for the Digits dataset, train it, and then evaluate its performance. The best pipeline will be exported to a Python file, which can be used for future predictions.

Advantages of Using TPOT

- **Ease of Use**: TPOT provides an intuitive interface that requires minimal code to get started, making it accessible to both beginners and experts.
- **Automation**: TPOT automates the tedious aspects of machine learning, such as model selection, hyperparameter tuning, and preprocessing, allowing users to focus on the high-level aspects of the project.
- **Integration with Scikit-Learn**: TPOT is built on top of Scikit-Learn, meaning you can use the wide array of Scikit-Learn models, transformers, and evaluation metrics in your pipeline.

- **Optimization and Exploration**: TPOT uses genetic algorithms to search the space of possible pipelines, allowing it to discover novel combinations of models and features that might not have been considered manually.
- **Model Export**: TPOT allows you to export the optimized model as Python code, which is great for deployment or further fine-tuning.

TPOT is a powerful tool that brings AutoML to Scikit-Learn, making it easy to optimize machine learning pipelines without manual intervention. By leveraging genetic algorithms, TPOT automates model selection, preprocessing, and hyperparameter optimization, saving time and improving efficiency. Whether you are a beginner looking to automate machine learning tasks or an experienced data scientist wanting to experiment with different models and features, TPOT provides a seamless solution for building high-performing models with minimal effort.

14.3 Applying AutoML with H2O.ai and Auto-Sklearn

As machine learning continues to evolve, there has been an increasing demand for automating the process of selecting the right models, optimizing hyperparameters, and preprocessing data. While tools like TPOT have made significant strides in automating machine learning (AutoML) tasks, there are also other prominent AutoML libraries, including H2O.ai and Auto-Sklearn, which have gained attention for their robust capabilities in automating the end-to-end machine learning pipeline. In this section, we will explore both H2O.ai and Auto-Sklearn, examining how they can be used to automate model training and hyperparameter tuning, and how they compare to Scikit-Learn-based AutoML libraries like TPOT.

H2O.ai: Automating Machine Learning at Scale

H2O.ai is an open-source software platform designed for data science and machine learning. It focuses on providing high-performance, distributed machine learning algorithms, making it a great choice for big data applications. One of its most well-known products is H2O AutoML, a platform that automates the entire machine learning pipeline, including data preprocessing, feature engineering, model selection, and hyperparameter tuning. H2O.ai is particularly known for its ability to scale across large datasets while maintaining high accuracy in model training.

Key Features of H2O AutoML:

- **Wide Range of Algorithms**: H2O AutoML supports a variety of machine learning algorithms, including generalized linear models (GLMs), gradient boosting machines (GBM), random forests, deep learning models, and more.
- **Automatic Model Selection**: H2O AutoML runs a comprehensive search across different models and finds the best performing one based on the dataset and task.
- **Ensemble Learning**: It generates multiple models and combines them in an ensemble to improve performance, often resulting in better generalization and accuracy.
- **Distributed Computation**: H2O AutoML can scale to handle large datasets efficiently by leveraging distributed computing capabilities, making it well-suited for big data applications.

How to Use H2O AutoML:

To use H2O AutoML, follow these steps:

Install H2O.ai:

H2O.ai can be installed with pip:

```
pip install h2o
```

Import Libraries and Initialize H2O:

```
import h2o
from h2o.automl import H2OAutoML
from h2o.estimators import H2ORandomForestEstimator
from sklearn.model_selection import train_test_split
```

Load and Prepare the Data:

H2O requires data to be in H2O-specific format (H2OFrame). You can easily convert a pandas DataFrame into an H2OFrame.

```
# Initialize H2O cluster
h2o.init()

# Load the dataset (Example: Iris dataset)
import pandas as pd
df = pd.read_csv('iris.csv')
```

```
h2o_df = h2o.H2OFrame(df)
```

```
# Split the dataset into training and testing sets
train, test = h2o_df.split_frame(ratios=[.8], seed=42)
```

Run H2O AutoML:

With H2O AutoML, simply call the train() method and pass in the dataset and target variable. H2O will automatically select, train, and evaluate various machine learning models.

```
# Set the target and predictor columns
x = df.columns[:-1]
y = df.columns[-1]
```

```
# Run AutoML
automl = H2OAutoML(max_models=20, seed=42)
automl.train(x=x, y=y, training_frame=train)
```

View Results:

After the AutoML process is complete, you can inspect the performance of the models and the leaderboard to identify the best performing model.

```
# View leaderboard of models
lb = automl.leaderboard
print(lb)
```

```
# Get the best model
best_model = automl.leader
```

Make Predictions:

You can now use the trained model to make predictions on the test set.

```
# Make predictions on the test set
predictions = best_model.predict(test)
print(predictions)
```

Advantages of H2O AutoML:

- **Scalability**: H2O is built for distributed computing, making it a great choice for large-scale data analysis.
- **Flexibility**: Supports a wide variety of machine learning algorithms, allowing users to try different models.
- **Ensemble Learning**: H2O AutoML generates ensembles that often improve predictive accuracy by combining the outputs of different models.
- **Open-Source**: H2O.ai offers an open-source version that is free to use for smaller-scale applications.

Auto-Sklearn: A Scikit-Learn-Based AutoML Framework

Auto-Sklearn is another powerful AutoML library built on top of Scikit-Learn. It is an open-source Python library that automates the process of model selection and hyperparameter tuning. It leverages Scikit-Learn's rich ecosystem of machine learning algorithms while adding optimization techniques to improve model performance.

Key Features of Auto-Sklearn:

- **Auto Model Selection**: Auto-Sklearn uses a meta-learning algorithm to select the best models based on the dataset and task.
- **Hyperparameter Optimization**: It automatically tunes the hyperparameters of models using Bayesian optimization, ensuring that the chosen model is fine-tuned for the dataset.
- **Ensemble Learning**: Like H2O, Auto-Sklearn also generates an ensemble of models, which improves generalization and predictive performance.
- **Scikit-Learn Compatibility**: Since Auto-Sklearn is built on Scikit-Learn, it integrates seamlessly with Scikit-Learn's API, making it easy to use for users already familiar with Scikit-Learn.

How to Use Auto-Sklearn:

Install Auto-Sklearn:

You can install Auto-Sklearn using pip:

pip install auto-sklearn

Import Libraries and Load Data:

```
import autosklearn.classification
from sklearn.datasets import load_digits
from sklearn.model_selection import train_test_split
```

Load and Split the Data:

```
# Load the Digits dataset
digits = load_digits()
X = digits.data
y = digits.target

# Split the data into training and testing sets
X_train, X_test, y_train, y_test = train_test_split(X, y, test_size=0.25, random_state=42)
```

Train the Auto-Sklearn Model:

```
# Create an Auto-sklearn classifier instance
automl = autosklearn.classification.AutoSklearnClassifier(time_left_for_this_task=60,
per_run_time_limit=30)

# Train the model
automl.fit(X_train, y_train)
```

Here, the time_left_for_this_task specifies the total time allowed for model training, while per_run_time_limit sets the time limit for each individual model training process.

Evaluate the Model:

Once the model is trained, you can evaluate its performance on the test set:

```
# Evaluate the model
print("Test Accuracy: ", automl.score(X_test, y_test))
```

Get the Best Model:

Auto-Sklearn also provides access to the best model found during the search process:

```
# Access the best model
best_model = automl.show_models()
print(best_model)
```

Advantages of Auto-Sklearn:

- **Scikit-Learn Integration**: Auto-Sklearn integrates smoothly with Scikit-Learn, allowing users to use familiar tools while automating model selection.
- **Efficiency**: Auto-Sklearn uses Bayesian optimization to efficiently search the hyperparameter space and select the best-performing models.
- **Ensemble Generation**: Auto-Sklearn generates an ensemble of models, which improves performance by combining the strengths of multiple models.
- **Active Learning**: Auto-Sklearn employs a meta-learning approach to improve model performance on unseen datasets.

Both H2O.ai and Auto-Sklearn are powerful AutoML frameworks that streamline the machine learning process by automating model selection, hyperparameter tuning, and feature engineering. While H2O.ai excels at handling large-scale datasets and provides distributed computation capabilities, Auto-Sklearn is an excellent choice for users already familiar with Scikit-Learn, thanks to its tight integration with Scikit-Learn and its efficient search for optimal models. By incorporating these AutoML tools into your machine learning workflow, you can save time, improve accuracy, and make machine learning accessible even to non-experts.

15. Best Practices and Common Pitfalls in Scikit-Learn

Many machine learning projects fail due to common mistakes such as data leakage, improper feature scaling, and overfitting. In this final chapter, we cover best practices for debugging, optimizing, and evaluating ML models to ensure they perform well in real-world applications.

15.1 Avoiding Data Leakage in Machine Learning

In the field of machine learning, data leakage refers to the unintentional inclusion of information from outside the training dataset that influences the model's predictions. This can result in overly optimistic performance metrics during model evaluation and lead to poor generalization when the model is deployed to unseen data. Avoiding data leakage is crucial to ensure that a model performs well in real-world scenarios and is able to generalize properly to new, unseen data.

In this section, we will explore what data leakage is, the different types of data leakage that can occur during a machine learning workflow, and how to avoid it effectively.

What is Data Leakage?

Data leakage occurs when the model is exposed to information it should not have during the training process. This information could include data that would not be available at the time of prediction or features that have an indirect relationship with the target variable. As a result, the model becomes "cheated" into making better predictions than it would if it were trained only on the data it would realistically have during real-world predictions.

There are two primary categories of data leakage:

Train-Test Data Leakage: This type of leakage occurs when the training data includes information from the test set. This causes the model to "see" the test data during training, leading to an overestimation of the model's performance.

Feature Data Leakage: This occurs when features used for training contain information from the future or include variables that are related to the target variable inappropriately.

This leakage can artificially increase the model's accuracy and give it an unfair advantage.

Types of Data Leakage

Leaking Information from the Test Set to the Training Set

The most common type of leakage happens when information from the test set is inadvertently included in the training process. This could occur when the same data is present in both the training and test sets or when preprocessing steps, such as scaling or imputation, are done improperly.

Example: Imagine you scale the data using the entire dataset (training + test set) before splitting it into training and testing subsets. This means the scaling process "leaks" information from the test set into the training data, and the model becomes exposed to this information. The model may perform exceptionally well, but only because it "knows" the scaling parameters for the test data.

Solution: To avoid leakage from the test set, always perform the following steps in the correct order:

- Split the dataset into training and test sets first.
- Apply any preprocessing techniques, like scaling, encoding, or imputation, separately on the training set.
- Once the model is trained on the training data, apply the same transformations to the test set.

Leaking Information from the Future

Data leakage can also occur when features are introduced that contain information that would not be available during prediction. This type of leakage happens when features include future values or outcome-related data that should not be known at the time of prediction.

Example: In a time series forecasting task, imagine using future data, such as the closing price of a stock at the next time step, as a feature when predicting the current price. Since this data is from the future, it should not be included as a feature for prediction.

Solution: In time series problems, be sure to avoid using future data when making predictions. Make sure the features are derived only from past or present information at the time of prediction.

Feature Engineering Leakage

Another form of leakage occurs during feature engineering when you create features that are too strongly correlated with the target variable or when the feature directly depends on the target.

Example: Suppose you're building a model to predict customer churn, and one of the features is the target variable itself, such as "whether a customer has churned in the past." This feature obviously carries direct information about the outcome, leading to leakage.

Solution: During feature engineering, make sure that the features you create do not directly include information about the target variable. It's important to carefully analyze and ensure that your features are only based on the information that would be available at the time of prediction.

Leaking Information During Cross-Validation

Data leakage can also happen when cross-validation is not implemented properly, especially when preprocessing steps like scaling or encoding are applied before splitting the data into folds.

Example: If you scale your entire dataset before performing cross-validation, information from the test fold will influence the training process in each fold. This violates the principle of keeping training and test data independent during cross-validation.

Solution: When performing cross-validation, apply any transformations like scaling, encoding, or imputing missing values within each fold separately. In other words, fit the scaler or encoder on the training fold, then transform the validation fold with the fitted scaler.

How to Avoid Data Leakage

Now that we understand the types of data leakage, let's discuss strategies for avoiding it:

Carefully Split Data Before Preprocessing: Always split your dataset into training and test sets before performing any preprocessing steps. This ensures that no information from the test set is used to influence the model during training. Once the data is split, you can apply feature engineering, scaling, or other preprocessing techniques on the training set and then apply the same transformations to the test set.

Use Cross-Validation Correctly: In machine learning workflows where cross-validation is used, you need to apply preprocessing steps like scaling and imputation within each fold of the cross-validation process. The data used for validation should never "leak" into the training process. This ensures that the model is validated on data that it has not seen during training.

Be Mindful of Temporal Order in Time Series Problems: In time series forecasting or any problem involving sequential data, it is essential to ensure that features do not "leak" future information into the model. Time series data should be processed so that features are derived from past or current observations, never from future values. Additionally, time series cross-validation techniques (such as walk-forward validation) should be used to maintain the integrity of the temporal structure.

Check Feature Engineering for Target Leakage: Always inspect your features to ensure they do not directly involve or correlate with the target variable inappropriately. If you're using domain-specific knowledge to create features, make sure these features are only derived from available data at the time of prediction.

Use Pipelines to Avoid Leakage: In Scikit-Learn, you can use pipelines to automate the process of applying preprocessing steps, ensuring that no data leakage occurs during preprocessing. With pipelines, you can chain the steps of feature extraction, scaling, model training, and evaluation in a manner that avoids the pitfalls of leaking information between training and test sets.

```
from sklearn.pipeline import Pipeline
from sklearn.preprocessing import StandardScaler
from sklearn.ensemble import RandomForestClassifier
from sklearn.model_selection import train_test_split

# Example pipeline
pipeline = Pipeline([
    ('scaler', StandardScaler()),
    ('classifier', RandomForestClassifier())
])

# Split data into training and test sets
```

```
X_train, X_test, y_train, y_test = train_test_split(X, y, test_size=0.2, random_state=42)

# Fit the model
pipeline.fit(X_train, y_train)

# Evaluate the model
score = pipeline.score(X_test, y_test)
print("Test Accuracy: ", score)
```

Perform Thorough Validation: Regularly check your model's performance on a separate validation set, and always keep the test set for final evaluation. If you notice unusually high performance on the validation set, investigate potential leakage.

Careful Handling of Imbalanced Data: When dealing with imbalanced datasets, be cautious of techniques such as oversampling or undersampling that might lead to leakage if not applied carefully. For example, oversampling techniques like SMOTE should be applied only to the training data, as applying them to the entire dataset before splitting would lead to leakage.

Data leakage is one of the most common pitfalls in machine learning that can lead to overoptimistic results and poor model generalization. By ensuring that data preprocessing is done in the right order, being mindful of temporal order in time series data, and using pipelines and cross-validation effectively, you can avoid the negative impact of data leakage. Preventing leakage ensures that the performance metrics of your model accurately reflect its ability to generalize to unseen data and helps in building robust, production-ready machine learning systems.

15.2 Debugging Machine Learning Models in Scikit-Learn

Debugging is an essential step in the machine learning workflow. It ensures that the model performs as expected, and it helps to uncover issues that might lead to poor performance, such as incorrect data processing, parameter choices, or algorithmic inefficiencies. In Scikit-Learn, debugging a machine learning model can be tricky, especially for beginners, as the model's behavior might not be immediately clear or the source of problems can be difficult to pinpoint. In this section, we'll explore strategies for debugging machine learning models in Scikit-Learn, including how to troubleshoot common issues, interpret errors, and systematically improve model performance.

1. Start with the Basics: Check Your Data

Before diving into complex model issues, always start by verifying the quality of your data. The most common issues with machine learning models arise from the data itself.

Common Data Issues:

- **Missing or NaN Values**: These can affect model training and lead to inaccurate predictions.
- **Incorrect Data Types**: Models expect certain data types for each feature (e.g., numerical vs. categorical).
- **Outliers**: Extreme values in the dataset might disproportionately influence the model's performance.
- **Class Imbalance**: If the target variable is highly imbalanced, the model might be biased towards the majority class.

How to Check for Data Issues:

Missing Values:

```
import pandas as pd
# Check for missing values
data.isnull().sum()
```

If there are missing values, you can either impute them or drop them depending on the problem and the size of the missing data.

Data Types: Ensure that each feature has the correct data type.

```
data.dtypes
```

You can use pd.get_dummies() to handle categorical variables and convert them into numeric features.

Outliers: Visualize your data using box plots to detect outliers.

```
import seaborn as sns
sns.boxplot(data['feature_name'])
```

If outliers are present, you may need to use robust scaling or remove the outliers entirely.

2. Check Model Inputs and Parameters

Once you've verified that the data is in good shape, check that you are passing the right inputs to the model and that you are using appropriate hyperparameters.

Common Issues to Look For:

Incorrect Input Shapes: Ensure that the shape of your feature matrix (X) matches the expected input shape of the model.

print(X_train.shape)
print(y_train.shape)

Feature Engineering Issues: If feature extraction or transformation steps are not carried out correctly, the model may struggle to learn meaningful patterns. Be sure that all preprocessing steps (e.g., scaling, encoding) are applied consistently across training and test data.

Hyperparameter Choices: Choosing the wrong hyperparameters, like an overly small or large learning rate, can negatively impact model performance. Some models are more sensitive to hyperparameters than others.

3. Assess Model Performance with Metrics

Evaluating the model's performance with appropriate metrics is key to debugging. Depending on the type of model and task (classification or regression), Scikit-Learn provides a variety of performance evaluation metrics, such as accuracy, precision, recall, F1-score for classification, and mean squared error (MSE), R^2 for regression.

For Classification Models:

Accuracy: Check if the accuracy score is as expected.

from sklearn.metrics import accuracy_score
print(accuracy_score(y_test, y_pred))

Confusion Matrix: This helps identify if the model is confusing certain classes.

from sklearn.metrics import confusion_matrix
print(confusion_matrix(y_test, y_pred))

Classification Report: This provides a more detailed view of precision, recall, and F1-score.

from sklearn.metrics import classification_report
print(classification_report(y_test, y_pred))

For Regression Models:

Mean Squared Error (MSE):

from sklearn.metrics import mean_squared_error
print(mean_squared_error(y_test, y_pred))

R² Score:

from sklearn.metrics import r2_score
print(r2_score(y_test, y_pred))

Analyzing Model Metrics:

- A high accuracy for a classification problem with a class imbalance might be misleading (due to the model just predicting the majority class). In such cases, precision, recall, or F1-score can provide better insights.
- A low R^2 score for a regression model indicates poor fit, meaning the model is not explaining the variance in the target variable.

4. Visualize Model Results

Visualizing predictions can provide insights into where the model is failing or succeeding.

Plotting Predicted vs. True Values (Regression):

```
import matplotlib.pyplot as plt
plt.scatter(y_test, y_pred)
plt.xlabel('True Values')
plt.ylabel('Predictions')
plt.show()
```

Confusion Matrix Heatmap (Classification):

```
import seaborn as sns
cm = confusion_matrix(y_test, y_pred)
sns.heatmap(cm, annot=True, fmt='d', cmap='Blues')
plt.xlabel('Predicted')
plt.ylabel('True')
plt.show()
```

These visualizations help in identifying areas where the model is not performing well. For example, if a regression model's predicted values are scattered without any clear relationship to the true values, this might indicate an issue with the model choice or feature selection.

5. Use Cross-Validation for Stability

To check the robustness of your model, perform cross-validation using Scikit-Learn's cross_val_score function. Cross-validation splits the data into multiple folds, training the model on different subsets and testing on others. This helps you to assess how well the model generalizes to unseen data and prevents overfitting on a single train-test split.

```
from sklearn.model_selection import cross_val_score
scores = cross_val_score(model, X, y, cv=5, scoring='accuracy')
print(f'Cross-validation scores: {scores}')
```

6. Handle Overfitting and Underfitting

Two of the most common model performance issues are overfitting (where the model performs well on training data but poorly on test data) and underfitting (where the model does not capture the underlying patterns in the data).

Overfitting:

Solution: Reduce model complexity by using simpler models, applying regularization (e.g., Lasso or Ridge for linear models), or increasing the amount of training data.

Underfitting:

Solution: Use a more complex model, add more relevant features, or reduce regularization to allow the model to fit the data more closely.

7. Debugging Hyperparameters with GridSearchCV

If you suspect that hyperparameters are the source of the issue, use GridSearchCV to perform an exhaustive search over a specified parameter grid to find the optimal hyperparameters. This process automatically tests all combinations of hyperparameters and identifies the best-performing ones.

```
from sklearn.model_selection import GridSearchCV

param_grid = {
    'max_depth': [5, 10, 15],
    'min_samples_split': [2, 5, 10],
}

grid_search               =               GridSearchCV(estimator=DecisionTreeClassifier(),
param_grid=param_grid, cv=5)
grid_search.fit(X_train, y_train)

print(f'Best parameters: {grid_search.best_params_}')
```

8. Examine Learning Curves

Learning curves are a useful way to track how the model's performance improves with additional data. If the training performance improves, but validation performance remains flat or worsens, this could be a sign of overfitting. On the other hand, if both training and validation performance are poor, the model may be underfitting.

```
from sklearn.model_selection import learning_curve
import matplotlib.pyplot as plt

train_sizes, train_scores, val_scores = learning_curve(model, X_train, y_train, cv=5)

plt.plot(train_sizes, train_scores.mean(axis=1), label="Training score")
plt.plot(train_sizes, val_scores.mean(axis=1), label="Cross-validation score")
plt.xlabel('Training Size')
plt.ylabel('Score')
plt.legend()
plt.show()
```

Debugging machine learning models in Scikit-Learn requires a structured approach to identify the source of issues and improve model performance. Start by carefully inspecting your data and preprocessing steps, evaluate model performance with appropriate metrics, visualize the results, and use cross-validation to assess generalization. Additionally, handling issues of overfitting and underfitting, tuning hyperparameters with GridSearchCV, and using learning curves can guide you in improving model performance. By methodically addressing each component of your machine learning pipeline, you will be able to debug and optimize your model effectively.

15.3 Optimizing Model Performance

Optimizing machine learning models is a crucial step to ensure that your model achieves the best possible performance on unseen data. Optimization goes beyond simply fitting a model to your training data; it involves tweaking various aspects of the machine learning pipeline, including preprocessing, feature engineering, model selection, and hyperparameter tuning, to achieve better generalization and minimize errors. In this section, we will discuss different strategies and techniques for optimizing model performance using Scikit-Learn.

1. Understanding the Model Performance

Before diving into optimization techniques, it's essential to understand the performance of the current model. Model evaluation metrics depend on the problem at hand—classification or regression.

- **For Classification**: Use accuracy, precision, recall, F1-score, and confusion matrix to understand how well the model classifies the target variable.
- **For Regression**: Evaluate with metrics like Mean Squared Error (MSE), Mean Absolute Error (MAE), and R^2 score.

Identifying whether your model is underfitting or overfitting is key to deciding on the optimization direction:

- Underfitting occurs when the model is too simple to capture the patterns in the data. Signs include high bias and poor performance on both training and testing sets.
- Overfitting happens when the model learns the noise in the training data, resulting in high variance and excellent performance on the training set but poor performance on unseen data.

2. Feature Engineering and Selection

Feature engineering plays a crucial role in optimizing model performance. The quality and relevance of features greatly affect the outcome of your model.

- **Feature Extraction**: Extract meaningful features that enhance the model's predictive power. For example, in time-series data, you might want to extract temporal features such as the day of the week or month.
- **Feature Scaling**: Many machine learning algorithms, such as logistic regression, support vector machines (SVM), and k-nearest neighbors (KNN), are sensitive to the scale of features. Standardizing or normalizing features ensures that the model treats all features equally.

```
from sklearn.preprocessing import StandardScaler
scaler = StandardScaler()
X_train_scaled = scaler.fit_transform(X_train)
X_test_scaled = scaler.transform(X_test)
```

Feature Selection: Selecting the most important features can reduce overfitting and improve model accuracy. Methods like Recursive Feature Elimination (RFE) or tree-based models' feature importance can be used to select the best features.

```
from sklearn.feature_selection import RFE
from sklearn.linear_model import LogisticRegression
model = LogisticRegression()
selector = RFE(model, n_features_to_select=5)
selector = selector.fit(X_train, y_train)
```

Handling Categorical Data: Ensure that categorical variables are encoded properly (e.g., one-hot encoding, label encoding) to ensure that machine learning algorithms can handle them correctly.

3. Choosing the Right Model

The choice of model has a significant impact on performance. A model that works well for one type of data might not work well for another. Experimenting with different types of models and comparing their performance is an essential part of the optimization process.

Try Different Models: Scikit-Learn provides several machine learning algorithms. When optimizing performance, consider testing multiple models and comparing their results.

- For classification tasks, consider models like Logistic Regression, Decision Trees, Random Forests, SVM, and k-NN.
- For regression tasks, experiment with models such as Linear Regression, Ridge, Lasso, Decision Trees, and Random Forests.

Example:

```
from sklearn.ensemble import RandomForestClassifier
rf_model = RandomForestClassifier(n_estimators=100)
rf_model.fit(X_train, y_train)
```

Ensemble Methods: Ensemble techniques like Random Forest and Gradient Boosting can improve predictive accuracy by combining multiple weak learners into a stronger model. They reduce overfitting and bias.

Random Forest combines multiple decision trees to increase the model's robustness by averaging predictions (for regression) or using majority voting (for classification). It's a great choice for tackling complex datasets with high variance.

Gradient Boosting (and variants like XGBoost) sequentially builds trees, each one correcting the errors of the previous one, and is often more accurate than random forests, though it may require more careful tuning.

4. Hyperparameter Tuning

Tuning the hyperparameters of a model is one of the most critical aspects of optimizing performance. Hyperparameters are settings that govern the learning process, such as the learning rate, the number of trees in a random forest, or the regularization strength in a regression model.

GridSearchCV: This technique exhaustively searches over a specified parameter grid to find the best hyperparameters. It's ideal for small to medium datasets.

```
from sklearn.model_selection import GridSearchCV
param_grid = {'n_estimators': [50, 100, 200], 'max_depth': [10, 20, 30]}
grid_search           =           GridSearchCV(estimator=RandomForestClassifier(),
param_grid=param_grid, cv=5)
```

```
grid_search.fit(X_train, y_train)
print(grid_search.best_params_)
```

RandomizedSearchCV: For large datasets or when the parameter grid is too large, RandomizedSearchCV allows you to search over a random subset of the parameter space, which can be more efficient than grid search.

```
from sklearn.model_selection import RandomizedSearchCV
param_dist = {'n_estimators': [50, 100, 200], 'max_depth': [10, 20, 30]}
random_search    =    RandomizedSearchCV(estimator=RandomForestClassifier(),
param_distributions=param_dist, n_iter=100, cv=5)
random_search.fit(X_train, y_train)
```

Bayesian Optimization: For more advanced optimization, you can use Bayesian Optimization, which builds a probabilistic model to predict the best parameters. Libraries like Optuna or Hyperopt can help with this process.

5. Cross-Validation for Model Evaluation

To ensure that your model's performance is stable and generalizable, always use cross-validation. It involves splitting the data into several subsets (folds) and training the model on each subset, testing it on the remaining data, and averaging the results.

K-Fold Cross-Validation: Use k-fold cross-validation to evaluate model performance. This approach provides a better estimate of model performance compared to a single train-test split.

```
from sklearn.model_selection import cross_val_score
scores = cross_val_score(rf_model, X, y, cv=5)
print(f'Cross-validation scores: {scores}')
```

Stratified K-Fold: In classification problems with class imbalance, Stratified K-Fold ensures that each fold has a proportionate representation of each class, improving model evaluation.

6. Regularization Techniques

Regularization is a technique used to prevent overfitting by penalizing large model parameters. It helps the model generalize better to unseen data.

L1 Regularization (Lasso): Lasso regression applies L1 regularization, which adds the sum of the absolute values of the model's coefficients to the loss function. This encourages sparse solutions (i.e., many coefficients are zero).

L2 Regularization (Ridge): Ridge regression applies L2 regularization, which adds the sum of the squared values of the coefficients to the loss function. It discourages large coefficients but doesn't set them exactly to zero.

ElasticNet: A hybrid of L1 and L2 regularization, ElasticNet allows you to control the mix between both types of regularization.

Regularization is particularly useful in high-dimensional datasets or when the model has many features. For linear models in Scikit-Learn, you can use Ridge, Lasso, or ElasticNet classes, which allow you to control the regularization strength with the alpha parameter.

7. Ensemble Methods and Stacking

Ensemble methods such as bagging, boosting, and stacking can improve the performance of machine learning models.

Bagging: Methods like Random Forest aggregate predictions from multiple models (decision trees in the case of Random Forest) to improve stability and accuracy.

Boosting: Techniques like Gradient Boosting and XGBoost sequentially build models to correct the errors of previous models, which usually leads to better performance than bagging.

Stacking: Stacking involves training multiple models and then using a meta-model to combine their predictions. It's an advanced ensemble technique that can outperform individual models.

8. Model Evaluation and Final Adjustments

Once optimization techniques have been applied, assess the final model using cross-validation and appropriate performance metrics. Compare the results with the baseline model and ensure that improvements are not merely a result of overfitting.

Fine-tune your final model based on its performance on the validation set and its generalizability to new, unseen data. Visualizations, like learning curves and confusion matrices, can be useful here.

Optimizing machine learning models is a multifaceted process that involves fine-tuning data preprocessing, feature engineering, model selection, and hyperparameters. Understanding where your model is struggling—whether it's underfitting or overfitting—will guide you toward the most appropriate optimization techniques. Leveraging ensemble methods, using cross-validation for robust evaluation, and applying regularization to prevent overfitting are powerful strategies to improve model performance. With careful iteration and evaluation, you can achieve a highly optimized machine learning model in Scikit-Learn that generalizes well to unseen data.

15.4 Future Trends and What's Next in Scikit-Learn

Scikit-Learn has become a fundamental library in the field of machine learning, particularly for developers and researchers working on classical machine learning algorithms. Over the years, Scikit-Learn has evolved significantly to accommodate a wide range of functionalities, from simple linear regression models to complex ensemble methods. As machine learning and data science continue to advance rapidly, the future of Scikit-Learn will be shaped by emerging trends in artificial intelligence, cloud computing, data processing, and the development of more efficient algorithms. In this section, we will explore potential future trends in Scikit-Learn and its evolving role in the data science ecosystem.

1. Integration with Deep Learning Frameworks

While Scikit-Learn excels in classical machine learning algorithms, it is not specifically designed for deep learning tasks such as training neural networks. However, many users of Scikit-Learn also work with deep learning frameworks like TensorFlow and PyTorch. In the future, we can expect even more seamless integration between Scikit-Learn and these deep learning libraries to allow for hybrid workflows.

Possible Developments:

- **Scikit-learn and TensorFlow/Keras Integration**: There is already some integration between Scikit-Learn and Keras (via wrappers like KerasClassifier and KerasRegressor), but we may see more extensive features such as automatic model tuning and deeper interoperability for neural network models within Scikit-Learn.
- **End-to-End Pipelines**: A stronger focus on enabling hybrid pipelines where Scikit-Learn can handle feature engineering, preprocessing, and traditional machine

learning, while deep learning frameworks can be integrated for more complex tasks (e.g., CNNs for image classification or RNNs for time-series forecasting).

By leveraging the strengths of both traditional machine learning and deep learning, Scikit-Learn could become an even more powerful tool in a machine learning engineer's toolkit.

2. Support for AutoML and Hyperparameter Optimization

AutoML (Automated Machine Learning) has gained significant attention in recent years as a way to automate the process of model selection, hyperparameter tuning, and feature engineering. While libraries like TPOT, Auto-sklearn, and H2O.ai have already introduced automated machine learning pipelines, Scikit-Learn could integrate these approaches to make machine learning even more accessible to a broader audience.

Possible Developments:

- **Built-in AutoML Capabilities**: Scikit-Learn may expand its functionality to include AutoML features for model selection and hyperparameter optimization. The integration of grid search, random search, and Bayesian optimization could be streamlined into Scikit-Learn's core API, making it easier to apply automated search strategies for model tuning.
- **Integration with Automated Machine Learning Tools**: Scikit-Learn could deepen its collaboration with popular AutoML libraries like TPOT, Auto-Sklearn, and H2O AutoML, providing an out-of-the-box way to automatically generate high-performing models with minimal user input.

AutoML is especially valuable for non-experts in machine learning who want to apply machine learning to their problems without needing deep domain expertise. As a result, Scikit-Learn's potential adoption of AutoML techniques would make it an even more user-friendly tool.

3. Expanded Support for Unsupervised Learning Techniques

While Scikit-Learn already offers a wide array of supervised learning algorithms, the library has historically provided fewer options for unsupervised learning. However, with the increasing interest in clustering, anomaly detection, dimensionality reduction, and unsupervised representation learning, Scikit-Learn is expected to extend its capabilities in this area.

Possible Developments:

- **Advanced Clustering Algorithms**: New and more advanced clustering techniques, such as Gaussian Mixture Models (GMM), Spectral Clustering, and DBSCAN, may be incorporated into the library or enhanced for better performance on large datasets.
- **Unsupervised Feature Learning**: Support for unsupervised learning techniques, such as autoencoders or self-organizing maps (SOMs), might be added to help uncover hidden structures in data without labels.
- **Dimensionality Reduction**: Dimensionality reduction methods such as t-SNE, UMAP, and PCA could be enhanced or optimized for even more scalable, efficient processing of high-dimensional datasets.

These advancements could enhance Scikit-Learn's support for unsupervised learning, enabling researchers and practitioners to unlock more insights from unlabeled data.

4. Better Handling of Large Datasets

Machine learning practitioners often deal with large-scale datasets that do not fit into memory. Currently, Scikit-Learn provides several techniques for scaling and working with large datasets, such as incremental learning and support for sparse matrices. However, as datasets continue to grow in size, there will be an increasing demand for efficient processing and distributed learning.

Possible Developments:

- **Distributed Computing**: Scikit-Learn could implement better support for distributed machine learning, allowing users to scale models across clusters of machines. Integration with distributed computing frameworks like Dask or Apache Spark would enable Scikit-Learn to handle massive datasets seamlessly.
- **Streaming Data**: As the demand for real-time analytics increases, there may be enhancements to Scikit-Learn's support for online learning—the process of training models incrementally on streaming data—allowing practitioners to update models as new data arrives.
- **GPU Acceleration**: While Scikit-Learn is primarily CPU-based, there is potential for integration with GPU libraries (e.g., CuML from RAPIDS) to speed up computation, especially for operations involving large datasets or computationally intensive models like SVMs and neural networks.

These improvements would make Scikit-Learn a more robust tool for large-scale machine learning applications, ensuring it can handle the data needs of future machine learning tasks.

5. Better Support for Time-Series Data

Time-series data is increasingly being used in various industries, including finance, healthcare, and e-commerce. While Scikit-Learn has basic support for time-series forecasting tasks, there is potential for more advanced time-series features to be added to the library.

Possible Developments:

- **Time-Series Forecasting Models**: Scikit-Learn could incorporate more time-series models, such as ARIMA, Exponential Smoothing, and other models that are specifically designed to handle temporal dependencies.
- **Temporal Cross-Validation**: Scikit-Learn could improve its time-series cross-validation tools to ensure that models are validated using a temporal hold-out approach rather than random splitting of data, which does not respect the temporal order of observations.

By adding more time-series functionality, Scikit-Learn could serve as a comprehensive tool for practitioners working with sequential data.

6. Improved Interpretability and Model Explanation

Interpretability of machine learning models is increasingly important, especially in fields like healthcare, finance, and legal applications, where model decisions need to be transparent. While Scikit-Learn provides basic tools for model evaluation, there is an ongoing need for more advanced methods for explaining model predictions.

Possible Developments:

- **Model Explainability Tools**: Scikit-Learn could integrate model-agnostic explainability techniques such as LIME (Local Interpretable Model-agnostic Explanations) and SHAP (Shapley Additive Explanations) directly into its pipeline. These tools would allow users to understand how a model is making decisions, which is critical for high-stakes applications.

- **Visualizations for Feature Importance**: Scikit-Learn could enhance its visualization tools to provide clearer insights into feature importance, model behavior, and decision boundaries.

Improving interpretability would increase trust in machine learning models and enable them to be used more effectively in real-world applications where understanding model decisions is essential.

7. Continual Learning and Model Updates

In many applications, machine learning models need to be updated as new data arrives. This process, known as continual learning, is important in dynamic environments like e-commerce, healthcare, or fraud detection, where patterns in the data evolve over time.

Possible Developments:

- **Incremental Learning Models**: Scikit-Learn could enhance its support for models that can be updated incrementally without requiring retraining from scratch. For instance, adding more efficient incremental learning algorithms for ensemble methods, neural networks, and clustering would be beneficial.
- **Online Learning for Evolving Data**: Online learning techniques that allow models to adapt as new data is available without the need for re-training from scratch may be integrated.

This would make Scikit-Learn a better fit for environments that require models to adapt continuously to new information.

The future of Scikit-Learn looks promising, as it continues to evolve and adapt to the changing landscape of machine learning. From deeper integration with deep learning frameworks to enhancing its AutoML capabilities, supporting unsupervised learning, and handling larger datasets more effectively, Scikit-Learn is poised to remain an essential tool for both beginners and advanced practitioners. As more demand for explainability, time-series processing, and continual learning arises, Scikit-Learn will likely integrate these advancements to meet the growing needs of the data science and machine learning communities. The continued development of Scikit-Learn ensures that it will remain an indispensable tool for machine learning in the coming years.

Machine learning is transforming industries, and Scikit-Learn is one of the most powerful and accessible tools to build intelligent systems. Mastering Scikit-Learn: Practical ML for Everyone provides a structured, hands-on approach to understanding and applying machine learning using Python's leading ML library.

From fundamental concepts to advanced techniques, this book takes you on a step-by-step journey, covering data preprocessing, model training, hyperparameter tuning, and real-world applications. You'll learn how to implement linear models, tree-based algorithms, clustering methods, and ensemble techniques, while also mastering pipelines, feature engineering, and model deployment.

Whether you're a beginner exploring machine learning for the first time or an experienced professional looking to refine your skills, this book equips you with the knowledge and tools to build high-performing ML models with confidence. Through practical examples, case studies, and best practices, you'll develop the expertise needed to tackle real-world AI challenges.

As the fifth book in the **AI from Scratch** series, this guide is part of a structured learning path designed to take you from foundational AI concepts to advanced mastery. If you're ready to elevate your machine learning skills and harness the full potential of Scikit-Learn, this book is your ultimate resource.

Your journey to mastering Scikit-Learn starts here! 🚀

-

Dear Reader,

Thank you for joining me on this journey through **Mastering Scikit-Learn: Practical ML for Everyone**. Writing this book has been a labor of love, and knowing that you chose to invest your time in learning from it means the world to me.

Machine learning is a vast and ever-evolving field, and I truly appreciate your curiosity, dedication, and willingness to explore it with me. Whether you're a student, a data scientist, a developer, or just someone passionate about AI, your pursuit of knowledge is what drives innovation and progress.

I am deeply grateful for your trust in this book as a guide to your learning journey. I hope it has provided you with the clarity, confidence, and practical skills to apply machine learning in meaningful ways. More importantly, I hope it has inspired you to keep learning, experimenting, and pushing the boundaries of what's possible with AI.

To my readers, supporters, and the amazing machine learning community—thank you for your encouragement, feedback, and enthusiasm. Your support fuels my passion for writing and sharing knowledge.

If this book has helped you in any way, I would love to hear about your journey! Feel free to connect with me, share your thoughts, and continue the conversation.

Wishing you all success and breakthroughs in your machine learning endeavors. Keep building, keep innovating, and keep mastering AI!

With gratitude,

Gilbert Gutiérrez